The Ferrell
of Baseball

6/23/06

DEAR LU & CLYDE,

CONGRATULATIONS ON
ACHIEVING A SIGNIFICANT
MILESTONE IN YOUR
LIVES - #50 YEARS
OF WEDDED BLISS!
WE'LL JOIN YOU IN
SEPTEMBER - 1956
WAS A GOOD YEAR!

LOVE & BLESSINGS
NANCY & RALPH

The Ferrell Brothers of Baseball

DICK THOMPSON

McFarland & Company, Inc., Publishers

Jefferson, North Carolina, and London

LIBRARY OF CONGRESS CATALOGUING-IN-PUBLICATION DATA

Thompson, Dick, 1955–
    The Ferrell brothers of baseball / Dick Thompson.
        p.   cm.
    Includes bibliographical references and index.

    ISBN 0-7864-2006-5 (softcover : 50# alkaline paper) ∞

    1. Ferrell, Rick, 1905–1995.   2. Ferrell, Wes, 1908–1976.
    3. Baseball players—United States—Biography.   4. Brothers—
    United States—Biography.   I. Title.
    GV865.A1T467   2005
    796.357'092'2—dc22   2005001730

British Library cataloguing data are available

©2005 Dick Thompson. All rights reserved

No part of this book may be reproduced or transmitted in any form
or by any means, electronic or mechanical, including photocopying
or recording, or by any information storage and retrieval system,
without permission in writing from the publisher.

On the cover: Rick (left) and Wes Ferrell, Sportsman's Park, 1930 (Wide
World Photos)

Manufactured in the United States of America

McFarland & Company, Inc., Publishers
    Box 611, Jefferson, North Carolina 28640
    www.mcfarlandpub.com

In memory of Kevin A. Breen —
a book lover and a Red Sox fan

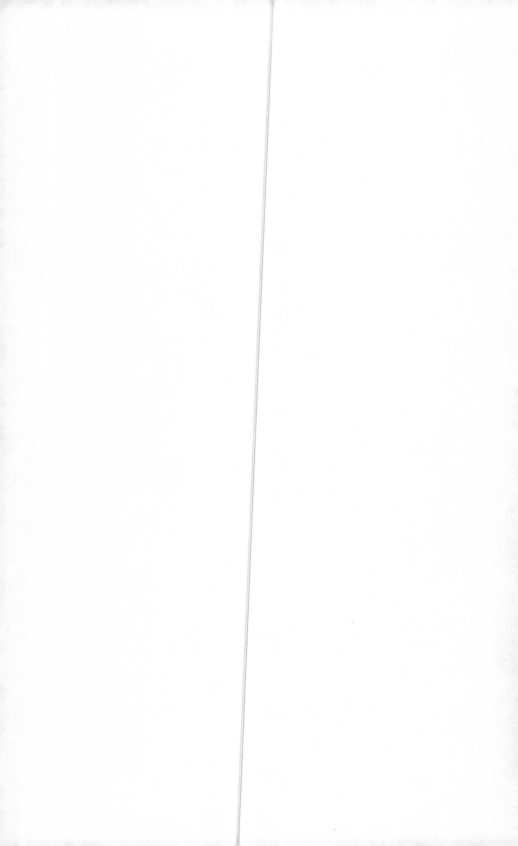

Acknowledgments

So many people have provided me assistance with this book that I am certain I will leave someone off of this list. For those who sent me material and do not see their name, please accept my apologies.

First and foremost, I must thank my wife Barbara, whose love and support was crucial to me during this project, and my daughter and her husband, Eve and Jason Gates, whose technical support of my semi-illiterate computer skills saved many a day.

The Ferrell Family graciously opened their archives and provided data that I would not have located without them. That effort, coordinated by George W. Ferrell, included James R. Ferrell, Gwen Ferrell Gore, Wes Ferrell, Jr., Maureen Ferrell, Marva Ferrell Flowers, Pam McReynolds, Mrs. Beverly "Deta" Ferrell, Kerrie Ferrell, Eleanor Ferrell Hoover, John Ferrell, Eddie Waynick and Barbara Nusbaum.

The following list of former major league players and baseball historians, many of whom are members of the Society for American Baseball Research, provided me with material, advice and support. They are Ross Adell, Mark Alvarez, Mark Armour, Elden Auker, Gerry Bierne, John Bennett, Dick Beverage, Charlie Bevis, Al Blumkin, Bob Broeg, Bill Carle, Roger Craig, Harrison Daniel, Mike Emeigh, Scott Flatow, Sean Forman, Mike Foster, Frank Geishecker, Steve Gietschier, Rick Harris, Joe Harring, Bobby Hicks, Ralph Hodgin, Ralph Houk, Jim Kaplan, Maxwell Kates, Kerry Keene, Francis Kinlaw, Rich Klein, Len Levin, Dan Levitt, Jim Leyland, Ted Lukacs, Ron Marshall, Scott Mayer, Richard McGrath, John McHale, Mike McKee, David Nemec, Rob Neyer, Bill Nowlin, Marc Okkonen, John Pastier, Pete Palmer, Bob Richardson, Branch Rickey III, Ron Selter, Tom Shieber, Dave Smith, Lyle Spatz, Steve Steinberg, Glenn Stout, Adie Suehsdorf, Stew Thornley, Bobby Thomson, Dixie Tourangeau, Jules Tygiel, David Vincent, Charlie Wagner, Rob Wood and Tom Zocco.

Marie Lowrey Armstrong, the archivist at the Oak Ridge Military

viii   Acknowledgments

Academy, and Dave Walters, the Sports Information Director at Guilford College, provided me information regarding the early baseball movements of the Ferrells. The historical societies of Douglas, Massachusetts, and Guilford County, North Carolina, did the same.

Four libraries were used during the compilation of this research so I wish to thank the staff members of the Widener Library at Harvard University, the Boston Public Library, the Maxwell C. Clement Library at Bridgewater State College and the Bridgewater, Massachusetts, Public Library. I am especially grateful to the reference staff at the Bridgewater Public Library—Mary O'Connell, Jane Murphy, Susan Scott and Dale Sheehy—for their efforts in obtaining microfilm and magazine articles via interlibrary loan.

A project of this type could not be completed without research at the National Baseball Hall of Fame at Cooperstown, New York. I always turn to Bill Deane when my projects lead me there, and once again Bill came through like the clutch-hitter he is. The statistical playing records of the Ferrells, found in the appendix, come courtesy of Ray Nemec, the foremost expert on minor league playing affiliations of players.

I would be remiss not to mention Harold Paretchen and the late Thomas P. Shea, mentors who took me under their wing more than 20 years ago and molded my passion for baseball history

I would also like to mention three current or recently retired North Carolina sportswriters. Though I have never met or had contact with Wilt Browning, Bill Haas or Al Thomy, I found their frequent and detailed material on the Ferrells very helpful.

Table of Contents

Preface

The inspiration for this book can be traced back to 1980 when I read Donald Honig's *Baseball When the Grass Was Real*, an oral history of 18 major league players whose careers ran from the 1920s to the 1940s. The opening interview was with Wes Ferrell, and I was immediately taken with both his confidence and his humbleness.

The 1930s was a great time for baseball brother acts. In addition to Wes and Rick Ferrell, there were Dizzy and Paul Dean, Paul and Lloyd Waner, Bob and Roy Johnson, and Joe and Vince DiMaggio. The Ferrells were a battery — Wes did the pitching and Rick the receiving. They had grown up on a dairy farm in North Carolina, obsessed with the game as soon as they were old enough to toss a ball. There were seven brothers in the family and all were great ballplayers. Trying to out-hit, out-pitch and out-run each other was a way of life for the siblings, and the competition for best player on the Ferrell farm was likely more intense than any game Wes or Rick contested on a major league diamond. Not that they didn't try and outdo each other there as well, for Wes always took great delight in putting Rick out, and Rick loved to get a hit off Wes.

Even as teammates the pair was often at odds with each other. Both liked to tell the story of a low-hit shutout Wes tossed against the Detroit Tigers — likely a two-hitter on May 3, 1936. "Throw any damn thing you please," Rick told Wes after arguing about pitch selection. "You can't fool me no way. I know you well enough." The Detroit hitters were quickly forgotten for the battle became brother against brother. "Me winning all those games, and he thinks he's going to catch me without signs?" Wes said of his brother/catcher to Donald Honig. "I kicked the mound around a little, pulled my cap down tight on my head. They I fired him a curveball — one of the best I'd ever thrown, I swear — and he just reached down across his body and caught it backhanded with that mitt of his. Showboating. I'd throw him my best fastballs and he'd catch them soft — you know, wouldn't

1

let it pop." Following the game — after watching Wes being congratulated by his teammates and the writers — Rick finally spoke. "Well," he said, "you pitched a pretty good game. But damn you, if you'd listened to me, you'd of pitched a no-hitter."

Intensity and competitiveness were inherent traits of the Ferrells. Nine members of the family played professional baseball and all had it to some degree, especially the six members of the first generation — brothers Wes, Rick, George and Marvin, and their cousins Bev and Charlie. Wes was Hollywood-handsome, tempestuous and fiery on the field, likely the greatest hitting pitcher of all time and capable of bashing the ball a country mile. Rick was the classy fielding backstop. He possessed the same passion that Wes did, and though his fuse was slower to burn, his punch carried just as much, if not more, wallop.

Beneath the exterior bravado of being major league stars, both men were of simple country stock. They were shy: honest and straightforward if their opinions were asked for, but stingy by nature with their words. Any battle on the field was left there, and family loyalty was of the utmost importance. Both were among the top stars of their era. Wes was a luminous baseball nova, a superstar player — hitter as well as pitcher — whose time on top was cut short by a sore arm. Rick was a top strategist, a master-handler of pitchers and recognized by his peers as a dangerous clutch hitter. He stayed in the game in the executive branch following his playing days, helping to run the Detroit Tigers for several decades.

Neither Ferrell played for great teams or appeared in a World Series. Devoid of that media exposure, and not being colorful figures like Dizzy Dean or Yogi Berra, both quickly faded from the eye of the baseball public. Neither, however, was ever forgotten by the men who played with and against them.

The Ferrell name was brought back into the public eye when Rick, then a vice-president of the Tigers, was named to the Hall of Fame by the Veterans Committee in 1984. That decision was applauded by baseball men who were aware of Rick's sixty years of service, but not understood by the less informed. One sportswriter, apparently trying to be funny, suggested that the committee members had confused the brothers and thought they were actually voting for Wes instead of Rick. Twenty years later that story still makes the rounds. It is insulting not only to the Ferrells, but to the men on the committee who were well aware of whom they were voting for.

Several years ago I became involved in a hot-stove discussion with my friend Kerry Keene. He has authored several baseball books and is both interested and knowledgeable about players in the Hall of Fame. Kerry asked me whom I thought had been overlooked for enshrinement and I replied with Wes Ferrell's name. That discussion morphed into an article on Wes that appeared in the 2001 edition of *The National Pastime*, a publication of the Society for American Baseball Research (SABR). I was fortunate enough, while researching that article, to come in contact with several members of the Ferrell family and quickly realized the wealth of information that was available. What started as a biography of one baseball pitcher has grown into the saga of a family whose accomplishments in professional baseball seem largely forgotten by today's generation of fans.

This is simply a story of that family.

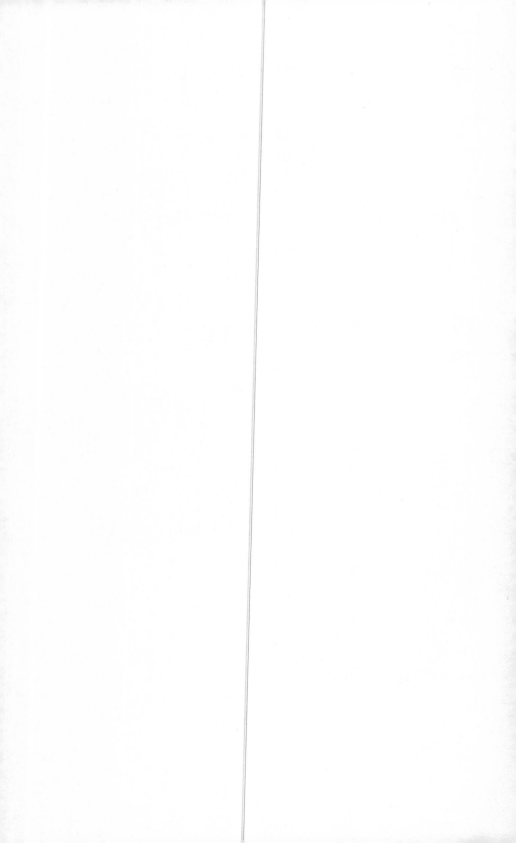

◆ 1 ◆

The Flesh and Blood
Frank Merriwell

There were two outs in the bottom of the seventh inning and the bases were loaded as Rick Ferrell walked to the plate at Fenway Park on July 1, 1935. The Boston backstop was swinging a hot stick. The previous afternoon he had slapped a homer, two doubles and a single to drive home four of Boston's runs in a 10–9 loss to the Athletics. Now working the count to three and two, he planted the next pitch off the left field wall for a bases-clearing double.

Tom Yawkey was in his third year as owner of the Boston Red Sox and the young and wealthy millionaire was hungry for baseball success. His first move when purchasing the perennial cellar-dwelling Boston club in 1933 had been to hire Eddie Collins as general manager. Collins' instructions were simple; build a winner, money was no object.

Collins had added four stars by 1935. His first big purchase in 1933 was acquiring Ferrell from the St. Louis Browns. The 1934 season saw the Red Sox debuts of Lefty Grove and Ferrell's younger brother Wesley, two of the premier pitchers in all of baseball. Joe Cronin, the leading shortstop and boy-wonder manager of the American League, was purchased from Washington for the 1935 season.

A pre-season poll of 194 members of the Baseball Writers Association of America (BBWAA) had projected the Red Sox to finish fourth and so far the polls weren't far off as Boston began July in fifth place with a 32–33 record, eight and a half games behind the front-running New York Yankees. If the Red Sox were to make a move, now was the time to do it.

The month began inauspiciously as the Washington Nationals scored a run in each of the first three innings off Boston starter Wes Ferrell. The first run—credited as earned on Ferrell's tally sheet—came when Boston third baseman Bill Werber, settling under a foul pop-up, ran into

5

WHY THEY CALL HIM "IRON MAN RICK"

July 16, 1935 — Rick Ferrell at the peak of his game (reprinted courtesy *The Boston Globe*).

a photographer who wasn't paying attention to the action. The ball dropped untouched and the sequence of events led to a Washington run that wouldn't have been scored had the play been completed.

Ferrell was unfazed for he was, as the Boston *Post* noted, "one hurler who doesn't become panic-stricken over a few enemy hits. It's a real pleasure for Boston fans to watch a pitcher who can defy opposition, nullify the sting of a heavy attack, never lose his self-possession or confidence and emerge triumphant."

Ferrell settled down and kept the Nats in check while his teammates came back for an 8–3 victory. Wes drove in a run with a second-inning single. Cronin's two-run homer in the fifth inning and Rick Ferrell's double in the seventh iced the game. The contest ended with Cronin going deep into the shortstop hole, "snaring a sizzling bounder and making a long throw to nip the runner at first base."

Maybe July would be a good month after all.

Boston swept the three-game series with Washington and left for a holiday doubleheader in New York against the Yankees where Cronin opened with his other ace, the redoubtable Lefty Grove. The Red Sox had purchased Grove from the Philadelphia Athletics and expected him to anchor the rotation in 1934. Instead, Grove came up with a sore arm that limited him to just eight victories.

Grove's arm was the big question of 1935 and Cronin started him off slowly. By mid-season the metamorphosis was complete. Gone was the overpowering fastballer and in his place was the complete pitcher, one who relied on his head just as much as his heat. Rick Ferrell played a role in that change. When Grove abandoned Philadelphia he also left behind his long-time catcher, Mickey Cochrane.

"Of course I'm sorry I no longer will have Mickey Cochrane catching me," said Grove. "But Rick Ferrell is one of the greatest receivers in the game and I am thoroughly satisfied."[1] When asked in 1936 about his comeback from his sore arm, Lefty gave much of the credit to Ferrell. "I owe it all to that trainer and Rick Ferrell, my catcher. Ferrell helped me learn to mix 'em up."[2]

The Bronx Bombers tagged the "Lonaconing Lion" for three runs in the opening frame on the Fourth of July but Grove shut them out the rest of the way for a 4–3 victory. New York hammered out a 7–1 win in the nightcap.

Grove and Wes Ferrell's contribution of 45 wins would top all other American League teammate tandems in 1935 and trail by two the total notched by the Dean Brothers of the St. Louis Cardinals. The benchmark of a standout pitching season has traditionally been 20 wins, and Lefty and

Wes already had 11 such seasons between them. They rivaled Dizzy Dean and Carl Hubbell as the two best pitchers in the game, and in 1935 the Red Sox would go only as far as the arms of Grove and Ferrell would take them.

Wes Ferrell beat Philadelphia 6–4 at Fenway Park on July 6 for his league-leading twelfth win. With Wes staked to a 6–0 lead, the Athletics scored four times in the sixth inning on three doubles and a home run. Ferrell then allowed just one hit over the last three innings.

A doubleheader on July 7 was the last action before the All-Star game planned for the next afternoon in Cleveland. Boston took the 13-inning opener by the score of 7–6 with Grove working spectacularly in relief, allowing just one hit over five innings to pick up the win. The hitting stars were Cronin, who scored four runs on three hits, and Rick Ferrell, who tallied five RBI on four hits. The nightcap was a 3–1 Philadelphia victory that was called after eight innings due to darkness. Immediately after the game the Red Sox All-Star contingent consisting of Cronin, Grove and Rick Ferrell plus Philadelphia's squad of Jimmy Foxx, Bob Johnson, Roger Cramer and (coach) Dave Keefe left for Cleveland.

Wes Ferrell had been the American League's leading pitcher since the season had opened and his spot on the All-Star team had frequently been discussed. In late May, J.G. Taylor Spink of *The Sporting News* opined that "Dizzy Dean and Ferrell doubtless will start as opposing hurlers." As late as a week before the game *The Sporting News* projected the American League's pitchers to be Johnny Whitehead of the White Sox, Tommy Bridges of the Tigers, and Ferrell. Wes, who had a 10–8 record, wasn't named to the squad when Mickey Cochrane announced the 20-player team on June 28, but Grove, with a 6–6 mark, was.

"Well," noted Dan Daniel in the *The Sporting News*, "the league picks the players, and there is Lefty Grove on the team again, while guys like Wes Ferrell and Ted Lyons are not even mentioned. This does not sit well with the customers but there is a good reason for picking Grove … the power of the National League is left-handed. So the American League says we gotta have two crooked-arms to shoot at Terry, Vaughan, Ott, Moore, and Paul Waner."[3]

All-Star teams have always been debate magnets. Cochrane left Hank Greenberg, his own first baseman and eventual league MVP, off of the team. "Greenberg is leading the league in home runs, total bases, runs batted in and playing a great game in the field," said Mickey, "but the other managers voted for Lou Gehrig, the theory probably being that Lou's superior experience makes him more valuable."[4]

Joe Cronin was feeling the strain of running the Red Sox and wasn't performing to his normal standards either at bat or in the field, hitting just .262 (53 for 202) with two home runs and 25 RBI when named to the all-star team. "Joe Cronin of Boston has been anything but an all-star shortstop this season," wrote the Chicago *Herald and Examiner*'s Warren Brown in the July 4 issue of *The Sporting News*. Wes Ferrell's batting average was .443 (27 for 61) at the same time and he had two home runs as well.

Ferrell voiced no complaints about being left off the squad. Instead, he let his arm do his talking, firing a two-hit shutout against the third-place Chicago White Sox on July 10 to open the second half of the season.

"There was never a time in the whole afternoon excepting the seventh when the White Sox had the ghost of a chance of making trouble for Boston's great right-hander," wrote the *Post*.

Chicago's Tony Piet dumped a single into center field in the fourth inning and led off the seventh with an infield hit that hugged the third-base line. A "looper" and a "topper" was how the Boston *Globe* described the hits. The Red Sox supported Wesley in fine fashion, scoring seven times on 14 hits. Rick Ferrell drove home the first Boston run in the second inning and Wes clouted a long homer over the left-field wall in the fifth.

The teams split a doubleheader the next afternoon. Grove allowed the White Sox five hits and three runs but held them scoreless after the third inning in a 4–3 win in the opener. He chipped in a couple of hits and scored the winning run in the ninth inning. Chicago took the second game 10–2, knocking out Boston starter Johnny Welch in the first inning before he could retire a batter. In the series finale the next afternoon, Chicago chased the Red Sox starter in the second inning and coasted to a 13–2 win. "That the Red Sox without Wes Ferrell or Lefty Grove are like a ship without a rudder was again demonstrated," said the *Globe*.

The Cleveland Indians came into town the next day and beat veteran Rube Walberg by a 4–2 score. Cronin sent Wes Ferrell and Fritz Ostermueller to the hill in a Sunday doubleheader on July 14 and Boston's three-game skid ended in the first game as Wes and his teammates routed the Indians, 14–3. Every Boston starter but Wes Ferrell had at least one hit. Rick Ferrell scored four runs with his four safeties.

"The opening contest, with the great Wes Ferrell starring, and incidentally hanging up his fourteenth victory of the year," wrote Boston scribe Paul Shannon, "was featured by a terrific demonstration of batting by the locals. Ferrell won in a canter, never being forced to bear down in a contest where he proved to his one-time teammates that he was again the Wes Ferrell of old."[5] Cleveland scored only in the third inning, after Boston had built up an 11–0 lead, and Wes called this his easiest game of the year.

The second game ended after ten innings as a 2–2 tie. Rick Ferrell caught both ends of the doubleheader and started the Boston ninth with a base hit. He was tearing around the bases when Babe Dahlgren's towering shot looked like it was going to hit the wall. The Cleveland left fielder caught the ball while crashing off the Fenway facade and fired the ball back to the infield to double up the Boston backstop.

While the Cleveland club waited in Boston, the Red Sox traveled to Bangor, Maine, for an exhibition game on July 15. There a reporter inquired about Boston's interest in yet another Ferrell brother — George — who was playing for the Richmond, Virginia team in the Piedmont League. "Ferrell's sensational hitting with Richmond is certainly impressive to say the least," said Tom Yawkey. "To tell you the truth, I was a little surprised when I saw the official figures today. I've talked it over with Joe and while I have nothing to promise or announce, it seems about time that he be given another crack at the big time."[6]

"I've had my eye on Ferrell for a long, long time," added Cronin. "I knew all about him — that is, his baseball career — before I left the Washington club, and I have been watching him ever since. Personally, I think he is the outstanding prospect in the minors so far this season."[7]

Nineteen thousand fans watched the Red Sox sweep a doubleheader, 13–5 and 3–1, from the Indians on July 17 to leap over Walter Johnson's club into fourth place, just two games behind the White Sox. The Boston starter couldn't get past the second inning in the first game but Rube Walberg pitched seven innings of effective relief to pick up the win. Rick Ferrell had three hits, including a double and a home run. He scored three runs and knocked in the same.

Grove was his usual self in the second game allowing eight hits and one run. Boston scored their three runs on just five hits. Moe Berg, Boston's backup catcher, knocked in all three runs for the Red Sox. Berg was one of the game's most eccentric characters, quirky enough to warrant several biographies. He relished the lifestyle, but not the physical aspect, of major league baseball. The standard joke about the well-educated Berg was that he could speak a dozen languages but couldn't hit in any of them.

"Joe Cronin's locker was two down from mine," recalled Rick Ferrell. "We'd play a doubleheader in Boston and Moe'd come over to my locker after I caught the first game and say, 'Rick, you're the greatest catcher in the American League. Joe, let's not change the lineup.' So I'd catch two games. I didn't care. He didn't want to play unless he had to."[8] Berg always referred to Rick as "the dandy little catcher" and the phrase quickly caught on with the Boston writers.

Wes Ferrell opened a big series with Detroit on Thursday, July 18. Manager Mickey Cochrane had the Tigers back on track after a slow start, and over the course of July they would climb from third to first place. Ferrell, looking for his fifteenth win, was beaten by Schoolboy Rowe, who scattered five singles in the 8–0 contest. The Boston defense made three errors that gave Detroit six unearned runs. "Rowe carried off the verdict and deserved it," said the *Globe*, "but the score by which the Tigers won does not do justice to the splendid account of himself rendered by Ferrell."

With a runner on first base and one out in the second inning, Cronin fumbled a routine double-play ball so badly that not even a single out could be recorded. Rowe followed with a triple and the Tigers scored three times in the inning. Ferrell walked Rowe to start the fifth inning. A base hit and an outfield error left runners on second and third. Wes fanned Cochrane and Cronin cut down Rowe at the plate on a ground ball. Hank Greenberg, whom Wes had fanned in his previous at-bat, was the next hitter and he singled to right on a three and two count to drive in two runs.

Detroit scored three more times in the ninth when Cronin let another potentially inning-ending double-play ball roll through his legs for his second error. "While two of the Detroit markers must go down in the books as earned runs, it is easy to see where the Tigers would have been held scoreless too if his mates had done right by Ferrell," read the *Globe*'s recap of the game.

Fritz Ostermueller and Tommy Bridges were Friday's starters and the Boston hurler was driven from the mound in the sixth inning when the Tigers scored five runs. Bridges left after allowing three runs in the bottom of the inning. The game ended in a 9–7 victory for Detroit.

Alvin Crowder was Cochrane's choice on Saturday afternoon. Cronin countered with Gordon Rhodes, whom the Tigers jumped on for four runs in less than two innings. Reliever Walberg pitched effectively and held Detroit scoreless until the seventh inning when he allowed a run that increased the lead to 5–1. Boston rallied in their half of the inning when pinch-hitter Wes Ferrell crashed a double high off the left-field wall that plated a run and knocked Crowder out of the game. Oscar Melillo followed with a hit and two more Boston runs were home. Wes stayed in to pitch and the Red Sox tied the game in the eighth. Charlie Gehringer singled with one out in the ninth and stole second as Ferrell fanned Greenberg. Goose Goslin singled in the game-winner and Boston's ninth inning rally—leaving the tying run on third—fell short.

Lefty Grove was Cronin's last hope. The Red Sox needed a win on Sunday to avoid a sweep. Cochrane came back with Tommy Bridges on just a day of rest. The scoring seesawed back and forth. Boston tallied once in the opening frame but Grove gave up two in the second inning, issuing two passes—one with the bases loaded—after a couple of scratch hits and Detroit took a 2–1 lead. Boston went ahead in the fifth inning on Rick Ferrell's triple, Cronin's single and a double by Dahlgren. Detroit tied it in the top of the eighth before Boston went back up by a run in the home half.

The ninth inning was something to behold. Pete Fox led off with a double before Grove retired Gee Walker on strikes and Gehringer on a fly ball. Greenberg, the league's RBI leader with 110, came to the plate and with the left-handed hitting Goslin next in the batting order, Cronin opted to walk him. Grove was not happy with this strategy and told Joe so. He wanted to face Greenberg, whom he felt he could strike out.

Neither of Cronin's aces was happy with the manager's input.

"Word from Boston," noted *The Sporting News*, "that the two veteran pitching stars of the Red Sox, Bob Grove and Wes Ferrell, have not been taking any too kindly to Joe Cronin's instructions on how to pitch to certain hitters. Having been around the American League for quite a spell, they feel they should know a little more about the weaknesses of opposing hitters than young Joe."[9]

Grove followed instructions and walked Greenberg. Goslin and Billy Rogell followed with singles and Detroit was back up by a run. Ray Hayworth—Detroit's right-handed hitting catcher—had been lifted for a runner in the eighth inning, so Cochrane, who rarely faced left-handers, was up next. He doubled to score Goslin and Rogell was cut down at the plate for the final out.

Grove was livid, heaving his glove into the crowd as he walked toward the dugout, and clawing at his uniform blouse. For a finale, he picked up one of Cronin's game bats and smashed it to pieces on the edge of the dugout.

Cronin led off the last of the ninth and the fans let him have it with a chorus of boos. Unfazed, he rapped out his third hit of the day. Werber followed with a single and Dahlgren laid down a sacrifice bunt. Boston now had runners on second and third with one out. A base hit could tie the game.

Wes Ferrell came up to pinch-hit for Grove. First base was open and Cochrane decided to walk him. Bridges argued with his manager, wanting to face Wes. They had history. They had squared off three times as opposing starters thus far in their careers with Ferrell winning them all and blasting homers off the Detroit righty in each contest. Bridges told Cochrane he would handle Ferrell. Cochrane deferred to his pitcher. It was a bad move, for Wes sent the first pitch over the left-field wall on to Lansdowne Street for a three-run, game-winning homer.

Boston had avoided the sweep and remained in the first division. Grove had his twelfth win of the year. The 24,000 fans in Fenway Park were ecstatic, several jumping from the stands near third base to escort Wes home. Cronin greeted Wes with a big hug as he crossed the plate. Cochrane was last seen dropkicking his catcher's mitt into the Detroit dugout.

Grove was down in the clubhouse, and he wasn't in a good mood.

"So we all rush into the clubhouse, laughing and hollering, the way you do after a game like that," Wes told historian Donald Honig. "And here's Lefty, sitting there, still thinking he's lost his game. When he saw all the carrying-on, I tell you, the smoke started coming out of his ears.

'I don't see what's so funny,' he says. 'A man loses a ball game, and you're all carrying on.'

"Then somebody says, 'Hell, Lefty, we won it. Wes hit a home run for you.'

"Well, I was sitting across the clubhouse from him, pulling my uniform off, and I notice he's staring at me, with

Wes saves the day for Lefty (reprinted courtesy *The Boston Globe*).

just a trace of a smile at the corners of his mouth. Just staring at me. He doesn't say anything. I give him a big grin and pull my sweat shirt up over my head. Then I hear him, 'Hey, Wes.' I look over and he's rolling a bottle of wine across to me — he'd keep a bottle of one thing or another stashed up in his locker. I picked it up and thanked him. At the end of the season I brought it back to Carolina with me and let it sit up on the mantel. It sat up there for years and years. Every time I looked at it I thought of old Left. He rolled it over to me."[10]

When several Boston writers approached Grove and jokingly said that they had decided to credit the win to Wes instead of him, Lefty responded, "You can bet your life that's all right with me."

St. Louis was in town next and Wes started against Dick Coffman the following afternoon. The Browns had been in last place all season but had just taken three out of four from the faltering Yankees in New York. Coffman, despite 15 years in the majors and a couple of World Series appearances, is best remembered for his 1–0 shutout of the Philadelphia Athletics in 1931 that snapped Grove's 16-game winning streak.

Coffman allowed eight hits and Wes seven as the game went to the last of the ninth knotted at 1–1. On a one and two count, Wes launched his second consecutive walk-off homer. The ball, which landed on the roof of a building across Lansdowne Street, was hit so hard that the Browns' left fielder didn't even move.[11]

"Leave it to the great Wes Ferrell to furnish the fans at Fenway Park with their meed of thrills!" wrote the Boston *Post*. "Leave it to the Red Sox pitching ace to show the rooters that his offensive value is nearly as great as his cleverness and experience on the mound!"

"A flesh and blood Frank Merriwell — that's Wesley Ferrell, pitching and hitting star of the Boston Red Sox," was how the New York *World-Telegram* started off their recap of Ferrell's weekend.

Boston dropped the next two games to St. Louis before traveling to Philadelphia where Cronin started Grove and Wes in a doubleheader on July 27. The first game was a 7–6 Philadelphia victory in 15 innings. Grove went the distance, allowing 21 hits and six walks. The Red Sox didn't do much offensively although Rick Ferrell had three hits. Grove, never proficient with the stick, hit a bases-loaded home run in the second inning. Lefty drove in just five runs in 1935 and four of them came on this one swing.

Johnny Marcum, the Athletics' ace, faced Wes in the second game and Mack's only lineup change was a different catcher. Rick Ferrell, who caught all 24 innings for Boston, handled his brother's 2–0 three-hit shutout. Wes was dominant, allowing only an infield single through the

BOSTON   POST,   MONDAY.   JULY   22,   1935

Let's Have That Spotlight!   -:-   *By Bob Coyne*

Pinch hitter extraordinaire (*The Boston Post*).

first seven innings. He scored the only run he would need when he came around after starting off the sixth inning with a single.

Wes' last game of the month was on July 31 at Washington's Griffith Stadium. He gave up four runs on 12 hits but offset those numbers with his bat, belting a three-run homer into the "distant left field bleachers" in the fourth inning and a solo shot in the seventh. "So hard hit," was the second ball, "that Left Fielder Heinie Manush didn't even deign to watch it as it passed over his head and landed near the top of the concrete stands." Both blasts came off Bobo Newsom. The final score was 6–4.

Griffith Stadium was not an easy place to hit home runs and only 30, sans three inside-the parkers, were hit there during the entire 1935 season. Only four members of the home club managed to hit a ball over the fence at Griffith all year. That's four men hitting one homer each! A list of home runs hit there by visiting players reveals the expected names. Gehringer led all hitters with three. Lou Gehrig, Foxx, Tony Lazzeri, Hal Trosky and Wes Ferrell hit two. Hank Greenberg, the league's co-leader in home runs that year, didn't hit any. Ferrell was the only man to hit two in one game.[12]

"Wesley Cheek Ferrell seems to be conducting a one-man debunking campaign against the popular belief that pitchers can't hit or are not supposed to hit," wrote celebrated Washington scribe Shirley Povich. "Four home runs in his last four games indicate that Ferrell is one pitcher who uses his bat for something else other than to knock the dirt out of his spikes."[13]

Tremendous home runs had long been Wes' forte. He had launched a ball 470 feet in Birmingham, Alabama's Rickwood Field on April 7 as the Red Sox moved north from spring training.[14] Rick Ferrell loved to tell a story that emphasized Wes' strength. Back on the farm the other Ferrell siblings would load four 100-pound bags of seed — two on each of his shoulders — and Wes would carry them 100 yards over the roughly hewn fields that had been prepared for sowing.

The Red Sox finished July with a 17–11 record. They had made their move but so had the Tigers (20–8) who moved past the faltering Yankees (12–13) and Indians (8–19). The White Sox (19–9) found themselves in the middle of a pennant race.

The Ferrell Brothers, or more precisely, the Ferrell Family, were at their peak. Wes led the Red Sox in pitching wins (7) and home runs (5) in July and at season's end would trail only Hank Greenberg in the league's MVP balloting. Rick, topping Boston hitters in batting average (.355) and RBI (18) for the month, had been named to all three American League All-Star squads since the game's inception in 1933. George Ferrell would win both the 1935 batting title and MVP award in the Piedmont League. Brother Marvin Ferrell had already played as high as the American Association and Cousin Beverly Ferrell's contract was owned by the Baltimore Orioles. All told, nine members of the family would eventually play professionally. Baseball was a game the Ferrells were born for.

* * *

◆ 2 ◆

Guilford County

Guilford County was established in 1770 and named in honor of Francis Lord North, the first Earl of Guilford and Prime Minister of Great Britain from 1770 to 1782. Located in the heart of North Carolina's Piedmont, Guilford County sits midway between the Smoky Mountains and the Atlantic Ocean. The first settlers, consisting of Scotch-Irish, German and English Quakers, arrived around 1750. Greensboro, established in 1808 as the county seat, is currently the third largest city in the state.

Guilford County holds a unique place in American history for on March 15, 1781, Major General Nathanael Greene, Southern Department Commander of the Continental Army, squared off against the British Army under Lieutenant General Charles Cornwallis at the Battle of Guilford Courthouse. Purposely avoiding a confrontation until his army could reach maximum strength, General Greene turned to face Cornwallis in the North Carolina countryside. British casualties suffered at Guilford Courthouse, plus an overextension of his supply line, caused Cornwallis to retreat from the Carolinas into Virginia. His surrender that fall at Yorktown ended the war. The action at Guilford Courthouse is often referred to as the "beginning of the last act of the Revolution."[1]

✶ ✶ ✶

Destiny appears to have dictated that the lives of the Ferrell Brothers and Lefty Grove would be intertwined as Grove's biographer, Jim Kaplan, noted that Grove's great-great-grandfather served in the Continental Army and fought in the battle of Guilford Courthouse.[2]

✶ ✶ ✶

Rufus Benjamin Ferrell was born in 1873 and grew up in Durham County, about 10 miles east of Durham proper. To friends, neighbors and relatives he was known as Lonnie. Lonnie's parents died when he was 18 and he became responsible for his 11 younger siblings. Ferrell supported his family as best he could; working as a farmhand or in a lumber mill. In 1898 he married Clora Alice Carpenter, who taught him how to read, write and do arithmetic. When Lonnie's siblings were old enough to take over the farm, the couple moved to Greensboro, where he took a job working for the railroad. The family lived at 508 Houston Street, close enough to the railroad tracks so Lonnie could wave down passing engines and catch a ride to the railroad roundhouse.

Lonnie worked for the Southern Railroad for 25 years, first as a fireman and then as an engineer. He survived several train wrecks; one in 1911 trapped him under his overturned engine for several hours.

Lonnie purchased property circa 1910 in the countryside approximately six miles south of the Guilford Courthouse Battleground and over the next several years he and his growing brood of sons built the family a home. "We built a two-story frame house right out on Highway 421," recalled George Ferrell late in his life. "It had a big oak tree in the front by the driveway. There was a well out there too. It had the best water. People would stop and water their horses and get a drink of water out of that well on their way to and from town. That was when the road was sand-clay, not paved. Before the house was finished in 1912, we'd come out in the summer time. We'd hook the team up and leave Houston Street about six o'clock in the morning coming out to work the farm. It would take us about two hours to get out there." Originally six to eight miles west of the Greensboro city limits and two miles from the campus of Guilford College, the site of the former Ferrell farm currently sits within the borders of Greater Greensboro.

Guilford County has never had an official township called Guilford. A small community surrounded the college campus and another village two miles away near the railroad station, called Guilford Station, maintained the local post office. The inhabitants referred to themselves as being from either Guilford College or Guilford Station. For tax and voting purposes, the populations of Guilford College and Guilford Station fell under the jurisdiction of the township of Friendship, North Carolina.

Lonnie and Clora Alice's seven children were all boys. Basil was born on November 16, 1900; William Kermit on February 8, 1902; George Stuart on April 14, 1904; Richard Benjamin on October 12, 1905; Wesley Cheek on February 2, 1908; Isaac Marvin on December 1, 1910; and finally Thomas Ewell on August 13, 1912. The second, sixth and seventh sons went by their middle names and Basil and Kermit were known by family and friends as "Slats" and "Pete." The exact origin of Wesley's middle name — which comes from the common North Carolina surname Cheek — is unconfirmed but a cousin conversant on family genealogy feels it was to honor Lonnie's

The Ferrell brothers on the family farm in the spring of 1928. From left: Ewell, George, Rick, Pete, Marvin, Slats, Wes (George W. Ferrell).

aunt, Sara Vickers Cheek Holloway, who took in some of Lonnie's siblings when Wes' grandparents died.

Only three of the brothers— George, Wesley and Marvin — have births recorded in Guilford County. George did not have a birth certificate until 1964 when Guilford County issued him one based on data he provided from a now misplaced family bible. The two older brothers were born in Durham before the family moved to Greensboro and all were thought to have been born at home or, like Rick, at the home of relatives in Durham where the boys spent time growing up.

Lonnie thought he had left farming behind when he started to work for the railroad, but he hadn't counted on his ambitious sons. "Dad worked on the railroad and we worked on the farm," said George. "We had several cows. We'd milk those cows and had a lot of milk. So I started selling some milk to the people in south Guilford, our neighbors. I'd sell them a gallon of milk and they'd pay me on Saturday. Pretty soon I told Dad what I was doing and he said that sounded pretty good. He got to thinking about a dairy and selling milk and butter in town.

"I reckon it was about 1918, 1920, somewhere along in there. We gradually built up until we had 55 head of cows and we milked them all by hand. I imagine that helped our wrists a whole lot. All that milking helped our grip. We all had pretty good wrists with the bat. We had to saw wood, chop wood, split wood and plow with mules."

Wes also recalled his boyhood fondly, especially the baseball. "But more than anything else we raised ballplayers on that farm," he said. "We'd go out into the fields after harvest time and hit for hours. Just hit an old beat-up nickel ball far as it'd go and chase it down and throw it around. Saturday and Sunday were our big days, of course. That's when we play team ball, around the countryside here."[3]

All seven of the brothers played baseball at Guilford High School, the older four boys being together on the 1918 squad. While little documentation survives of their high school play, the five older brothers performed regularly in the Guilford County League, a weekend circuit which received good coverage in the Greensboro papers of the 1920s. Rufus Smith, Dave

The 1918 Guilford High School baseball squad. Pete Ferrell sits at the center of the bottom row. Slats Ferrell is standing second from left. Rick Ferrell is the small boy in the center of the photograph (James R. "Little Rick" Ferrell).

Harris and Dave Barbee, local contemporaries of the brothers, also played in the County League before reaching the majors.

First names were not always included in the County League games, so keeping track of the brothers is a little confusing. The Greensboro *Daily Record* of July 30, 1924, in reporting a Greensboro All-Star team loss to Siler City, described the Greensboro pitcher (apparently Wes) as, "one of the rather numerous Ferrells, this one the hurler for the Guilford highs."

County League game accounts usually showed Slats at first base, Pete at third or shortstop and Rick catching. George could and did play any position and Wes was just as likely to show up in the outfield or at second base as he was on the pitcher's mound.

The County League was made up of clubs representing Guilford County townships. The Glenwood team, with Rick catching and Wes pitching them to a 2–1 victory in the championship game, won the 1921 pennant. Rick's Pomona team lost out to George's Buffalo squad for the 1922 title. Slats, Pete, George and Wes copped the 1924 flag for Glenwood and Slats, George and Wes played together for Jamestown in 1925. Slats and Wes won another championship for Glenwood in 1926 and finally Slats, going it alone after his brothers had turned pro, played on the Revolution pennant winner in 1927.

Many County League games were played at Cone Mills Park in Greensboro.[4] The Cones were a wealthy, civic-minded, Greensboro family and the ball field was initially built as a recreational device for the company mill workers. Professional games had been played at Cone Mills Park as early as 1902, and the Greensboro Piedmont League clubs called it home until moving to War Memorial Stadium in 1930.

George's son — George Wesley Ferrell — himself a minor-league outfielder in the 1950s, recalls how his father and uncles first became enamored with baseball at Cone Park. "Slats would take his brothers across town to the Cone Mills Park to watch the games. They had to walk to the park which was eight miles from their home. This is where they really got their desire to play. One day Slats found a season's pass lying on the street. He used the ticket and went inside. He then put the ticket in a cigar box and threw it over the fence behind the bleachers and then the next brother would use the ticket to get in. This one ticket and box was used until all of his brothers got into see the game."

"We were just like any other bunch of kids, I reckon," said the elder George Ferrell in a 1936 interview, "excepting that we made up our minds early that we all were going to make professional ball players. We talked, slept and ate baseball. And I can't remember when there wasn't a lot of balls and bats laying around the house."[5]

George discussed his two older brothers in the same interview. "Slats," he said, "was one of the best natural hitters I ever saw. But he got married and decided to settle down on the farm. He never played professional ball, but might have done pretty well with it. Pete played in the county leagues and semipro. I thought he might get somewhere, too, for he could really play short. But he gave it up before he ever got a tryout."[6]

The Greensboro *Daily News* published a story about Pete shortly after World War Two. "They use to say Pete Ferrell was the best baseball player in the fabulous Ferrell family 20 or 25 years ago, but one of the saddest memories Pete has today is that he didn't take time out to prove it. Now 46, living at Guilford College, Pete reflects back and says, 'My highest ambition in life was to become an outstanding baseball player, but things just didn't work out for me that way. I just stayed around the farm and helped my father instead of following up on my ability.'"[7]

Pete's son — James Richard Ferrell — was also a catcher and known to family and neighbors as "Little Rick" to distinguish him from his famous uncle. "I know less about my dad," recalls Little Rick, "than Rick, Wes, George, Marvin, Slats and Ewell. He seemed to work all the time, mostly nights. Guess with five children he had to. Always heard he was the best player of the bunch. Also told he first caught, but Rick came along and wanted to catch, so my dad turned it over to Rick and moved to third base. He married in 1922 and lived on the farm several years. He moved into Greensboro and started to work on the railroad, then for Clegg Baking Company and later Duke Power Company. He did not have the opportunity to play, having to stay on the farm and work. Then came the Depression. He would have been a great player but he had no chance to play."

George was the first brother to take his game to a higher level, playing at Guilford College for two years where he made the baseball squad in 1922 as a pitcher. Rick appeared in the Guilford College lineup beginning in 1924 and would be the team's catcher for three seasons before turning pro. Neither brother received a degree but both are in the Guilford College Athletics Hall of Fame, Rick being elected with Ernie Shore in the inaugural class of 1970 and George ten years later in 1980.

George and Rick boxed semiprofessionally while in college to earn money, Rick fighting under the alias "Kid Corbett." He mentioned his boxing career in various interviews, citing his record as 18–1 and indicating he made $35–$50 per fight.[8] His fighting weight was 135 pounds and he was once set to face W. L. "Young" Stribling, the Georgia professional who fought and lost a world heavyweight fight to Max Schmeling in 1931, but the contest was canceled at the last minute.

The 1926 Guilford High School basketball squad. Wes Ferrell sits front and center, holding basketball (Wes Ferrell, Jr.).

Bob Doak, the Guilford College baseball coach, predicted in 1925 that both Rick and his battery-mate, a left-handed pitcher named Rufus Smith, would soon be drawing the attention of professional scouts.[9] Rufus "Shirt" Smith was the son of Guilford County deputy sheriff Lucian Smith, a local legend who led the Southern Association in pitching while with New Orleans in 1896.

Rick and Shirt spent the summers of 1924 and 1925 playing semipro in South Carolina. When the team needed players, Rick convinced the manager to take a look at his brother. "Rick got me a job in Newberry, South Carolina, in 1925 as an outfielder," recalled George many years later. "I'd been pitching all the time. They sent for me to come down. I made the ball club, in the outfield."[10]

George, Rick and Wes had also established themselves as skillful basketball players. George and Rick were forwards for Guilford College and Wes was a dominant center for the high school team. He scored 13 points in Guilford's 28–9 win over Winston-Salem on January 15, 13 points in a

25–19 win against Bessemer on February 27, and 18 points in a 25–18 win against Leaksville on March 1. Guilford claimed the high school championship of western North Carolina when Wes scored 12 points in an 18–12 win against Chandler High School on March 6, 1925. The following day, Wes led the tiny Guilford squad to the North Carolina state high school basketball championship game in Chapel Hill. Durham beat Guilford, 17–15. Wes scored nine points.

* * *

Charlie Carroll managed the Piedmont League's Greensboro Patriots from 1920 through 1924 and then the Winston-Salem squad in 1925. One of his first moves upon being named to manage the Monroe, Louisiana, club in the Cotton States League in 1926 was to sign George Ferrell to a contract. Carroll had given George a tryout with Greensboro in 1924 but George's season was derailed before he was officially a team member when he collided with the club's catcher, "Railroad" Ray, and sustained a broken jaw.

The first mention of the Ferrell name in *The Sporting News* was in the Cotton States gossip column in the April 1, 1926 issue. "Farrell (sic) has been hitting and looks to be a finished fielder. In all probability he will draw the left field assignment." George's 35 doubles and 20 homers led the league and his .355 average placed him third. In late August, he was sold to Memphis in the Southern Association.

* * *

Shirt Smith was the captain of the 1926 Guilford College basketball team that competed against such fast company as Wake Forest, Davidson and North Carolina State. Rick Ferrell averaged 7.5 points per game; scoring 18 points in a 35–29 win over the University of Richmond on February 13.

Rick opened his 1926 college baseball season by doubling in the only run that Shirt Smith would need as Smith fanned 15 batters and shut out the U.S. Marine Corps team from Quantico, Virginia, 1–0, on March 22 at Cone Mills Park.

The Quantico coach was Tom Keady, a Dartmouth graduate who had played minor league baseball for Jesse Burkett at Worcester, Massachusetts, in the New England League fifteen years earlier. A noted college football coach, Keady also served as a Boston Red Sox scout and immediately wired the Boston club recommending that they sign both Ferrell and Smith.[11]

The local papers reported that a number of major league teams were following the progress of the Ferrell and Smith battery. The Detroit Tigers,

The 1924 Guilford College baseball team. Rick Ferrell is sitting third from left in the bottom row. Shirt Smith, who played for the Detroit Tigers in 1927, is standing in the top row, second from right (Guilford College).

Philadelphia Athletics, Washington Nationals and New York Yankees were mentioned as interested parties. Scouts Mike Drennan, Eddie Herr and Joe Engel were hot after Smith, but Shirt was listening to his father's advice to finish his college degree first.

The Guilford College Quakers finished their season in late May. Ferrell hit .360 (27 for 75), second best on the team, from the cleanup spot.[12] Rick announced on May 22 that he would forgo his senior year at Guilford and sign with the Detroit Tigers. He expressed his disappointment at not being able to fulfill his responsibility as captain-elect of the upcoming season's basketball team. He thanked all involved with his development at the college, especially Coach Doak. Speculation was that Ty Cobb would start Rick off with one of the Virginia League teams.

Rick made his professional debut on May 24 for the Kinston Eagles in the Virginia League. Kinston was in North Carolina and with a population of less than 10,000 was the smallest city in the country to host a Class B baseball team.[13] Rick hit .266 in 64 games, missing the entire month of July with an apparent injury. At the end of the Virginia League schedule, Rick advanced to the Columbus team in the American Association, where he appeared in five games before season's end.

* * *

Wes' 1926 season began on the basketball court, leading Guilford high school to the final four in the twelfth annual North Carolina State High School Basketball Championship Tournament before losing to Winston-Salem in the semis on March 2.

The local papers only reported one of Wes' high school baseball games but 19 of his contests for Glenwood in the County League were published. In addition to his 11–3 record as a pitcher, Wes, who batted cleanup, hit .355 with seven home runs. Slats Ferrell, hitting third in the order, stroked .405 with 8 doubles and two home runs. After Wes tossed a no-hitter against the Colfax team on June 12 in which he fanned 14 batters, the Greensboro *Daily News* called him "one of the smartest and most effective hurlers in North Carolina amateur baseball circles."[14]

After losing the opener of a three-game playoff series for the Greensboro City League title in late August, the Vick Chemical Company brought in Wes to face the North Carolina Public Service company team in game two. Ferrell fanned 16 in a 6–1 win and the only batter to do any damage was the leadoff hitter, a third baseman named Allen Jessup who went three for four. Three days later Wes won again, 7–1, for the championship, fanning 12 and sending Jessup back to the bench on strikes four times. Constantly making adjustments to batters would be an essential part of Ferrell's pitching makeup.

Glenwood faced Colfax in the County League finals. Wes won 3–1 on September 4 and 12–1 eight days later. Glenwood's manager — W. G. Harrell — issued a game challenge to any amateur team within a 75-mile radius of Greensboro. On September 18, the Travola Manufacturing company team responded and so did Ferrell, defeating George Euliss, who had won 17 games in the Piedmont League in 1924, 3–2. Wes' final baseball game in 1926 came on October 2 when he pitched Glenwood to a 1–0 victory over an all-star team made up of other Guilford County League players. Dave Barbee and Dave Harris, both having already played in the major leagues, were home in time to enter the game. Slats Ferrell drove in the only run his little brother required with a first-inning double.

* * *

The Ferrell Brothers began 1927 on the basketball court. Marvin Ferrell had taken Wes' spot on the Guilford high school team. Rick, George and Wes played on an independent team called the Guilford All-Stars. Wes was also playing for the Oak Ridge Institute.

The Oak Ridge Military Academy — as it is known today — was established in 1852. It is located about 15 miles northwest of Greensboro. Wes attended Oak Ridge for the school season of 1926-1927 when it was a college preparatory school known as the Oak Ridge Institute. A few years after Wes attended, the name was changed to the Oak Ridge Military Institution and eventually two years of junior college were added. Currently the school provides education only through the high school level. Marvin Ferrell was a student at Oak Ridge in 1929-1930.

The Oak Ridge basketball team ran up a 20–3 record that season before losing in the second round of the Southern Preparatory School Tournament at Washington and Lee University in Lexington, Virginia, on March 5. Oak Ridge's schedule consisted of games against other prep schools and college freshman teams. Wes, a forward/center, scored 22 points in a 50–21 win over Benedictine College on March 3 and 14 points in a 41–40 victory over North Carolina State on March 22.

The Oak Ridge baseball squad started practicing in March and Wes was listed as an outfielder. John White was the team captain and pitching ace for Oak Ridge.[15] He had an overpowering fastball but poor control. Cleveland Indians' scout Bill Rapp, who signed both White and Ferrell to contracts, swore that White was faster than Lefty Grove.[16]

Wes played right field and batted fourth as White defeated the Virginia Military Institute on March 26, 10–4, allowing all four runs on walks. On April 13, Wes pitched against Duke University's freshman squad, whose shortstop and cleanup hitter was Bill Werber, losing 4–3, while fanning 10. White struck out 17 batters on April 22 as Oak Ridge won the North Carolina prep school championship. On May 5, White again faced the Virginia Military Institute, this time sitting down 20 without contact.

Coach Earl Holt ran a strong baseball program at Oak Ridge and sent a number of players to the major leagues. Pitcher Jakie May played 14 seasons. Catchers Al Evans and Ray Hayworth lasted 12 and 15 years respectively. Another catcher, Hayworth's brother Myron, plus pitchers Ben Shields, Chubby Dean and Maxie Wilson were Oak Ridge alumni, as was first baseman Dick Burrus. Wilson, who fanned 23 and 25 batters in Oak Ridge games, played for the American Baseball Congress team in England during the summer of 1937.[17] E. Frank Mayberry, a much-beloved mathematics instructor at Oak Ridge who died in a 1929 auto accident at age 40, pitched nearly 20 years of minor league baseball.[18]

The Hayworth Brothers were from nearby High Point and frequently crossed paths with the Ferrells. Ray Hayworth graduated from Oak Ridge in 1924 and, like Rick Ferrell, signed his first contract with the Detroit Tigers. Hayworth was usually one step ahead of Rick on the climb to the major leagues. When Hayworth was called up from Columbus to Detroit late in the 1926 season, Rick took his spot on the Columbus roster. There were four Hayworth brothers who played professional baseball and all were catchers.[19]

Bill Rapp had been a Cleveland scout since 1916 and before that a catcher for eight minor league seasons. Working out of Washington, D.C., he covered the southern states for the Tribe. Rapp and Holt were life-long friends and Holt invited the scout to Oak Ridge to look White over.

"White is the man you want," Holt told the scout. "Ferrell is a fine ball player, but he looks better in the outfield than he does as a pitcher. You'll make no mistake on White." Rapp, though, was immediately taken with Wes' size, his fastball and his easy pitching motion. Ferrell told Rapp that he did not intend to play professional baseball, saying instead that he hoped to become a doctor. He planned on playing semi-pro ball to earn money to pay for his education.[20]

* * *

Wes spent the summer playing baseball in the Blackstone Valley League for the East Douglas, Massachusetts team. The Blackstone River Valley is approximately 50 miles long and runs from Worcester, Massachusetts to Pawtucket, Rhode Island. America's first mechanized factory was established along the Blackstone River in Pawtucket in the late 1700s and over the next century a number of textile mills and factories— with power generated from the dammed river — had sprung up among the area towns.

The Blackstone Valley League of the 1920s and 1930s was one of the strongest semiprofessional baseball leagues in the country. It would be comparable to today's Cape Cod League with one exception; professional players were eligible to play. The great Holy Cross baseball teams of the 1920s often outdrew both Boston major league teams. With Brown University in Providence, Rhode Island, sitting at one end of the Valley and Holy Cross at the other — and with professional baseball banned in Massachusetts on Sundays in the 1920s— the region's best baseball was frequently found in the Blackstone Valley League. The East Douglas team was its perennial kingpin.

Walter E. Schuster loved baseball. When he died in 1932 he was the president or treasurer of two banks and four woolen mills. He had been involved in local and Massachusetts state politics and was among the richest men in the Blackstone Valley. Schuster had supported the East Douglas baseball team for 30 years, employing professional scouts who directed a steady stream of the best amateur, college and professional players to East Douglas.

"Employees of three woolen mills at East Douglas and Millbury, Massachusetts, all owned by Schuster & Hayward Company, played ball on a company field, but their baseball interest centered on a pro team that Walter E. Schuster hired to represent the company," wrote historian Dr. Harold Seymour. "Its games, most of them played at home in the company park at East Douglas, began at 5:15 P.M., and many workers who watched had supper at the park. Attendance at these games in 1928 averaged 4,300 paid admissions, which covered part of Schuster's operating costs. For important games, Schuster added a player for the minors or majors. Once Schuster guaranteed Lefty Grove $300 plus $10 for every batter Grove struck out. He made $490 on the deal, so he must have fanned nineteen men!"[21]

The Grove game occurred in October 1927 and another version had Schuster paying Grove $500 plus $10 per strikeout for a total of $690. The game was for the "semi-pro championship of central Massachusetts" and both lineups consisted of professional players. Danny MacFayden pitched and lost the 4–0 game for the opposing Clinton team. "I am kind of sore that McFayden (sic) couldn't have held our side scoreless, too, so that the game might have gone into fifteen or sixteen innings," said Grove, thinking of the ringing cash register every time he punched out a batter.[22]

Winfield Schuster, Walter's son and heir, earned an MBA from Harvard in 1930 and an undergraduate degree from Brown University in 1928 where he had captained the baseball team under Coach Jean Dubuc. A veteran of nine big league seasons, Dubuc also guided the East Douglas team for which Winfield Schuster played third base. The younger Schuster was involved in Massachusetts politics, owned a daily newspaper in Worcester and backed a minor league hockey team operated by Dubuc in the 1930s.

Throughout the 1930s and well into the '40s, major league teams frequently played exhibition games in East Douglas. When Ted Williams wrecked his car driving to a Red Sox game in East Douglas in 1946, Schuster simply bought him a new one. For good measure he bought one for Joe Cronin as well. Schuster, just before the arrival of Tom Yawkey, had an interest in buying the Red Sox.

"Winfield A. Schuster, 26-year-old millionaire of East Douglas, Mass.," wrote *The Sporting News* in 1932, "was quoted last week as saying he would like to take control of the Boston Red Sox with a group of other men, but that the price asked by Bob Quinn was too high. He said Quinn was asking $1,200,000 for the club, not including the Fenway Park property. At about the same time Quinn denied any negotiations had been started although tacitly admitting he would like to get out. 'I know nothing about Schuster's plans,' he said, 'although his father, the late Walter E. Schuster, at one time was considered as a possible purchaser.'"[23]

So how exactly did Wes Ferrell find his way from a North Carolina dairy farm to Massachusetts? Well, apparently Dubuc was employing ringers on his Brown baseball team, and one in particular was Shirt Smith, Rick Ferrell's old battery-mate at Guilford College.[24] "After high school," recalled Wes," I went to a military school in Oak Ridge, not far from home. I was playing ball, too, of course, and looking pretty good. What happened was, some college boy down here saw me pitch and told me I ought to go up to East Douglas, Massachusetts, and pitch for that club in the Blackstone Valley League. Semipro ball. So I did that. I was getting $300 a month, plus free lodging and free food. That was in the summer of 1927."[25]

Shirt Smith played with Wes on the East Douglas squad in 1927 and Dubuc employed five pitchers who had or would have major league experience in Ferrell, Smith, Tim McNamara, Bots Nekola and Haskell Billings. Even the club's batboy, Henry Coppola, eventually pitched in the big leagues. Other major league players such as Irving "Bump" Hadley, Gene Desautels and Hank Greenberg played for East Douglas around that time.

Only a handful of Ferrell's games for East Douglas were located. He reported his pitching record as 7–1 and many years later recalled that he had pitched against Satchel Paige while with East Douglas. He also played right field and first base. Billings, who played on the same high school baseball team in Sommerville, Massachusetts, that produced MacFayden and Shanty Hogan — and who pitched for Dubuc at Brown University — was the team's ace. In addition to playing for East Douglas in 1927, Billings also pitched for the Falmouth team in the Cape Cod League.

Dubuc was also working as a scout for the Detroit Tigers and East Douglas was essentially a de facto Detroit minor league squad. Several years later Dubuc tried to steer Greenberg away from other New York area scouts by hiding him in East Douglas. Greenberg, in his autobiography, recalled the East Douglas lineup being so strong that he had trouble cracking it.[26] The Tigers soon signed Billings and Smith to contracts. Billings debuted with a 6–2 win over the Red Sox on August 17 and Smith's only major league appearance came at the end of the season.

Frank Shaughnessy, later the president of the International League and the man who introduced the minor league playoff system — the "Shaughnessy Playoffs"— scouted the college and industrial teams of New England for Detroit in the late '20s.

"I was doing my turn around the New England colleges in the spring of 1927 when I spotted a big fellow who could fire the ball, on a mill team near Providence," recalled Shaughnessy in 1960. "His name was Wes Ferrell. As Detroit was coming into Boston to play the Red Sox in a few days,

I wired [Frank] Navin that I would deliver Ferrell in Fenway Park, so that George Moriarty, the manager, could look him over.

"When I got to Fenway, Moriarty asked me to put on a uniform and sit on the bench with him. Ferrell worked out and Moriarty liked him. I told Wes to dress and wait in the clubhouse for me, and after the game we would go to the hotel and sign a contract.

"During the game, a whale of an argument broke out between Marty McManus, third baseman, and Moriarty. Moriarty took him out and fined him $500. The argument was even hotter in the clubhouse after the game. When I got Ferrell out of there, he apologized to me, but insisted he simply would not play for Detroit. Apparently the boy hadn't cared for the argument. I couldn't do a thing about it."[27]

When Cleveland scout Charlie Hickman approached Wes in East Douglas, the youngster told him that he had given his word that if he signed it would be with Bill Rapp. Hickman informed Cleveland and Rapp then inked Wes to a contract.

Wes spent the last two months of the 1927 season with Cleveland. His only appearance was on September 9, when he pitched the last inning of a 6–1 loss to the Red Sox at Fenway Park.

"We always said that we were going to make baseball players of ourselves," Wes told historian Donald Honig. "That was what we wanted to do. It was just a dream back then, of course, but it turned out to come true. And it happened so doggone fast, too. It seemed that one day I was thinking about my boyhood hero, Babe Ruth, and then almost overnight I was standing on the mound in Cleveland trying to strike him out. Overnight isn't far from the fact either. Spring of '27 I was still living on the farm, and in the fall I pitched a few innings for Cleveland."[28]

While Wes reached the major leagues at age 19 without having spent any time in the minors, Rick and George were taking the more conventional route. George hit .292 in 120 games playing for Clyde Milan at Memphis in the Southern Association, touching former Cleveland Indians star Ray Caldwell for an opening day home run. Rick hit .249 in 345 at-bats for Columbus in the American Association where he was the team's starting catcher.

The Ferrell Brothers were on their way.

◆ 3 ◆

The Free Agent

Rick Ferrell and Carl Hubbell were in the Detroit Tigers' spring training camp in 1928. George Moriarty, having let Wes slip through his fingers the previous summer, now repeated the blunder with Hubbell. Not yet famous as "The Meal Ticket," Hubbell was left behind with the Beaumont club in the Texas League where later in the season he was purchased by the New York Giants. Imagine a Detroit rotation led by Hubbell and Wes Ferrell?

Detroit sent Rick Ferrell back to Columbus in early April. This time, however, they apparently did not send him on option. Instead they sold, or at least claimed to have sold the catcher's contract outright to Columbus.[1]

Rick's manager at Columbus was Nemo Leibold, a 13-year big league veteran who had played in four different World Series. Leibold stressed plate discipline, encouraging his batters to take as many pitches as possible.[2] Rick drew 44 walks and struck out just four times in close to 400 plate appearances, establishing a pattern that he would show throughout his career. Ferrell, as former Red Sox pitcher Charlie Wagner echoed in 2002, was "a tough out."

Rick hit .333, tenth best in the American Association.[3] Expected to miss a month after a spike wound to his hand on May 8, Rick was back in the lineup just 12 days later. He was especially hot in May and June, hitting .402 (51 for 127) with 14 doubles, two triples and a pair of homers. He slowed down in mid-summer, hitting just .223 in July and August, but finished up nicely by poking .431 in September.

Ferrell was expecting a late-season call-up to either Detroit, the club he originally signed with, or the Cincinnati Reds, the parent club of the Columbus Senators. "I took a bus on an off day to see (Detroit owner) Frank Navin and asked what kind of plans he had for me," said Rick. "He told me that I should continue to have a good year, he'd bring me up at

Rick Ferrell signed with St. Louis after being declared a free agent by Judge Landis (George W. Ferrell).

the end of the season. It was just another promise, so I next paid a visit to Cincinnati, the parent club of Columbus. Again, only promises."⁴ His suspicions aroused when Cincinnati called up catcher Hugh McMullen from Minneapolis, Ferrell traveled to Chicago to see Commissioner Kenesaw Mountain Landis after the season closed. "I waited around for a day or two and finally got to see the commissioner's assistant, Leslie O'Connor. He heard my story, and told me to put it in writing."⁵

Cincinnati had purchased the Columbus club in February 1927. At the time Columbus has 34 players under contract who immediately became property of the Reds. The Senators had finished last in 1927 and seventh in 1928 and the only significant players on the roster were Ferrell and "Jersey Joe" Stripp. Cincinnati called up Stripp at the end of June 1928 when he was thumping American Association pitchers to the tune of .419.

"Of course, Cincinnati has said nothing at all about taking Ferrell," noted an unidentified newspaper clipping from a Ferrell family scrapbook, " but then they said nothing about annexing Mr. Stripp until the 'deal' was actually made. Ferrell is without a doubt the possessor of one of the greatest throwing arms in the history of the American Association. He catches runners at second base without an apparent effort and seems to have more enthusiasm in his work than at any other time since joining the Senators....

"Class is written all over him and when all is said and done it might safely be said that he is a better major league prospect than even Joe Stripp. It's laughable the way he picks runners off as they attempt to steal bases."⁶

The reason that Cincinnati couldn't call Rick up from Columbus was simple, they didn't own his contract. "Ferrell didn't belong to Columbus," wrote *The Sporting News*. "The previous management of the Senators had entered into some sort of cover-up arrangement regarding this promising young catcher and he got wind of it not long ago. He took his case to Judge Landis and the commissioner made him a free agent last week, thereby causing many a groan in Red offices."⁷

Cincinnati manager Jack Hendricks, lamenting the loss of Ferrell, estimated Rick's value at approximately $50,000. *The Sporting News* thought that high and guessed that Rick might draw a bid of $10,000. Landis ruled that Detroit, Cincinnati and Columbus were barred from bidding, but Rick was free to negotiate with any other team in professional baseball. The Yankees, Red Sox, Browns, White Sox, Pirates, Giants and Washington Nationals were all reportedly interested.

The Ferrell Brothers all understood the business end of baseball and none of them ever underestimated their worth. Rick quickly turned down an $18,000 offer from the Red Sox. He wired John McGraw, proposing a

$25,000 deal. Earlier in the season McGraw had attempted to secure Rick from Columbus, claiming that Ferrell had spent time with Detroit in May 1928 and was thus eligible for drafting. Landis investigated this and found McGraw's contention held merit. Obviously Rick did not appear in any American League games for Detroit, but the timing of McGraw's claim did correspond with his "spike wound."[8]

The St. Louis Browns topped the other offers and Rick signed a three-year contract worth $25,000 in addition to a $20,000 signing bonus.[9] *The Sporting News* praised Landis' decision in an editorial on November 22, citing the irony of Ferrell signing with St. Louis, for the previous season Landis had declared a catcher named Thompson a free agent when the Browns and Milwaukee had conspired in a similar fashion.

Browns' business manager Bill Friel made the trip to Greensboro with Rick's bonus check. Fifteen years later Ferrell found out that Friel was authorized to go as high as $35,000 if Rick proved stubborn. "I thought I was doing the smart thing to sign with the Browns," Rick said. "They had just finished third in 1928, and they had a couple of old-timers, Steve O'Neill and Wally Schang, catching. I figured I could step right in and take over the catching job."[10]

* * *

George Ferrell played for Doc Prothro at Memphis in 1928. He hit well in games against major league teams in the spring but lost his starting job to Johnny Frederick; attributing his lack of playing time to a beaning in 1928 and a foot injury sustained late in the 1927 season that robbed him of his foot speed.[11] "Tagged the bag with the wrong foot," said Ferrell. "Twisted my ankle and instep and tore it up. I was in Atlanta. This club owner, Tom Watkins, he wanted to get me back in the lineup too quickly. This doctor had one of those instep braces in there. He had it made out of steel and they put it in my baseball shoe and made me play."

The Southern Association was a hitting league in 1928. The Memphis team batting average was .315 and Prothro fielded a strong outfield. Frederick hit .359 with 221 hits, and his 52 doubles for the Brooklyn Dodgers the next season remains the major league rookie record. Left fielder Danny Taylor hit .374 and eventually spent nine years in the majors. Center fielder Tex Jeanes, who hit .373 in 120 games, wandered the minor leagues after debuting for the Cleveland Indians in 1921. He had brief major league stops with Washington and the New York Giants but is basically remembered for two things; he was Tris Speaker's nephew,[12] and he had trouble finding roommates because he always kept pet snakes in his room.[13]

George hit .292 in 69 games and played wherever needed; third base, catcher, pinch-hitter, and all three outfield spots. He had nine extra-base hits in a 12-game span in July while subbing for an injured Jeanes.

* * *

Wes reported to the Indians' spring training camp in New Orleans on February 22. The 18-year-old Mel Harder and Ferrell's former Oak Ridge teammate, John White, were also on the squad. Roger Peckinpaugh was the new Cleveland manager in 1928. "Peck" had grown up in Cleveland and was a well-respected baseball figure, with seventeen big league seasons and an American League Most Valuable Player Award to his credit. This was his first managerial post except for a short stint as interim manager of the New York Yankees in 1914.

One of Peck's coaches was Grover Hartley, a 39-year-old catcher and baseball lifer who began his professional career in 1910. Hartley played for John McGraw on two different occasions and later worked in a coaching capacity under Rogers Hornsby and Mel Ott. He often referred to Christy Mathewson and Eddie Plank — hurlers he had handled — as the greatest right-handed and left-handed pitchers of all time.

Wes frequently drew comparisons to Christy Mathewson and Hartley appears to have been the first to make that observation. "He looks more like Matty than any young pitcher I ever saw," said Hartley. "He's got the same simple easy motion Matty had. He just goes up like this and down like this and lets the ball go without any effort, but when he lets it go it's got plenty on it. He's a big swell-looking kid, and the way he's put together he couldn't be anything but a pitcher. They turned him over to me, so's that I could teach him something about pitching, but nobody has to teach him much. He was born with it, I guess, just like most really good pitchers are. Now and then, of course, I have to teach him something, but I have to tell it to him only once."[14]

Ferrell's smoothness on the hill was not visible just to Hartley. "The opinion around this camp is that a year in fairly fast company will make the tall southerner about as formidable a pitcher as the club owns," wrote Gordon Cobbledick in the Cleveland *Plain Dealer* on March 22.

Wes made the opening day roster but Billy Evans, Cleveland's general manager, soon farmed him to Terre Haute in the Three-I League where he debuted in Peoria on May 7 and finished the season as the circuit's top winner with a 20–8 record. He lost two 1–0 games, one to Paul Derringer on the Fourth of July, and clouted a pinch-hit home run in the ninth inning on June 23. Decatur took the postseason series from Terre Haute (4–1 with one tie) and Ferrell, though his team's leading batter with three hits, lost the opening game 4–3 in 10 innings on September 12. Decatur won the second contest and was leading 5–2 in bottom of the ninth inning in game three before Wes saved the day (the game ended as a tie) with a pinch-hit triple plating two runs. He won 8–1 on September 16, fanning nine batters, to notch Terre Haute's only win in the series.

Cleveland, whose anemic lineup was held to a single run or less ten times in September, went 4–20 to end 1928 in seventh place. Wes started two games after his recall from Terre Haute. On September 28 he lost a 1–0 game to the Red Sox in which he allowed just five hits. The Tribe managed six hits and the only one for extra bases was Ferrell's three-bagger. "He slipped just once," wrote Cobbledick of Ferrell, "and that when he was pitching to (George) Loepp, the rookie leadoff man of the Red Sox, in the first inning. Loepp, who hasn't shown himself to be that kind of a hitter, slapped one over George Gerken's head in left field for three bases and scored the only run of the game on an infield out."[15]

◆ 4 ◆

1929 — The Prodigy

Wes Ferrell arrived at the Indians' training camp in New Orleans in 1929 throwing every pitch at top speed. The result was a sore arm that limited him to just two spring games. That was enough for Peckinpaugh who said, "Ferrell is another I'm counting on. He's as good looking a youngster as I've seen in a long time."[1]

All doubts — if Peck had any — disappeared after an exhibition game with the Cincinnati Reds on April 13. Ferrell entered the game with one out and one on in the sixth after the Reds had pounded Ken Holloway for thirteen hits and six runs in five innings. Wes allowed a hit to the first man he faced but set Cincinnati down in order in the seventh, eighth and ninth innings. Gordon Cobbledick suggested that Ferrell was, "as completely baffling as anyone the National Leaguers are likely to face all summer."[2]

No one expected much from the Indians, who were projected to finish anywhere from fourth to seventh place. The Yankees were the odds-on-favorite to win the pennant and Detroit had the best hitting in the league. The Tigers, along with the Athletics and Yankees, were the only clubs to manage 100 homers. Cleveland hit 62 homers, Washington 48, St. Louis 46 and Chicago 37. The last-place Red Sox managed just 28 home runs, a total that was fewer than Babe Ruth, Lou Gehrig, Al Simmons and Jimmy Foxx hit as individuals.

Wes debuted in the season's second game against the Tigers at Cleveland's Dunn Field.[3] Detroit pounded out 18 hits and 15 runs. Peck's starter gave up five hits and five runs and didn't survive the second inning, and Cleveland's third pitcher, who came in after Wes was pinch-hit for, gave up ten hits and eight runs in three innings. Wes allowed a hit in the second inning and two more in the third, but Detroit couldn't touch him in the fourth, fifth or sixth. "The big kid has a terrific fast ball and a fine curve, together with excellent control," wrote Cobbledick. "Moreover, he uses his head while he's out there in the box and there isn't much more than that a pitcher needs."[4]

Many years later Wes recalled how these games made an impression on Peckinpaugh. He also remembered how nervous he was. "We were playing Detroit and our starter got in trouble. They waved me into the bull pen to warm up, and I'll never forget how scared I was. My pitching was just automatic. I hardly knew I was throwing the ball, and all I can remember is the catcher telling me to throw faster, faster, faster. Then they waved me into the game. I'll never know how I got to the mound, everybody yelling like mad. I just floated in. I

Wes Ferrell in his early Cleveland days. He was immediately compared to Christy Mathewson (Gwenlo Ferrell Gore).

didn't give them a hit for two or three innings—I can't remember how long exactly—and from that day on I was made."

Wes picked up two quick wins in relief, working the last two innings against Detroit on April 19 for his first career victory—allowing just an infield single and an unearned run—and then on April 23, where he closed the game with two scoreless innings against Chicago.

His first start came in Detroit on April 26. "Well," said Peckinpaugh just before the game, "We'll get one game out of this series. Ferrell is going to pitch today."[5] Peck's conviction in the youngster, who won 11–5, had not escaped Cobbledick. "The performance the youngster gave," he wrote, "cannot be measured by the number of hits he allowed, which was twelve. It was the way he worked on the Detroit sluggers with men on the bases that made his pitching stand out as the best the Indians have enjoyed this season."[6] Wes had two hits in the game and drove in a run. Detroit's Dale Alexander hit two triples early in the game. When he came to bat in the eighth, Wes fed him two wide ones before pumping three straight fastballs across the plate. Alexander never took the bat off his shoulder.

Ferrell's next start came against Alvin Crowder and the first-place St. Louis Browns on May 1 and he only allowed one hit over the first three innings. After a 30-minute rain delay St. Louis tagged him for a run in the fourth and three more in the fifth. The final was a 4–3 win for Crowder.

Wes allowed five earned runs in less than five innings in a 5–4 loss to the Red Sox on May 7 and the *Plain Dealer* observed that "Ferrell, after looking unbeatable for two innings, was battered from the box in the fifth. A couple of cheap hits had fallen just out of the reach of Wes' fielders, and the inexperienced hurler came unraveled."

An inning of relief work against the Philadelphia Athletics on May 11 gave Wes his first opportunity to see Lefty Grove in action. Like virtually everyone else who faced Grove, Ferrell referred to him as the greatest, as well as the fastest pitcher he ever saw. The Philly lefty mowed down batters for seven innings but the Tribe staged an eighth inning rally. Lew Fonseca, after three straight hits, beat out a bunt only to be called out for running outside the basepath. When Peck raced out to argue and was tossed from the game, pop bottles immediately started to fly from the stands. One hit umpire Red Ormsby, knocking him out cold, and Cleveland GM Billy Evans had to come onto the field to quiet the crowd so the game could continue. Wes came on to pitch the top of the ninth and fanned two batters. Cleveland started the home ninth with two more hits to knock out Grove. They scored another run but left the bases loaded when Glenn Myatt, batting for Wes, popped out to end the game.

Ferrell worked twice more in May, both times against St. Louis and neither time effectively. He pitched five innings of middle relief on May 17, allowing only two runs but walking six, and absorbed a 7–6 loss. In his start on May 23 he was relieved in the fourth inning after allowing 10 hits and all seven runs in a 7–5 defeat.

Peckinpaugh moved Wes back to the bullpen for three weeks. The hitters had adjusted to Ferrell and now he would have to respond in kind.

Cleveland had jumped out to an 8–0 lead at Yankee Stadium on June 6 but Huggins' crew roared back to score seven times. Wes was called into the game in the ninth, with runners on first and third and no outs, to preserve a 9–7 lead. Lou Gehrig watched as the young man looked wild taking his warmup tosses. The first two pitches were wide and called balls. Wes then fired across a knee-high fastball for a called strike. Next came two curves. Gehrig flailed wildly and missed the first one. Wes froze him with the second and the Iron Horse could do nothing but watch helplessly as it broke over the plate for strike three. He heaved away his bat in disgust on his way back to the bench. Ben Paschal ended the game by hitting into a double play.

"The Yankees," reported *The Sporting News*, "kept on plugging until they had a chance to win in the last inning. But Leader Peckinpaugh hurried young Ferrell to the rifle pit and the latter covered himself with glory by striking out the mighty Gehrig with a wide curve ball."[7]

Wes pitched five innings of scoreless, three-hit relief against Washington on June 9 and then a short appearance in a 10–9 win over Philadelphia on June 16 in which he picked up the victory.

Fats Fothergill and Dale Alexander accounted for six of Detroit's ten hits on June 22, but Wes scattered them well enough for a 4–3 complete-game win over former Holy Cross pitching sensation Ownie Carroll. Five days later Carroll had the last laugh as Roy Johnson hit a grand-slam off Ferrell in the second inning of a 6–2 Detroit win at Navin Field. Wes pitched one more time that month, allowing two runs in one inning of relief against Detroit on June 29.

By the end of June it was evident that Philadelphia—with a 48–17 record—had supplanted the Yankees (38–26) as the best team in the American League. The St. Louis Browns (41–26), who defeated the Athletics ten times that year, appeared to be the only team capable of catching the front-runners. The Tigers were in fourth place (38–33) and the Indians sat fifth (31–34). Washington (26–37), Chicago (23–46) and the Red Sox (22–48) were the trailing clubs. Ferrell had conducted himself well during the first half of the season. The 21-year-old had gone 5–5 with a 4.77 ERA in 66 innings. Three of his wins had come against the Tigers and three of his losses were to the Browns. He had shown flashes of brilliance but his inexperience was still evident.

Wes started against the White Sox on July 3. He took a 3–2 lead into the ninth before giving up the tying run. Wes recorded two outs in the tenth before Chicago scored three times for a 6–3 final. Ferrell had two hits in the game as a batter, one a double. He scored one of the Tribe's runs and drove in another.

On July 7, Wes lost a 3–0 game to Ed Morris and the Red Sox in Cleveland. It was the second game of a doubleheader and the contest was halted after five innings due to rain. Wes worked the first four innings before being lifted for a pinch-hitter. None of the Boston runs were earned.

In its July 11 issue, *The Sporting News* identified Lefty Grove—his record at 13 wins and 2 losses—Rube Walberg (12–3) and George Earnshaw (10–3) as the top American League pitchers. Ferrell's record stood at 5–7, but from then until the end of the season he would go 16–3 and draw accolades from everyone who watched him perform. The star had arrived.

Wes relieved Johnny Miljus on July 10 against Washington. Coming to bat in the bottom of the fourth with his team down by five runs, he belted a two-run homer off Bump Hadley for his first career home run. Ferrell worked 5⅔ innings of scoreless relief and picked up the win as the Indians won 9–7.

Howard Ehmke was still several months short shy of fanning 13 Chicago Cubs in the first game of the 1929 World Series when the Tribe knocked him from the box early on July 15. Wes allowed the league-leading Athletics five runs in the first four innings but then shut them down over the last five frames for an 8–5 victory. He fanned seven and held the meat of the mighty Philadelphia batting order — Cochrane, Simmons and Foxx — to just two hits in 12 at bats. Simmons never took his bat off his shoulder while watching three straight first-inning curve balls break over the heart of the plate and James Isaminger — Philadelphia's correspondent for *The Sporting News* — wrote in his weekly recap that Ferrell "is turning out to be a real pitcher."[8]

Cleveland played a doubleheader against the Yankees on July 19 and Wes laced a pinch-hit triple in the first game before beating New York ace George Pipgras in the nightcap. The final was 11–3 and Wes allowed a run in the first inning and then single runs in the eighth and ninth after the game had been put on ice. He fanned nine and walked five. The New York *Times* wrote that, "Wes Ferrell, raw-boned and rugged Carolina collegian right-hander, kept the Yanks stepping around and trying to find the ball whenever there were men on base."[9]

Two days later Ferrell relieved in the seventh inning, stranding two New Yorkers to snuff out a rally. He finished the game, allowing a run on three hits, to preserve a 6–4 win. The Yankees scored in the ninth on two infield hits and an error but left the bases loaded when Bill Dickey flew out to end the game.

Cleveland split a doubleheader in Philadelphia on July 23 and Wes touched Rube Walberg for a pinch-hit triple in the opener before pitching and winning the second game 9–3. The nightcap was tight before the Indians erupted for six in the top of the ninth. Ferrell allowed seven hits, though one was a home run by Jimmy Foxx that cleared the roof of the double-decked pavilion in left-center field in the eighth inning.

"I wish I had him," said Connie Mack of Ferrell after the game. "He's the finest looking young pitcher I've seen in years. A terrific amount of stuff, good control, plenty of nerve and, I'd be willing to bet, a pretty good noodle. He acts and pitches like a fellow who's thinking about the job."[10]

Wes pitched poorly in relief in Washington on July 28, allowing eight base runners and two earned runs in just two innings of work.

An 11–4 triumph at Fenway Park on July 30 was his tenth win of the season and while he allowed 13 hits, it was never a contest as his mates had scored six times in the first two innings.

Ferrell faced Herb Pennock at Yankee Stadium on August 4, and neither starter figured in the decision as New York tagged Wes for 10 hits and four earned runs in less than four innings. Cleveland trailed for most of the game before taking Wes off the hook with nine runs in the last frame of the 14–6 final. The highlight of Wes' day was a triple he hit off Pennock.

Ferrell next worked twice in relief against Detroit, picking up a win with 2⅔ innings of work on August 6 and a loss on August 8 when he allowed seven hits and five runs in two innings. He opened the ninth inning of the August 8 game with a 6–5 lead but was nicked for two infield singles with one down. Another slow roller produced an out but the runners were able to move up a base, causing Peck to call for a free pass to set up a confrontation between Wes and four-time American League batting champion Harry Heilmann. The Detroit outfielder doubled off the right-field wall to clear the bases.

Wes—just two days after he watched Babe Ruth hit his 500th career home run — took a tight duel from Fred Heimach on August 13. New York's two third-inning runs held up until the last of the ninth when the Indians scored a pair for a 3–2 win. Ferrell worked the heart of the Yankees' order well, holding Gehrig, Ruth, Lazzeri, Meusel and Dickey to two hits in 15 at bats. He passed seven — two intentionally and Ruth three times— and didn't strike out a batter. Cleveland's late rally, highlighted when Grover Hartley—a notorious pull-hitter—fouled up Miller Huggins by shooting one back up the middle after the New York skipper had shifted his outfield around to left, made Wes' record 12–8.

"Ferrell's tremendous improvement this year," noted *The Sporting News*, "Makes Peck's pitching for next season much easier. Wes not only has a lot of physical skill, but is a keen student of pitching and is bound to improve right along. Miller Huggins calls him the best pitcher to come into the league this year and one of the best prospects he has ever lamped."[11]

Lefty Grove opened a three-game series in Cleveland with a 17-inning, 5–3 triumph on August 14 in which he allowed 20 hits. Earnshaw, after a day of rain, beat the Indians 6–5 on August 16. Wes allowed Philadelphia just four hits the next afternoon, holding Mack's big hitters— Cochrane, Simmons and Foxx — to one safety in 11 at bats. He did not pass anyone and fanned four. Rube Walberg was just as good and opened the ninth leading 1–0; the only scoring coming in the fourth when Mickey Cochrane singled in a run with a hit to right on which the Cleveland outfielder fired a strike to the plate that catcher Luke Sewell couldn't handle cleanly and drew an error on. Wes then retired the final 13 batters in order and once again Grover Hartley came up big for Ferrell, driving in the tying run with a pinch-hit single in the ninth. Moments later a fly ball made Wes the winning pitcher.

"The finest change of pace in the country today!" wrote Sam Murphy, "That's what the players say of Wesley Ferrell of the Indians....

"Ferrell's most brilliant achievement this year was on last Saturday when he stilled the Athletics, letting them down with four hits. It was Ferrell's slow ball that halted Simmons and made Foxx look bad.

"There was a time that the older batters detected Ferrell's sudden switch from his slow ball to this fast ball, but of late he has masked his motion and that is the reason for his steady climb up to a place among the leading hurlers of the circuit."[12]

Lloyd Brown was the opposing starter on August 21 when Wes copped his fourteenth win with another four-hit gem. The final was 3–1 and the Cleveland hurler fanned five and walked three. Washington's lone run came in the third inning on two hits and a sacrifice fly.

The Red Sox came into town next, and though they had spent most of the season in the league cellar they took three games from the Tribe to go 12–6 on their western trip. Wes beat them 5–4 for his fifteenth victory in the nightcap of a doubleheader on August 25.

Ferrell ended the month with an 8–5 win over the White Sox at Comiskey Park on August 31, allowing nine hits and three earned runs. Cleveland ran up an 8–2 lead before he gave single runs in the sixth, eighth and ninth innings and *The Sporting News* reported that Wes was never in any trouble. The Cleveland *Plain Dealer* indicated he worked well around three Indians errors.

Earl Whitehill and the Tigers fell 7–2 to Ferrell on September 4. Detroit scored their tallies in the sixth by stringing together four consecutive safeties, two of which did not leave the infield. Wes walked two, fanned three and allowed 11 hits. At the plate he had two hits and scored two runs, lacing a double off the left-field fence to begin the third inning.

George Earnshaw — the American League's leading winner with 20 — bested Wes 6–5 in Philadelphia on September 10. Jimmy Foxx belted a long homer with two on in the first inning but Ferrell tightened up and allowed just three singles and two walks over the next six shutout innings. Hits by Cochrane, Simmons, Miller and Dykes in the eighth plated two runs, and in the ninth, after Wes retired the first two batters, a Mule Haas double and a Cochrane single won the game.

Ferrell limited the opposition to five hits in posting a 4–1 victory at Griffith Stadium on September 14. Joe Cronin heaved a potentially inning-ending double-play ball over the first baseman's head in the second. An intentional pass followed and when Washington pitcher Lloyd Brown tried to pump a fastball past his pitching opponent, Wes clouted it over the center fielder's head to knock in two runs. He tallied another run with a ninth-inning single as he ran his record to 18–9.

Ferrell's next two appearances came at Yankee Stadium. Peck's squad led 4–1 going into the ninth on September 16, but a triple by Gehrig and a double by Mark Koenig knocked out the Tribe's starter. Wes arrived from the pen and got Gene Robertson on a grounder and punched out Earle Combs to close the contest.

Wes started and lost the second game of a doubleheader on September 18. He carried a 2–1 lead through five innings but New York scored four times in the sixth on three hits, three walks (two intentional), a sacrifice and an outfield error. Ferrell was lifted for a pinch-hitter and the Indians' bullpen allowed New York seven more runs.

Wes relieved in the eighth inning on September 20 and snuffed out a Red Sox rally to preserve a 4–2 win. Two days later he recorded his nineteenth victory by downing the BoSox 7–4 in 10 innings.

Cleveland and St. Louis closed the season with six-game series—three games being in each city—that would determine third place in the standings.

Wes recorded his twentieth win with a brilliant two-hit shutout in Cleveland's last home game on September 29. He walked a batter in the second inning and allowed base-hits, both singles, in the third and fourth. No Brownie advanced beyond first base.

"Get the kid one run and it's all over," Lew Fonseca said after watching Wes for two innings. The game—which Cleveland won 4–0—was scoreless until the sixth inning and Ferrell put away the final 16 batters in order.

"No more than half a dozen times during the game did Ferrell fail to get the first strike across on the batter," wrote the *Plain Dealer*, "Mostly it was a curve ball, and placed where they couldn't hit it."[13]

The Sporting News said, "The day was dark and at times rain fell in a fine mist, which made Ferrell's fast ball and curve unhittable. Ferrell never worked better than that day and the Browns players declared he had more stuff than they had seen all season. His fast ball was breaking a foot and his curve snapping like a bolt of summer lightning."[14]

St. Louis' last hope for a piece of third-place money ended when Wes bested their top winner, Sam Gray, by a 3–2 score on October 5. The contest was tight with each team pushing across runs in the third and eighth innings and Wes himself drove in the winning run with a ninth-inning

Capable of laughing before game time, Wes (left) and Rick took great delight in outdoing each other once the contest began (Wes Ferrell, Jr.).

single. He held the Browns to nine hits and Rick Ferrell, catching for the Browns and facing Wes for the first time in big league action, went 0–3.

* * *

While Rick Ferrell knew he was the St. Louis catcher of the future, he expected and received no advice from his teammates. "You didn't get the help you do now," recalled Rick 60 years later, "You observed, and you corrected your own faults. You didn't have the coaching, and the ballplayers were a little different back then. You were there to get their jobs, so they didn't help you a great deal.

"You observed and watched the different catchers, the catchers from the other clubs. Mickey Cochrane was one of my favorites. I observed what they did, and how they did it, and more or less learned from observation."[15]

The two catchers in front of Rick were 39-year-old Wally Schang, who had caught almost 1,400 American League games spread over 16 seasons, and 32-year-old Clyde Manion, in the majors since 1920. St. Louis had come out of the gate fast and at times seemed the only team capable of handling Philadelphia. The middle of a pennant race did not present a lot of opportunities for a player of Ferrell's limited experience and he was used sparingly over the first half of the season.

Rick's debut came as a pinch-hitter on April 19 and two days later he hit safely for the first time off Earl Whitehill. Most of his playing time consisted of catching second games of doubleheaders and pinch-hitting. His biggest hit in the first half of the season was a pinch-hit double that drove home two runs in the eighth inning against the Red Sox on June 15.

A personal tragedy befell Manion when his wife was killed in an auto accident near Hamilton, Ontario, on June 27.[16] The Browns were in Chicago and he immediately left the team. Manion did not return until August and most of Rick's playing time came while he was away.

Rick caught Lefty Stewart's two-hit shutout of Cleveland on June 25, driving in two runs on two walks and a pair of hits. Stewart requested Ferrell as his regular catcher and on June 29 they combined for a 12–4 win over Chicago. Ferrell went two for four in the game, scoring three times and driving home two.

Manager Dan Howley began using Rick on a regular basis and he caught three games of a series in July with New York when the Yankees were vying with St. Louis for second place. He went two for three and drove in the Browns only run in a 3–1 loss to Herb Pennock on July 6. The next day he had two hits and an RBI in Alvin Crowder's 7–2 win over Waite Hoyt.

Rick took a pitch off his kneecap on July 20 and missed a week. He came back in early August to reach base 17 times over 30 plate appearances. He had five hits over three games against Philadelphia on August 5 and 6, catching two games and delivering a pinch-hit on August 5 when the Browns knocked out Lefty Grove.

St. Louis coach Bill Killefer — Grover Cleveland Alexander's favorite

catcher and a veteran of over 1,000 big league games behind the dish —
said that Ferrell was the only receiver he ever saw who arrived in the major
leagues already knowing everything that was needed to play the position.

* * *

By the end of his first full season Wes Ferrell was drawing comparisons to Christy Mathewson and Cy Young.[17] Columnist Ernie Lanigan of
The Sporting News — subsequently the first historian at the Baseball Hall
of Fame — wrote, "Every expert you see who has visioned Ferrell this year
raves about him."[18] Sam Greene, the Detroit correspondent for *The Sporting News*, noted in August that, "Ferrell seems to work best against the
hard-hitting teams. He has beaten the Tigers and Athletics three times
each and the Yankees twice. Miller Huggins said he was the best prospect
among the new pitchers who have come into the American league this season and the Tigers are ready to agree with the midget manager."[19]

Ferrell won 11 games against the three heaviest-hitting teams in the
league while Grove won only four. This is skewed, of course, because Grove
couldn't pitch against his own team, but the facts cannot be overlooked
that Ferrell pitched against tougher competition in 1929 than Grove did.
The following table shows the won-lost records of Ferrell and Grove versus opposing teams ranked in order of runs scored.[20]

Ferrell		Grove
5–2	Detroit	2–0
4–1	Philadelphia	0–0
2–1	New York	2–1
2–3	St. Louis	1–2
3–0	Washington	1–0
0–0	Cleveland	5–0
2–1	Chicago	2–2
3–2	Boston	7–1

Grove — spelled "Groves" while in the minors and during his first year
in Philadelphia — came into the American League with much fanfare in
1925 after running up a 108–36 record in five seasons at Baltimore in the
International League. Among the fastest pitchers ever, he had little idea
where the ball was going when he arrived in the major leagues.

"Last spring Jack Dunn, the wily manager of the Baltimore club, who
developed Groves, told me that he would win at least 20 games for Mack,
possibly 25," wrote American League umpire Billy Evans late in 1925.

"If Groves had come up to expectations and been a consistent winner for the Athletics as Connie Mack and Jack Dunn figured he would,
Washington would now be facing a far tougher task in repeating.

"Groves has shown me more stuff than any left-hander I have seen since the passing of Rube Waddell, but his control on the whole has been atrocious."[21]

Chief Bender, Mack's famous pitcher of the previous generation, said the same thing. "Grove's inability to win consistently in the American League this year can be charged to his lack of control, for he certainly has the stuff."[22]

Mack hired Kid Gleason—forever remembered as the manager of the Chicago Black Sox—in 1926 to work on Grove's control and he made a simple adjustment with the way Lefty held his hands prior to his windup. Years later Grove told author Donald Honig, "I enjoyed every damn year I was in baseball except the first year with the A's, when I was a rookie learning the ropes, and the first year in Boston, when I had a sore arm."[23]

Though generally regarded as the best pitcher in baseball by 1929, Grove had problems during the second half of the season. His record stood at 15–2 with an ERA of 1.83 in his first 157 innings, but after July 12 he was just 5–4 with a 4.10 ERA in 118.2 innings. Some of the New York players felt Mack was overworking his top three pitchers—Grove, Earnshaw and Walberg—and predicted a breakdown that would allow them back into the pennant race.[24] Over the last ten weeks of the season Grove won only four games, two each against Cleveland and Boston, and left games tailing seven times, only to see his team rally to take him off the hook.

"The decision of Connie Mack to keep Grove on the sidelines has been made clear," noted *The Sporting News* after the World Series. "Connie knew that Grove's pitching hand was not in good shape. Long before the season closed the lefthanded fireballer skinned his pitching fingers. He was able to breeze along for several innings but was not certain he could last the full nine."[25]

The American League did not have an official Most Valuable Player award in 1929 but *The Sporting News* published two unofficial polls. The first, in late October, was made up of an unspecified committee of BBWAA writers.[26] Cleveland's Lew Fonseca led the balloting and Jimmy Dykes of Philadelphia was second. Neither Grove nor Ferrell appeared among the 21 players who received votes, although three more of Grove's teammates—Foxx, Simmons and Cochrane—and Ferrell's rookie teammate Earl Averill, did.

In late December, the same eight-member committee of writers who made the 1928 American League selection was asked by *The Sporting News* to name a winner for 1929.[27] Al Simmons led this group of 25 named players and Ferrell finished eleventh, one vote behind Jimmy Foxx. Again Grove did not receive a vote.

The BBWAA's 187 members named *The Sporting News'* All-Star Team in early December.[28] Grove and Burleigh Grimes of the Pittsburgh Pirates were named as left-handed and right-handed pitchers. Grove dominated with 174 votes. Rube Walberg and Carl Hubbell were the only other lefties named and they received just one vote each. Grimes led the righties with 37 votes. He was followed by George Earnshaw (33 votes), Guy Bush (29), Red Lucas (26), Charlie Root (26) and Ferrell, who had 20 votes.

Ferrell was named as the pitcher on *The Sporting News'* All-Star Major Recruit Team.[29]

Bill Slocum, a longtime New York sportswriter and editor opined in an article about the American League's top freshman in 1929, that either Ferrell or Bill Dickey of the Yankees stood out as the best man.

"Ferrell," wrote Slocum, "has size, strength, a fast ball that is worthy of the name and he has acquired a change of pace that is remarkable in a pitcher so young. He has hung up impressive victories against the best clubs in his league and with even his brief experience in the majors, where pitchers usually need several years to learn what it is all about, he ranks in the top set of American League boxsmen."[30]

♦ 5 ♦

1930— The Best Pitcher
in Baseball

Cleveland offered Wes $7,000 for 1930 but the hurler wanted $12,000. "Ferrell is more of a business man than the average 22-year-old ballplayer," noted *The Sporting News*. A compromise was reached at $10,000 and Wes signed his contract on March 4. He went into conference with Peckinpaugh immediately upon his arrival in New Orleans and both emerged from the meeting smiling. Watching Wes toss for five minutes was enough to brighten Peck's day.

Ferrell began working out shortly after Christmas as he had the advantage of a ready-made baseball team right there on the farm. "In my opinion," he said, "my brother at St. Louis is a better ball player than I am, while I always thought that my brother at Memphis was better than either of us. We all thought that my oldest brother had more athletic ability than any other member of the family. He never had a chance. He had to work the farm."[1]

An article titled "The Phenomenal Ferrell" appeared in the March 1930 issue of *Baseball* Magazine. In it author F. C. Lane penned, "His teammates say that Ferrell has everything. That is a sweeping statement, but only a moderate exaggeration, at best, for he certainly has everything that he seems to require to pitch winning ball.

"His best ball, of course, is his fast ball. But he also has a most serviceable curve, such a curve as many pitchers fail to acquire in years of patient practice. And young and inexperienced as he is, he has developed a baffling change of pace."

Henry Edwards, a former Cleveland sportswriter and then the American League's public relations chief, also had a take on Ferrell. "Perhaps he is not as fast as Walter Johnson was in his prime but he can throw the ball past the batters, just the same. He does not, however, rely entirely

51

Wes Ferrell at his peak. His self-confidence and fastball rated with the best of them (Gwenlo Ferrell Gore).

upon his speed. He also owns a deceptive curve while no pitcher in the land has a better change of pace. His curve may be likened to that used by Dazzy Vance. He brings it down overhand and often the batter backs up, fearing he will be hit, only to see the ball curve right over the heart of the plate. Al Simmons declares he would rather bat against any other pitcher in the American League."[2]

Peck named Willis Hudlin his opening day starter and slotted Ferrell for the second game. Bad weather postponed much of the American League schedule, and only Philadelphia and New York got off on time, with Lefty Grove beating the Bombers by a 6–2 score on April 15. Anxious to get going after Charlie Gehringer voiced his doubts that the Cleveland hurler would win 15 games, Wes beat the Tigers 7–1 in Detroit on April 18, scattering five hits and two walks over the first eight innings. The Bengals' lone tally came in their final trip to the plate and *The Sporting News* wrote, "Wes Ferrell was the complete master of the situation." Cleveland scored three times in the second inning—one via a Ferrell double—and three more in the eighth. Gehringer was retired all four times he came to the plate.

Detroit won 6–4 the next afternoon despite Wes' pinch-hit in the eighth inning that plated two runs.

Twenty thousand fans at Cleveland's home opener on April 22 saw the White Sox score twice off Ferrell in the first on an error, a flare behind second base, a single to right and a grounder which bounced off third baseman Joe Sewell's chest. Wes pitched five more innings, allowing one run on six hits (two infield rollers), before being lifted for a hitter in the seventh inning. Cleveland tied the game before eventually losing 4–3.

Wes picked up a win with three scoreless relief innings in a 5–4 win over the Tigers on April 25. "It was Wesley Ferrell, who came on the scene in the eighth after the tribe had tied the score," noted the *Plain Dealer*, "and proceeded to make the Tigers look foolish for the succeeding three rounds.

"He set them down in order in the eighth. In the ninth they filled the bases after two were out and he bore down and struck out Elias Funk. And in the tenth he whiffed Jonathan Stone, Roy Johnson and Bill Rogell, three pretty fair hitters."

Detroit—highlighted by Gehringer's two-run shot—jumped on Ferrell for six hits and five runs in the first inning of a 7–1 game on April 27. The Tribe's batters were held to just six hits—the only one for extra bases was a third inning double off Ferrell's bat that the *Plain Dealer* described as, "a line smash directly over Center Fielder Funk's head, nearly to the score board...."[3]

Wes allowed a run on two hits — one a bad hopper over the first baseman — in tossing the last two innings to save a 5–3 victory against St. Louis
on April 29. Rick Ferrell lined a rope toward the left-field corner in the
ninth but third baseman Johnny Burnett speared it with a leaping catch.

The Carolina hurler copped his third game on May 2 with an 8–3 win
over the Red Sox in Boston. "Ferrell allowed only three hits in seven innings
but every one counted in the scoring," recapped the *Plain Dealer*. "A home
run by Phil Todt in the second coming on top of the only bases on balls
Wes issued gave the Sox a two-run lead. Two more hits, an error and an
infield out in the fifth gave them their third and final run."[4] Wes plastered
the ball off the left-field wall in the third inning but was held to a long
single. He was lifted for a hitter in eighth with Boston holding a 3–2 lead,
but Cleveland scored three runs in both the eighth and ninth innings. Joe
Sewell, fighting the flu for several days, was forced to remain in bed and
his consecutive game streak ended at 1,102.

Cleveland was sitting atop the American League standings with
Philadelphia after Wes beat the Yankees on May 6, though he needed help
from Mel Harder in the 7–6 contest. Earle Combs began the game with an
inside-the-park homer, then a fourth-inning double by Tony Lazzeri gave
the Yankees a 2–0 lead before Cleveland knocked out Yankees' starter
George Pipgras with four runs in the fifth. Ferrell tripled over Combs'
head to begin the seventh and when Eddie Morgan followed with a home
run the Tribe was up 6–3. The Yanks answered right back to score two on
a single, a triple and a double by Dickey, Combs and Ruth. Peck went to
Harder after Wes walked the leadoff hitter in the eighth.

The Athletics took three out of four from the Tribe beginning in
Philadelphia on May 9 with a 9–4 Grove victory. The Indians took a 25–7
blowout in the third game — a contest played in Cleveland due to a Sunday
ban in Pennsylvania — which Wes started opposite Eddie Rommel. The score
was 14–0 after four and Wes had a perfect day at the plate with two hits
and three walks. He retired the first nine batters before Philadelphia scored
four runs in the fifth on three walks, two errors, an infield hit and one clean
base hit. Peck figured the bullpen could handle the game after the sixth.

Wes dropped his second game in Chicago on May 17 by the score of
4–1. He limited the White Sox to seven hits and no passes but Ted Lyons
did better, blanking Cleveland until the last frame. Two of Chicago's runs
were unearned, coming in the sixth on a base hit and subsequent fumble
of a sacrifice hit back to the mound. Wes, who drew two errors on the play,
compounded the miscue by throwing the ball into right field. One of the
three hits Lyons allowed before the ninth was a double by Ferrell.

Peck called for his ace in the eighth inning of a doubleheader nightcap with the White Sox on May 20 with runners on first and third and the Tribe up 7–4, and he induced two ground balls to close out the inning.

Ferrell started the next afternoon against the Browns. He allowed only two hits over the first five frames and was working with a 1–0 lead in the sixth when Lew Fonseca threw a potentially inning-ending double play ball into left field. That unsettled the 22-year-old hurler who had a self-identified issue with bad reactions to fielding miscues, and three hits, sandwiched around an intentional pass, gave St. Louis a 4–1 lead before the inning ended. They scored again in the seventh when Fonseca, with the potential third out trapped in a rundown, committed another error. Mel Harder worked the last two innings but the 6–5 loss went to Ferrell.

The Browns beat the Indians for the third straight day on May 23. Ferrell came into the tied contest in the eighth inning and retired all three batters he faced but the sequence of the batters—grounder advancing a runner and then two fly outs—allowed St. Louis to go ahead. Wes led off the ninth inning with a walk but died on second base and the St. Louis battery of Lefty Stewart and Rick Ferrell were 5–4 winners.

Peckinpaugh and GM Billy Evans assessed the team's needs in late May. Fonseca, their defending batting champ, had a shoulder that chronically popped out of joint, but Peck compensated by using Eddie Morgan at first base. Joe Sewell was slow in recovering from his bout with the flu, but Johnny Burnett filled in nicely at third base. The pitching had been inconsistent but the biggest problem, Peck and Evans decided, was the Indians' lack of power, so on May 24 Evans announced that the fences in right and right-center fields would be altered to make an easier target for Earl Averill and Morgan. A ten-foot screen was removed from the top of the 35-foot wall in the 296-foot right-field corner and a screen in right-center, where the wall was 340 feet from home plate, would be removed, leaving only a twenty-foot concrete fence. "Since this season started I have seen at least a dozen balls hit by members of the Cleveland team that would have been home runs in any other park in the major leagues," said Evans, "Last season Averill must have hit twenty and Falk nearly as many."[5]

Ferrell's next start was the first game of a twin bill in Cleveland on May 26. Red Faber started for Chicago and pitched four hitless innings before going to pieces in the fifth when the Tribe scored seven times. Wes gave but five hits, four of them in the seventh when Chisox made all their tallies in the 7–3 final. When the game was tight he was especially stingy, allowing just a hit and a walk through the first six frames. Two errors and a walk left the bases jammed in the ninth but he punched out Johnny Watwood on three pitches to end the contest.

Peck looked to Wes for the final two outs in the ninth inning the next afternoon after the White Sox rallied for four runs to take a lead. He became the winning pitcher when Ted Lyons coughed up two runs in the bottom of the frame.

Detroit handed Wes his worst drubbing of the season on Memorial Day, beating him 9–6 and knocking him from the box with six hits and four runs in the fifth inning. With one down and a runner on second base, "Gehringer lifted a pop fly back of first that looked as if it should have been handled by Porter, but Dick didn't get there and Johnny Hodapp missed on a desperate try for the ball. It went for a triple. McManus then lifted a fly to Averill that would have been the third out with no runs scored had Gehringer's fly ball been caught. As it was, Marty's sky scraper scored Gehringer and then four more hits followed in succession to produce four runs."[6]

"That slip of the Cleveland defense," wrote the *Plain Dealer*, "proved to be just what the Tigers needed."

The first extended invasion of the eastern clubs into Cleveland came at the beginning of June and three of those teams — Washington, New York and Philadelphia — were shaping up as the teams the Tribe had to beat. The fourth club — the Red Sox — had just suffered through a 14-game losing streak. Ferrell beat the pathetic Bosox 8–3 on June 3, allowing just four singles and no runs over the first seven innings. "Wesley Ferrell did the pitching yesterday, and did it so well that he became the second American League hurler to win eight games," wrote the *Plain Dealer*. "The Boston batters made eight hits off Wesley, but four of them came in the eighth and ninth innings when they couldn't possibly do any good."

Next in town was Washington, whom manager Walter Johnson — with virtually the same roster that had finished fifth in 1929 — had in first place. Ferrell opened that series with a 3–2 victory on June 8. "Never before this year," wrote the *Plain Dealer*, "has Wes showed the full assortment of stuff that made him a twenty-game winner in 1929, but he had it yesterday — sizzling fast ball, down-breaking curve and perfect change of pace. He fanned eight Washington batsmen, including such robust hitters as Sam Rice, Goose Goslin, Joe Judge, Buddy Myer and Joe Cronin — the big gun of the Nationals' attack."

The contest was knotted at two with runners on first and third and one down in the ninth. Johnson ordered a pass to the number eight hitter which brought Ferrell to the plate. Gordon Cobbledick described what happened next.

"A dozen feet southwest of home plate there squatted a large and ever-so-earnest young man who made a dismal failure of concealing his impatience as he waited for that fourth ball to Burnett.

"He fidgeted nervously. He clenched his teeth. He curled back his lips in a rather ominous snarl. His ball game was at stake, and he wanted to hit. Oh, how he wanted to hit.

"Burnett took the fourth one and jogged to first. The large chap jerked himself to his feet, swung two bats in an arc over his head, then hurled one savagely toward the players bench.

"Down on the first base coaching line Roger Peckinpaugh, the Indians' manager, threw an anxious look toward the young man. The large young man looked back and suddenly the snarl vanished, along with the appearance of tense determination. In their place came a wide and cheerful grin and Mr. Peckinpaugh, satisfied, turned back to his job of admonishing the base runners to take modest leads.

"The large kid took his place at the plate, facing his youthful adversary, the honest but underhanded Ad Liska. A fast ball came sweeping up from somewhere between the submarine hurler's feet and the large one swung.

"There was the mellow crack of a well-hit apple. The ball shot straight to shortstop Joe Cronin, took one wicked hop, just tipped his up-stretched hand and went into center field, while Earl Averill sprinted in from third with the winning run."[7]

Another victory the next afternoon moved the Tribe within a half game of second-place but the price was high as catcher Luke Sewell broke a finger and was expected to miss three weeks.

The first-place Athletics followed the Nats into town and Peck sent Willis Hudlin against Grove on June 11. The Tribe, after increasing their lead to 6–1 after Grove left for a pinch-hitter in the eighth, looked like easy winners but the A's fought back to knock out Hudlin. Peck, with one run in and two runners on, called for Wes, who induced two ground balls—a fielder's choice and double play—to end the game. Cleveland won the next day also, giving Wes the opportunity, if he could capture his start on June 13, to move his team into a first-place tie with Mack's boys.

Rube Walberg wasn't around when Wes recorded the final out of the 15–2 game an hour and 55 minutes later. The victory was Ferrell's tenth and it made him the American League's top winner. "It was Wesley Cheek Ferrell, the young Carolina dairy farmer who drew the mountainous assignment of making it three in a row over the men of Mack yesterday," wrote Cobbledick, "Wesley Ferrell and the eight young batters who stood at his back." Ferrell was shaky early but settled down, allowing just three base runners over the final five innings and retiring the last ten batters in order. Wes— the batter — hit safely in both the seven-run sixth and three-run seventh when Cleveland broke open the game.

Cleveland's stay on top lasted but two days as the Yankees outscored them 43–19 in sweeping an ensuing three-game series. Overall, though — with about one third of the season played — the team was in a good position, as only percentage points separated the top four clubs.

Wes dropped a 7–2 game to Roy Mahaffey in Philadelphia on June 18. He was in a hole right away after his right fielder misplayed Max Bishop's fly into a triple to open the first. Moments later — "with a double play in front of him" — his shortstop booted Al Simmons' grounder. "Poor support," noted the *Plain Dealer*, "got Ferrell into trouble in the first inning and gave the A's three runs that they didn't deserve." Wes doubled to start the Cleveland third and scored the club's first run, but three consecutive home runs knocked him out in the fifth. "We hit him for three home runs in a row," said Al Simmons when recalling the game in 1945. "Bing Miller banged one in the lower deck. I dropped one upstairs, and Foxx cracked one over the roof.

"Three in a row, with Joe Boley coming up, and here's a chance to set a world record. So Boley bunts and beats it out. 'That's enough,' yells Ferrell, and he throws his glove into the stands. He had a tough time getting it back, because the fans passed it down slowly, from row to row so they could watch him stand there and burn.

"But that Ferrell was a great pitcher. Beat us nine times when we had our great teams in '29 and '30. In Cleveland they always wanted us to pitch Grove against him."[8]

Losses in the next three games to Grove, Earnshaw and Walberg ran the Indians' losing streak to seven before Ferrell stopped it with a 4–2 win over Bill Shores in Cleveland on June 22. He allowed seven hits and a walk and both of Philadelphia's runs were unearned. "To Ferrell goes the lion's share of the credit, for he hurled a beautiful game," wrote the *Plain Dealer*'s Sam Otis. "Yielding only seven hits he really should have had a shut out, but some very loose support in the second inning derived him of that. In three other sessions Wes bore down and prevented what appeared to be certain tallying, and then, getting better all the while, retired the leaders in order during the final three stanzas."[9]

Following Wes' June 13 victory that put them briefly atop the circuit, Cleveland proceeded to drop 20 of the next 23 games to prove decisively that they did not have the ability to compete with Philadelphia, Washington or New York. The Tribe won 27 and lost 39 games against those teams in 1930. They were 12–5 when Wes was the pitcher of record and 15–34 when he wasn't.

New York took four of five games from Cleveland beginning on Thursday, June 26, when they pounded Ferrell for eight hits and eight runs (they won 13–11) before Peck went to the pen in the fourth. Ferrell and Grove each had three poor starts apiece in 1930 — games in which they failed to go at least than six innings. Grove's games came against the Yankees and the White Sox (twice) while Ferrell's were versus Detroit, Philadelphia and New York. Grove received three no-decisions while Ferrell took three losses.

Cleveland won on Friday but the Yankees took two on Saturday, winning 13–1 and 14–2. Peck came back with Ferrell on Sunday and though he lost, the *Plain Dealer* felt, with the exception of two pitches, he threw a fine game. The final was 7–6.

Cleveland scored three in the first but New York got one back via a Tony Lazzeri triple. Ferrell retired the next nine batters before Gehrig touched him for a solo blast in the fourth. The fifth, however, was the disaster when two walks and a single preceded a grand slam by Jimmie Reese. Now trailing 6–4, Wes led off the Cleveland sixth with a single and the Tribe came back to tie the game. Lazzeri drove in the game-winner with a fly ball in the seventh.

The Indians' pennant hopes continued to sink as they dropped two of three to the Red Sox in early July. Wes—working in relief—retired the last batter in the eighth inning of a tie game on July 2 but immediately dug himself a hole by passing the first batter in the ninth. A sacrifice and intentional pass left runners on first and second and Bosox pitcher Ed Morris at the plate. Ferrell threw two curveballs that Morris hopelessly swung at. He put the third bender off the left-field wall to win the game.

Ferrell suffered his fourth loss in eight days in the opener of a doubleheader in Detroit on the Fourth of July. He was protecting a 1–0 lead when Charlie Gehringer began the Tigers' seventh with just their third — and second infield — hit of the game. Quickly a walk, a base-hit and a wild throw by the Cleveland shortstop resulted in three tallies. Cleveland came back and was leading 4–3 with two down in the tenth when pinch-hitter George Uhle—who looked bad on three straight swings—managed to make off-balance contact with Ferrell's curveball and roll it into left field. Roy Johnson followed with a double and Liz Funk sent a grounder back through the box that went into center field for a 5–4 Detroit victory.

Ferrell's record was 11–9 and the Indians' pennant flotilla was dead in the water. Speculation — with the Tribe having quickly dropped from first to fourth place — was that Peckinpaugh's job was on the line. The club would play better, going 48–39 from then until the end of the season, but the improvement was directly attributable to Wes' strong right arm. The Tribe was 37–40 when he ran off the first of thirteen consecutive victories on July 9. Seven weeks later on September 2, the morning after his thirteenth, they were 71–63.

The Tigers were pressing Cleveland for fourth place as they punched around their pitching staff for 21 hits in an 8–6 win on July 5. Wes ignited a ninth-inning rally by scorching a pinch-hit triple to the center-field fence, and though the Tribe went down, they at least went swinging.

"Wesley Ferrell was pitching as tightly as was necessary," noted the *Plain Dealer* as the tall Carolinian began his streak with a 9–5 win at home against St. Louis on July 9. The Browns scored twice (one unearned) in the second inning before the Indians notched four in the fourth and two more in the sixth when Eddie Morgan doubled in Wes and Johnny Burnett. Ferrell retired the side in the fourth, fifth and sixth innings before allowing two runs in the eighth and another in the ninth. Two of the ten hits he allowed didn't leave the infield. Rick Ferrell had a good day against his brother with a single and two of the four passes issued. The victory, his twelfth, made Wes, along with Ted Lyons, the league's top winner.

Milt Gaston of the Red Sox locked horns with the Tribe's ace in a 3–2 duel that Cleveland won on July 14. Phil Todt found Wes for a home run in the first and Boston tied it in the fourth when a walk, a single and a double produced their final run. Cleveland's defense made four sparkling plays for Ferrell and Charlie Jamieson knocked in the winning run in the ninth.

Wes put down Washington by a 5–2 score (one earned run) on a hot and humid July 19 at League Park. The only negative for the Tribe was a broken wrist suffered by Johnny Burnett. "Ferrell," noted the *Plain Dealer*, "was sailing along in high most of the distance, granting only seven hits, but one of which came prior to the sixth period. With men on he was just plain poison to the Nats, bearing down to emerge from every tight situation except one. He was inclined to be wild occasionally, but fanned seven of the visitors. Two of his strikeouts came with a pair on in the fourth and two more with another pair on in the eighth."[10]

Cleveland took four of five from the Yankees between July 20 and 23 and Wes took the final game by a 10–6 score. He had, as the *Plain Dealer* noted, " his troubles but bore down in the pinches with the result that the slugging easterners, though tallying in five of the nine innings, registered as many as two runs only in the third, when Reese doubled in between hits by Combs and Ruth. Wes got out of that jam and others, three times fanning Lou Gehrig with men on the pathways and breezing Lazzeri, Dickey, Pennock and Rice with runners waiting."[11]

The Athletics— scoring 32 runs in the process— took three in a row from the Tribe from July 24–26 with Grove winning a 14–1 laugher in the middle contest. Ferrell stopped the skid in the fourth game, winning 7–4 and keeping the Athletics off the board until he had a 5–0 lead. The victory pushed his record to 16–9, one more win than Ted Lyons and two more than Grove, who was 14–4. The *Plain Dealer* reported that Wes was the boss throughout. "He allowed seven hits and every one a single, and only once did he permit two blows to be grouped in an inning. It happened in this session, the sixth, and he also issued two bases on balls and these, together with an error by Jonah Goldman, made it possible for the Mackmen to score their four runs.

"But for that error with a made-to-order double play in sight, Wes would have had a shutout, but he won't be doing any crying about that because they don't pay any more for shutouts than they do any other kind of victory."[12]

Detroit was in town next and the Indians took four of five, with only Mel Harder dropping a 6–5 game on July 30. Trailing 6–2 in that contest, the Indians rallied for three runs in the seventh with Wes delivering a pinch-hit single to knock Waite Hoyt from the box.

Dale Alexander accounted for the only early damage done to Ferrell in his 5–3 victory over the Tigers on July 31 with a second-inning home run. Detroit tallied in the seventh on a single, their only free pass of the day and an infield out; and then again in the eighth when Roy Johnson — reaching on a soft flare into center and subsequently cut down stealing only to have the call reversed when an infielder dropped the ball — scored. Wes allowed nine hits in the game and Eddie Morgan came up big for Wes with a two-out, two-run shot in the ninth.

Ferrell, Grove and Lyons all worked on August 4. The 71–35 Philadelphia squad ran over the 36–69 Red Sox as Grove easily won his seventeenth game 13–4. Two days earlier Grove had picked up a win against Boston with an inning of relief work. A twelfth-inning home run by Charlie Gehringer denied Lyons his eighteenth victory.

Wes — with his club at 55–51 — beat the seventh-place Browns 5–2 in St. Louis for his eighteenth, and seventh win in a row. He stranded five base runners over the first six frames before three singles in the seventh and two doubles in the eighth allowed the Browns to tie the score. The Indians scored three times in the ninth. "Ferrell whiffed Goose Goslin in the fourth without permitting the slugger so much as a foul tip," wrote the *Plain Dealer*. "Goslin took three cuts and every one was aimed at the bleachers." Rick Ferrell was out of the lineup with a broken finger.

Wes' nineteenth was a 4–2 triumph in Washington on August 9 in which he allowed nine hits and kept the Nationals off the board until an infielder's two-out throwing error let in two unearned runs in the ninth.

Cleveland moved into Philadelphia for four games played from August 12–14. The A's took the opening doubleheader 9–1 and 7–0 behind Grove and Bill Shores, and Earnshaw continued the slaughter the next afternoon, triumphing 7–2. That left it to Ferrell, who allowed seven singles—just two after the fourth inning—in dominating the front-running club 15–0. The Tribe scored three runs in the first inning, two in the fourth, and broke it open with six in the fifth. "Wes Ferrell, of course," wrote the *Plain Dealer*, "did the pitching—else how could such a ball club as the A's have been whitewashed? It was his twentieth victory of the season and his ninth in a row and it placed him once more on the top of the big league twirling list after two days in which he was tied with Lefty Grove.

"Incidentally, it was the second shutout triumph of his major league career. Great pitcher that he has been—and there's no one who will deny his greatness now—something has always happened to spoil his bid for shutout fame."[13]

Ferrell was the hottest pitcher in baseball—and getting his due.

"Down the years through the game's history great pitchers have bobbed up overnight, flashing a natural ability that made years of experience unnecessary," wrote *The Sporting News*, "In these days of free hitting and mediocre pitching, such men apparently are getting fewer and fewer and may be considered rare specimens indeed. However, Wesley Ferrell is one of those exceptions."[14]

Ferrell's next game was a 7–2 triumph in Boston on August 17 in which none of the ten hits he gave were for extra bases. The Red Sox scored once in the fourth on two hits—one a Texas Leaguer—and a walk; and then an unearned run in the ninth. Wes had three singles as a batter.

"There are at least two pitchers in the American League who are getting back to the days of old-time consistency when Matty and Walsh and Johnson stepped along," wrote Grantland Rice, "Young Wesley Ferrell of Cleveland has won his 21st game with nearly six weeks to go...."[15]

Grove copped his twenty-first win on August 20, a 10–6 victory over Detroit, but the Cleveland ace moved back ahead with a 4–2 victory at Yankee Stadium on August 24 in which he fanned eight while allowing six hits. A walk and a double to start the sixth inning left Wes facing a pitcher's worst nightmare—two runners in scoring position with Ruth, Gehrig, and Lazzeri due up. The North Carolinian calmly punched out the Bambino on strikes before passing the Iron Horse to fill the bases. Lazzeri hit a come-backer to Ferrell, who threw home for the force, and Dusty Cooke fanned to end the inning.

"Not one of the four Yankee sluggers had hit a ball past the pitcher's box," wrote John Kieran of the New York *Times*. "That's pitching in a pinch."

Ferrell, who fanned Ruth three times, weakened in the ninth and gave up a double (to Gehrig), a triple and a single before retiring the final out. Until that last frame Wes had allowed just one earned run over his last 36 innings.

Ferrell's twelfth consecutive win came at the expense of the White Sox, 10–5, on August 28. At the dish Wes doubled in a run in the second, tripled to lead off the fifth, and singled to begin the eighth. Chicago scored two first-inning runs and then single runs in the fifth, sixth, and eighth innings.

Ferrell's 24th victory came in the 9–5 nightcap of a doubleheader in St. Louis on September 1. It was his fifteenth consecutive completed start, and he again showed less than his best stuff as the Browns scored twice in the second inning on two hits— one a line drive that bounced over outfielder Charlie Jamieson's head — a walk and an error. Two singles and a fly ball produced a St. Louis tally in the fourth and one more came in the seventh on a double and a single.

The Indians though, by that time, had scored nine runs and went into the eighth inning leading by five. Darkness was rapidly setting in as the Browns were making a last run at Ferrell. Three singles and a walk had plated a run and the bases loaded with two down as Wes blazed a third-strike fastball past pinch-hitter Ted Gullic. Umpire Brick Owens then called the game because of darkness.

Peckinpaugh intended to start Mel Harder against Ted Lyons in the first game of a twin bill with Chicago on September 6 but Wes— slated for the nightcap — insisted on working against the Chisox ace to avenge his May 17 loss.[16] The Chicago crowd was sparse, but the photographers were playing it up like the World Series and snapped several shots of Lyons and Ferrell before the game.

Cleveland had a great opportunity in the first inning when a single, a walk and two consecutive errors let in a run, but Lyons retired Charlie Jamieson and Luke Sewell with the bases loaded. That 1–0 score held up until the Chicago fifth, when Lyons tripled down the first-base line to begin the frame. Wes retired the next two batters, but Carl Reynolds singled to tie the score. Lyons, who allowed seven hits in the game, got a big break in the third when Eddie Morgan was cut down trying to stretch a base hit into a double. Instead of runners on first and third and one down, the situation was a man on third with two down, and Lyons retired the next batter on a fly ball. Reynolds beat out a one-down grounder in the eighth and two batters later Johnny Watwood, who hadn't had the ball out of the infield in his three previous at-bats, shot a line drive just inside the first-base bag and Reynolds came all the way around from first to score.

The game ended 2–1 and Ferrell's winning streak died at thirteen.

Years later Lyons, who recalled him as a "temperamental but wonderful guy," said that Wes stomped around the clubhouse, steaming and snorting for an hour, taking out his frustrations on a big potbellied stove.[17]

In addition to losing his first game in several months, Ferrell also dropped behind Grove as the league's top winner. Philadelphia, in first place with an 89–45 record, opened a four-game series at home against the 44–85 Red Sox on September 3. The A's had given Grove a 7–0 cushion in the opener, but Mack pulled his ace after Boston scored four in the sixth inning. Philadelphia went on to win the game 11–4 and Grove's record became 23–5. The next afternoon he won with nine innings of relief. Boston took the lead in the tenth on a Bobby Reeves homer, but Bing Miller slammed one out in the bottom of the frame to retie the game. Lefty gave up two more runs in the fourteenth but Al Simmons' two-run shot again saved him, and Philadelphia made him the winner in the fifteenth. Bill Shores had Boston limited to a single run on September 6, but Mack replaced him with Grove, who worked three hitless innings. Mickey Cochrane broke a 1–1 tie with a tenth-inning homer to make Grove 25–5.

So while Grove had overtaken Ferrell with ten wins between August 2 and September 6, six of them had come against the hapless Red Sox, a squad the Philadelphia left-hander actually pitched more innings against (18) over that four-day period in early September than he did against the hard-hitting Yankees (16.2) all season long. As a matter of fact, excluding his work against the Yankees in the opening week of the season (all in April), Mack used Grove against New York for a total of just 5.2 innings over the last six months of the season.

Ferrell dropped another game to the Yankees on September 10 in which he allowed 11 hits and six walks. The score was 7–2, and only three of the runs were earned, as he had to pitch around four errors. Ben Chapman led off the third with a double in front of a hot shot Earle Combs hit to first base. Eddie Morgan fired across the diamond to third base to nab Chapman, who was diving back for the bag. Chapman was called out but Jonah Goldman dropped the ball and was charged with an error. A fielder's choice by Lyn Lary that should have been the third out scored Chapman, and Ruth followed with a single to plate Combs. New York scored two more runs in the fourth inning on a clean single, a bunt single and made-to-order double play ball that — although ruled a hit — caught shortstop Ed Montague off balance and rolled into left field. A two-base muff of a routine fly ball by Charlie Jamieson in the eighth and a Ray Gardner throwing error in the ninth gave New York two more runs.

* * *

Thinking of the gate a Grove-Ferrell duel would draw, Billy Evans wired Connie Mack proposing such a pairing for Sunday, September 14.

"It happens that Ferrell and Grove have not opposed each other in the twenty games that have been played to date between our two teams," wrote back Mack. "To have them hook up in the final battle of the year would, I am sure, be a treat that would delight Cleveland fans and I hope that nothing will prevent my using Grove on that date, since it would be his regular turn to pitch."

The hype, like other great pitching duels throughout history, was page one material.

"A single game," wrote *The Sporting News*, "of course, is not a reliable criterion of comparative pitching ability, but nevertheless, the announcement that Ferrell and Grove are to clash, undoubtedly will bring more fans into League Park than many an important championship game.

"Ferrell and Grove have not been matched this year, a feature of the schedule that has brought some disfavor on both managers, certain fans contending that Mack and Peckinpaugh were 'picking the spots' for their prize pitchers. Even in this accusation were true it would carry no particular weight for the business of a manager is to win ball games; and if he thinks it better to save his outstanding hurler for a spot where he will be almost sure of victory than to risk defeat against another star moundsman, there certainly is no room for criticism of his judgment."[18]

Many of the sportswriters were likening Ferrell to Christy Mathewson but Mack, while praising him, pointed out that Wes had been in the show for only two seasons and several more should be required before that comparison could be made. The Cleveland media took this as a slight and put Connie on the spot, asking him if he had said that Ferrell was overrated or that Peck picked his spots. "If such an article appeared," Mack exploded, "It would be fake — pure and simple. I have said repeatedly that I believe Ferrell is a great pitcher, one of the greatest youngsters I have ever seen. His record proves conclusively that he doesn't need to have his spots picked for him. I have admired him deeply ever since I first saw him pitch, and I have expressed my admiration so often that I am surprised credence should be given to such a ridiculous statement as you say was attributed to me."[19]

"Suppose they did meet in Sunday's game," continued Mack, "What would it prove? They are both great pitchers, but one of them would have to lose. That wouldn't make him any less great.

"I will say this: If my team were in second place, with no hope of getting any higher, I might be inclined to agree to the thing as a sporting proposition. But I have other things to think of now — the World Series, I mean.

"Grove has been working extremely hard in the past two months. There has not been a time all summer when our pitchers began to show signs of weakening that Grove didn't ask permission to go in and save the game. He has worked in turn and out, and the time has arrived now to think about his condition in the World Series.

"Mind you, I haven't said that he will not pitch against Ferrell. I don't know myself when I will use him. It will depend on a number of things. But I want it understood that Grove works when I tell him to, not when he wants to. If I tell him to go to the box on Sunday he will be glad to go, but he knows as well as I do that it wouldn't prove anything."[20]

Philadelphia's record that Saturday morning was 94–47. Washington, 6½ games back at 87–53, was the only club with a remote hope of catching them. Earnshaw and Hudlin were the opposing starters and Philadelphia built up a 5–2 lead by the time Cleveland came to bat in the fifth. Charlie Jamieson had started the Cleveland first with a double but the next three batters went down in order. Johnny Hodapp singled off Joe Boley's glove in the second inning and Earnshaw was touched for two hits in the third and three in the fourth when the Indians scored twice. Grove went to the hill when Philadelphia took the field in the fifth and the fans, realizing there would be no Ferrell-Grove duel the next afternoon, hooted it up for a full five minutes. Although the boos continued for the rest of the game, some cheers of respect became evident, for Lefty set the Indians down over the final five innings with just one hit.

Philadelphia won 9–2 and the official scorer credited the win to Earnshaw. Several days later, however, the American League office overturned that ruling and it became Grove's twenty-seventh win. Mack had a habit of pulling his starters at what seemed like odd timing and Grove was on the receiving end of several other late-season gifts. A similar situation occurred on September 24, 1933, enabling him to record his twenty-fourth victory and tie Alvin Crowder for the American League lead in wins. Mack brought in Grove to start the fifth inning of that game with Washington despite an 8–3 lead and he worked the last five innings in the 11–4 final Even *The Sporting News* commented on the credibility of this type "gift" win.[21]

When Wes took the hill on Sunday, Mack's starter was Earnshaw. Jimmie Dykes hit a first-inning home run and the score remained 1–0 until hits by Simmons, Foxx and Mule Haas plated two runs in the sixth. Wes gave up three more runs in the top of the seventh and was lifted for a hitter when Cleveland came to bat. It was the first time in eighteen starts that he failed to go the route. The final was 7–1.

Did Mack exploit the situation, purposely stroking Grove's ego by putting him a situation where he couldn't lose? And at the same time could he have been toying with Ferrell, who had dominated the mighty Athletics with a 9–2 record and 2.73 ERA to that point in his young career?

Certainly Mack was aware that Grove and Ferrell were two of the toughest losers in history. Grove sulked after losses, not talking to teammates and sometimes making himself unavailable to the team. Jim Kaplan, author of *Lefty Grove: American Original*, noted this behavior in his biography. "Following a bad relief performance in a no-decision," Kaplan wrote regarding a 1931 incident, "Grove was idled for fifteen days with what he told Mack was a 'severe cold.' It is fruitless to speculate whether he was depressed, or whether he'd have won the three likely starts he missed. What's noteworthy is that Connie Mack accepted Grove's explanation without comment or question, the fatherly manager allowing his tempestuous pitcher his long leash. 'He hasn't felt like pitching and for that reason I permitted him to treat his cold his way,' Mack told reporters...."[22] Jimmie Dykes, in his autobiography, said that Grove's moody behavior "annoyed" his teammates and that Lefty "suffered the agonies of the damned every time he lost a ball game." Dykes told a similar tale to that of Kaplan's, this time citing Grove jumping the team after a loss and remaining away for five days.[23] Ferrell, after taking out his frustration on inanimate objects, usually wanted to get right back in action, often without proper rest.

"Billy Evans phoned me once to ask me to pitch Grove against Ferrell on a Sunday," recalled Mack in 1945. "I told him I didn't think I could accommodate him. I started Earnshaw and we got a big lead after five innings I put Grove in. Those Indians never had a chance."[24]

* * *

A 3–2 decision taken from Washington on September 18 became Ferrell's twenty-fifth win. Only three of the seven hits he allowed came after the third inning and errors accounted for both of the Nats' runs. Wes scored Cleveland's first run in the sixth inning and singled home their second in the seventh.

His last appearance of the season came in relief against the Red Sox on September 21. He tossed two shutout innings but trailed 4–2 as he walked to the plate with two down in the ninth. His base hit ignited a rally that allowed the game to go into extra innings but Boston scored five runs in the top of the tenth on four hits, a walk and two errors.

* * *

"Rick Ferrell is another one upon whom [manager] Killefer is placing a lot of dependence," remarked *The Sporting News* during spring train-

Arriving in the majors as a polished catcher with a weak stick, Rick was quickly recognized by his peers as a good man to have at the plate in a tough situation.

ing. "If Killefer's plans come out, it would not be surprising to see Ferrell as the Browns' first-string catcher. He has a great arm, and Bill believes he will hit when worked regularly. His one weakness is tagging runners at the plate. Ferrell is not a heavyweight who can smother the plate, or serve as a brick wall to thundering runners."[25]

Rick was named the starting catcher during spring training and was soon recognized as a master of applying the tag to players sliding into the dish.

"Killefer, who should know a catcher when he sees one, is enthusiastic over Rick Ferrell, who after only one year's experience, has been promoted to the first string catching job. Manager Bill believes the Tar Heel will show himself the best catcher to break into the American league since Mickey Cochrane came up."

The contrast between the two is worthy of note. While Ferrell came into the majors a polished catcher with a questionable stick, Cochrane — who didn't become a catcher until turning pro — arrived as a great offensive player but horrible catcher.

Shortly after Cochrane's playing career came to a crashing halt in 1937, Connie Mack recalled that he almost had to switch him to the outfield. "He was crude at receiving the ball. His stance and crouch were both wrong. And on foul balls he was simply pathetic. What can I do with that boy? He's trying his heart out, but he doesn't even look like a catcher."[26]

Rick hit his first career home run on June 14 against Washington. He was three for three for the day and drove in four runs in a 5–4 win. The homer, a two-run blast coming when the Browns were down 4–3, was the game winner. He went seven for ten with nine RBI during that four-game series with Washington.

When Lefty Grove beat the Browns 4–2 on August 16 for his twentieth win of the season, Ferrell touched Grove for a pair of singles and a free pass.

Rick had two hits on August 24 when St. Louis beat Detroit 7–5, snapping Earl Whitehill's 11-game winning streak. Tommy Bridges, a 7–5 winner in his first big league start the next afternoon, was knocked out following a bases-clearing triple by Ferrell in the ninth inning.

* * *

George Ferrell's contract was purchased by the Winston-Salem Twins in the Piedmont League in March. Following three full seasons in the Southern Association, he would now play the first of eleven in the Piedmont. While Rick and Wes were becoming nationally known, George was establishing himself as the local celebrity and the Greensboro *Daily News* joked that while his brothers had escaped to the big city, George would be fully expected by Father Ferrell to perform his share of the farm chores before heading off to play.

Winston-Salem finished in third place after a fast start by George kept them in the early running. "George Ferrell's bat may keep the Twins in the front pew," wrote the *Daily News* in late May, "but Winston right now does not seem to pack that stuff that comes out in July." George, who played center field and batted cleanup, clouted a home run on May 1 that was the longest anyone could ever recall hit in Winston-Salem. His contract was sold to Buffalo of the International League in June with the stipulation that he would finish out the current season in Winston-Salem.

Hank Greenberg played first base for the Raleigh Capitals that season, batting .314 with 19 homers and 93 RBI. Ferrell hit 12 home runs with 105 RBI and a .330 batting average. Raleigh beat Winston-Salem on August 16, with Ferrell being ruled out on a close play at first base in which Greenberg was pulled off the bag. The play, which ended the game, did not please the fans and they mobbed the umpire. The players, along with local police, had to clear a path through the crowd so that umpire could leave safely.

George Ferrell was inducted into the Greater Winston-Salem Baseball Hall of Fame on January 21, 2003.

* * *

There is no question that the title of best major league pitcher of 1930 belonged to either Wes Ferrell or Grove. Babe Ruth and John McGraw both named them to their personal All-Star teams. "As to the pitchers," said McGraw, "I quite agree with Ruth and his committee. Grove and Ferrell have been standouts all season. Their records alone would decide that choice."[27]

The first season of the BBWAA Most Valuable Player Awards was not until 1931, so while there was no (now recognizable) official title to bestow in 1930, both *The Sporting News* and the Associated Press did empower panels to name winners and Ferrell finished higher than Grove in both polls.

Joe Cronin and Al Simmons finished first and second in *The Sporting News'* MVP with 52 and 46 votes. Vying for third place were Charlie Gehringer (31 votes), Ted Lyons (30), Lou Gehrig (29) and Ferrell (29). Next in line were Ruth and Grove who drew nine votes apiece.[28] The Associated Press results were similar. Cronin drew 48 votes and Simmons and Gehrig were next with 39. Gehringer finished at 36, Lyons 26, Ferrell 25, Eddie Morgan 15, Mickey Cochrane 13 and Grove 8.

The Sporting News, polling 228 BBWAA members, announced its 1930 All-Star team on January 1, 1931. Ten players, encompassing both leagues, were selected. There was one player named for each position and a right-handed and left-handed pitcher. The hurlers were Grove, who received 218 votes, and Ferrell, who drew 163. Other pitchers named on more than two ballots were Lyons (41), Dazzy Vance (9) and Earnshaw (7), all right-handers. They were no other dominant lefties to siphon votes away from Grove.

Wes was referred to as the handsomest player of his time and the writers joked about the attention he received from female fans. Wes' only printed comment, coming in 1932, was "Blondes have always been good to me." (*Left:* courtesy Wes Ferrell, Jr.; *right:* courtesy Gwenlo Ferrell Gore).

Baseball Magazine named four All-Star pitchers. They were Grove, Ferrell, Lyons and Pat Malone.

So who was the better pitcher in 1930?

Grove put up impressive numbers, leading the league in wins, strike-outs and ERA. Ferrell was second in wins and ERA, and fourth in strike-outs. On the other hand, Grove played for a team of champions who were 74–47 after subtracting his 28–5 record while the Indians were 56–60 without Ferrell's 25–13 contribution.

Grove was supported by the best fielding squad in the American League — just 145 errors — while Ferrell's club committed a league high 237 miscues. Five different men put in significant time behind Ferrell at shortstop for Cleveland and none of them did a very good job. The deciding factor, though, like 1929, was that Ferrell faced tougher competition than Grove, who didn't have to face the best team in the league — his own — and rarely pitched against New York.

Ferrell worked 99.1 innings, roughly one third of his total assignment, against Philadelphia and New York, going 8–5 with a 4.44 ERA. Against the rest of the league he was 17–8 and 2.74. Against the top three clubs—

Philadelphia, Washington and New York — Ferrell was 12–5 while Grove was 3–1. This, of course, is skewed because Grove couldn't pitch against he own team, but it cannot be overlooked that the Philadelphia left-hander worked three times as often against the anemic Red Sox (53.2 innings) than he did against the bludgeoning Yankees (16.2 innings).

Ferrell was 9–2 with a dazzling 2.09 ERA against Philadelphia (5–2, 2.98) and Washington (4–0, 0.75), the first and second-place finishers. He had his trouble with the Yankees, against whom he was 3–3 with a 6.20 ERA in 45 innings, but then again, so did Grove who was 1–0 with a 4.86 ERA in his 16.2 innings.

What about dominant games? Grove tossed two shutouts and one other complete game in which he did not allow an earned run. Those games came against Washington, Boston and Detroit. Ferrell had one shutout but three other complete games in which he did not allow an earned run. Two of those games came against the first-place Athletics and two against second-place Washington.

How about control? Did Ferrell walk more batters than Grove due to shoddier control? No he didn't, he walked more batters due to strategic necessity, issuing 50 passes in 99.1 innings versus New York and Philadelphia, but just 56 in 197.1 innings against the rest of the league. Against the trailing clubs, Boston and Chicago, Grove walked 14 in 86.1 innings while Wes passed 12 in 81.1 innings.

Ferrell was the best pitcher in baseball at the conclusion of the 1930 season. It was a title he had held since the middle of 1929.

◆ 6 ◆

1931— Baseball's Greatest Hitting Pitcher

"Keep your eye on Ferrell's head as he throws that ball, see what he does with his head," Luke Sewell told a sportswriter in New Orleans in early April. When the writer said that he couldn't see anything, the Cleveland catcher replied, "That's just it. He keeps his head fixed in one position, like it was in a brace. And his eyes are always glued to the plate. That's what distinguishes him from most pitchers. Watch them. They wind up and either they're looking at the ground or twisting their head some way. Ferrell keeps his head like you have to when you hit a golf ball, fixed and eye on the ball. That's where he gets his control. He has a great delivery, with a perfect follow through. His motion is the same for all balls, for a fast one, a curve, a change of pace."

The Indians, expected again to finish fourth, opened the season against the White Sox on April 14 with Gordon Cobbledick laughing off suggestions of a recent jinx of Tribe opening day hurlers. "That's a joke to Ferrell. The only jinx he knows is the kind that can be overwhelmed by a fast ball up under the chin and curve ball knee high and on the outside corner. He says he can beat the White Sox, and he isn't a guy who boasts."[1]

Twenty-six thousand fans watched as he held the White Sox to eight hits in a 5–4 victory. "Wes could pitch the same ball game ten times and nine times it would be a shutout victory," noted the *Plain Dealer*. "Only two of the Chicago hits had that ring of real authority to them. Three were of the scratchiest kind of infield safeties. Two others were easy bounders that sneaked past first base, fair by no more than an inch or two, for two-baggers. Another was a fly which Bib (sic) Falk misjudged." At the plate Wes scored twice and knocked in two. Trailing by a run, he singled to tie the game in the eighth and later scored the winning run.

His second start was a 7–2 loss to Earl Whitehill and Detroit on April

Cleveland skipper Roger Peckinpaugh (left) greets his ace upon Wes' arrival in the Tribe's 1931 spring camp in New Orleans (Gwenlo Ferrell Gore).

19. "Ferrell had thrown no more than half a dozen balls in the first round, when it became apparent that he didn't have his usual assortment of stuff," wrote Cobbledick. "His fast ball wasn't fast, his curve wouldn't break and his slow one wouldn't go where he wanted it." The Tigers scored three times in the first inning and Ferrell was gone in the fourth. His lone at-bat produced a ground-rule double into the left-field crowd.

Two days later Ferrell picked up a win, relieving in the top of the ninth after Detroit scored four times to tie the game. He retired two batters with just three pitches. Coming to bat in the bottom of the frame with the winning run on second base and one down, Ferrell slammed one back at the box that bounced off the pitcher. Wes was thrown out but the runner moved to third and scored two batters later.

Wes had all his stuff in an 8–2 win in Chicago on April 24. "He allowed the Sox just five hits, three of which were out and out flukes— one pop fly and two weirdly hopping grounders," said the *Plain Dealer*. "Not until his mates had staked him to a four-run lead did Wes loosen up sufficiently to allow Simons to single and Reynolds to triple in the sixth. Then, with Reynolds waiting on third, he turned on the juice and fanned Fred Eichrodt for the second time."

"Wes had everything that he lacked in his shellacking by the Detroit Tigers last Sunday. His fast ball fairly blistered Luke Sewell's mitt, and his hook had the enemy swinging so wildly that eight of them went down on strikes." He drove in his club's fourth run with a double down the left-field line in the sixth inning.

Next for Ferrell were the visiting St. Louis Browns, whom he shut out 9–0 without a hit on April 29. "His fast ball, shot low around the batters' knees, could not be seen," wrote Stuart Bell in the Cleveland *Press*. "His curve ball broke on the corners of the plate sharply and with such control the Browns could not gauge their swings. And to make his speed and curves more effective, Ferrell interspersed a slow ball that came to the plate with unerring control and which kept the enemy hitters off stride thru the entire game."[2]

The contest opened with Cleveland's new shortstop, Bill Hunnefield, booting a routine grounder. Hunnefield had spent five seasons with the White Sox before the Tribe drafted him from Toledo late in 1930. He studied business at Northeastern and Colgate Universities and eventually dropped out of baseball to go into the cosmetics business. When several older sportswriters spotted Hunnefield watching a spring training game in 1963, and questioned him about his post-baseball life, Bill informed them he was retired, having just sold his business for $4.25 million.[3]

Wes, who fanned eight and walked three, blasted a two-run shot in the fourth but the actual location of the home run — described as a terrific clout — is uncertain. The *Press* described it as "a potent smash into the center field bleachers," but the *Plain Dealer* said it was "into the old wooden bleachers in left field."

Hunnefield, despite three fielding miscues, was actually a hero, fielding a bad-hop grounder in the second inning and nailing the runner with a long throw across the diamond, and then making a difficult over-the-shoulder snag in short left field in the third. The closest the Browns came to a hit before the eighth inning was a bullet that Goose Goslin shot back at Wes to start the seventh. Ferrell knocked the ball down and threw him out.

Cleveland scored three times in the bottom of the eighth with Wes' double off the right-field wall being the big blow, but the excitement had been in the top of the frame when, with two down, the responsibility of breaking up the no-hitter fell to Rick Ferrell. The Brownie backstop cracked a fastball on the ground toward left and the throng let out a groan as the ball passed under third baseman Johnny Burnett's glove, but Hunnefield snared the ball behind Burnett, turned, planted, and unleashed a long throw toward first. The crowd went silent.

"I could always run faster backwards than Rick could forward but he really surprised me this time," Wes told the Greensboro *Daily News* in 1974. "He hit the ball to deep short, and our man made a great play but he pulled the first baseman off with the throw, and the scorer gave him an error. I always felt Rick had the throw beat anyway, but it was scored an error."

Ed Bang of the *Press* was the official scorer. "From the press box I could see that Hunnefield's throw was wild," he said. "Without a thought of Ferrell's no-hit performance up to that time I yelled out 'error for Hunnefield' to the other newspaperman in the press box.

"To check up on myself and make perfectly sure I hadn't made a mistake in scoring the play, I talked to Umpire George Moriarty about it after the game. He told me I was correct in the scoring. Moriarty said he would have called the runner out had Hunnefield's throw to Fonseca been perfect.

"There's no doubt in my mind that Ferrell's performance was a 100 per cent no-hit pitching exhibition and I see no reason for any dispute about it."[4]

Hunnefield immediately erred again, but Wes fanned the next batter to end the inning. The Browns went down in the ninth on two ground ball outs sandwiched around a strikeout and a walk. None of the players on the field were aware of the ruling on Rick Ferrell's ball until after the game.

"John McGraw always claimed, and rightfully so, that no man could be a high class major league pitcher without a good fast ball," wrote former major league hurler Al Demaree in his syndicated baseball column on May 5. "Cy Young, Mathewson, Johnson, Alexander and Wes Ferrell, the great Cleveland righthander of today had and have great fast balls."

Joe Williams, writing in the *World-Telegram* on the same day, said, "You can add young Mr. Wesley Ferrell to your list of supremely self-confident athletes—along with the Cobbs, the Hagens, the Tunneys and the Tildens. Mr. Ferrell is good, knows it and admits it."

"Everybody," continued Williams, "tabbed him right off as the best young pitching prospect since Christy Mathewson's time ... they call him the Second Matty."

John Kieran of the *Times* said the late Miller Huggins only had to watch Ferrell twice before declaring him the best young hurler he had seen since Matty.

"Ferrell has come fast and is climbing high," continued Kieran. "Grove and Earnshaw are great pitchers, but it was a slower climb for them and they have always had a strong team behind them all the way. Grove had to learn control before he became a star in the major leagues. But Ferrell came up and stepped out as a winning pitcher from the very start. The test of his caliber was that he kept going and has climbed since."[5]

Earlier that spring, while watching George Earnshaw, Joe McCarthy wondered aloud if the Philadelphia hurler was the best right-hander in the circuit. Bill Dickey agreed but Earle Combs did not, suggesting it was Ferrell. "Ferrell is as good as they come when he is right," said Combs. "He's a chesty boy, too. Lots of confidence. But he always pitches the same way to us. I think he makes a mistake. He breezes that high hard one—look, up here—and when he gets you swinging up there and looking for another, he breaks the curve down across you."

"Yes," agreed Dickey. "And he has control, too. He'll chuck that curve ball in there on three and two."

"Good curve ball, has he?" asked McCarthy.

"Sure it's a good curve," replied Combs. "But his curve is like a gift after that high hard one of his. He sure slings that fast one through. I'll take the curve every time I can get it."[6]

Thirty-five thousand fans were on hand in Detroit on May 3 as Wes notched his fifth win with a 7–4 decision over the Tigers. Johnny Hodapp erred on a Charlie Gehringer foul ball with two down in the first inning, and given a second chance the "Mechanical Man" bounced one back up the middle. Dale Alexander followed with a double into the overflow crowd along the right field line and John Stone drew an intentional pass. Two more singles followed and Wes was down by three before getting out of the inning. All the runs were counted as earned despite the error. Ferrell retired the next 17 batters in a row, the next hit coming with two outs in the seventh inning when the score was 7–3 in his favor. Wes had two singles in four trips to the plate and scored the second Cleveland run.

Mel Harder started in St. Louis on May 5 and had an 8–5 lead before faltering in the seventh inning. The first relief pitcher retired one batter, threw a wild pitch, walked Rick Ferrell and allowed a single that filled the bases. When he went 2–0 to the next batter, Peck waved Wes into the game. He pitched the rest of the game and "was his usual invincible self." The only hit he allowed was a ninth-inning single by his brother, who had four in the game.

Ferrell had gone 46–17 since the middle of 1929 and was drawing comparisons to Cy Young and Walter Johnson as well as Mathewson. He was just 23 years old, with unlimited potential. Speculation was that he would shatter all existing pitching records, but what shattered instead was the Carolinian's right arm. The process was gradual, but the first crack was just days away.

Wes noticed a toothache-like pain in his shoulder while warming up to pitch against the Red Sox on May 8. He worked to three batters, allowing a double to the center-field wall, a double off the right-field screen, and a double down the left-field line. He glanced at his manager and walked off the mound.

Peck had the Tribe in first place but was continuously tinkering with his infield. Jonah Goldman, who had flunked out as the Tribe's shortstop the previous season, was brought back to replace Hunnefield and third baseman Willie Kamm came over from the White Sox in exchange for Lew Fonseca, allowing Eddie Morgan to play first base full-time. None of the changes would matter, though, if Wes couldn't pitch. "Cleveland, I don't believe," said Walter Johnson, "will be as dangerous all season as they have been figured. Outside of Wes Ferrell, they lack the pitching and the Indian infield is not any too strong."[7]

Ferrell's next start came on May 13 where he lasted until the fourth inning, giving ten hits and five earned runs in his first career loss to Washington. In his one trip to the plate he plastered the ball off the right-field screen. "It is true that a number of the Washington hits had about them a faint odor of camembert," wrote Cobbledick, "but Ferrell at his best always has something in reserve to check that kind of hitting as well as the real variety. Yesterday he had nothing, in spite of the fact that he reported himself fully recovered from the arm trouble that was bothering him a few days ago."

Cleveland had lost eight games in a row when Wes went against George Earnshaw on May 17 in a battle of the league's best right-handers. In three trips to the plate, Ferrell doubled off the right-field wall and homered into the left-field bleachers. "Wesley Ferrell, as great a pitcher as Earnshaw and probably a greater one, was Cleveland's starter," wrote Cob-

Ferrell's pitching motion was described as smooth and effortless (Gwenlo Ferrell Gore).

bledick. "He went out in the sixth with two home runs, five doubles and five singles charged against him, and all that terrific slugging of his mates was wasted."[8] Philadelphia won 15–10.

Despite five infield errors behind him, Ferrell put an end to Cleveland's 12-game losing streak with a 10–5 win over the White Sox on May 23. As a batter Wes had a single and two walks in five plate appearances. "While still a long way removed from his top form," wrote the *Plain Dealer*, "Wes was good enough yesterday to win behind the kind of offensive backing his teammates gave him.

"For three innings he was hit freely. In that time the Sox made more than half of their eleven hits and three-fifths of their runs. Thereafter Ferrell seemed to recover the stuff that has been mysteriously missing for a fortnight, and at the finish he was pumping the ball into Luke Sewell's mitt with all his old-time zip."[9]

Two days later Willis Hudlin beat Chicago, but required ninth-inning help from Ferrell, who had been warming in the pen for three innings.

The Indians were in sixth place with a 14–20 record on May 26. Wes started the next day against St. Louis and was a 5–4 winner thanks to a four-run Cleveland rally in the ninth. "Wes Ferrell was the Indian pitcher, and the victory was his seventh of the season," said the *Plain Dealer*. "Still far from the Ferrell who blanked the same team hitless four weeks ago, Wes still was good enough to hold them to eight hits and two earned runs.

"It was the two unearned runs, however, that threatened to ruin his day. They were the result of an error by Joe Vosmik in the opening inning, when, after Levey had singled, he allowed Goslin's single to roll through him to the bleachers, both runners scoring."

The Indians ran their win streak to seven on May 31 with a 6–4 victory over Detroit. When the Cleveland starter ran out of gas in the seventh, Peck rushed Wes to the hill. Umpire Bill McGowan allowed the hurler additional warmup tosses but stopped him after ten or a dozen. Ferrell protested that he wasn't ready, and when Luke Sewell and Peck argued Wes' case, the Cleveland manager was chased from the field. Wes threw another warmup toss and McGowan called it ball one. The *Plain Dealer* thought their pitcher within his rights, but the Detroit press viewed this as an example of Ferrell's temperament. When he finally went to work, Wes held the Bengals to one infield hit in the three innings, and his club was never in trouble again.

Detroit writer H. G. Salsinger elaborated at length about this in *The Sporting News*. "He is probably not a great pitcher because of his temperament, but he is temperamental because he is a great pitcher. He's probably got the idea that you cannot be established until you have temperament, artistic or otherwise.

"Temperament is one concession that baseball should grant Mr. Ferrell. The late Christopher Mathewson, to whom Mr. Ferrell has been likened, was also a man of temperament. Mr. Mathewson had it in abundance and his colleagues made allowances for it."[10]

Wes answered these charges at the end of the season. "Vague rumors have flitted about the circuit that Ferrell is 'swell-headed," wrote *Baseball* magazine. "That is not true. He is quiet, efficient and believes in attending to his own affairs. There is nothing of noisy braggadocio in Ferrell's nature. But he is and has every reason to be confident of his own abilities. Why Not? Are they not self-evident?

"Bragging never set well with me,' says Ferrell. 'But there's a difference between knowing what you can do and exaggerating what you can do. A pitcher must have confidence in himself or he's of little value to anybody. If I went in there with the feeling that I was going to get my ears knocked off, what success would I have? I am never sure of winning a ball game. I realized that baseball is too uncertain for that. But I have been sure many times of pitching a good game. That's my contribution to the club. If it's not enough to win for us, I can't help it."[11]

Ferrell finally came clean on his arm while the Indians were in Boston. "After several weeks of evasion and denial, Wesley Ferrell finally admitted to Manager Peckinpaugh today that his right shoulder is painfully sore and has been so almost ever since his no-hit performance on April 29.

"Wes doesn't know just what to attribute his trouble to, but rather suspects a tooth that has been bothering him for some time. Peck is going to send him to a dentist tomorrow, and if that doesn't reveal the root of the difficulty the star pitcher will be shipped off to a specialist in baseball arms and shoulders."[12]

Ferrell went from the dentist's chair to the mound in Fenway Park on June 4 to beat the hapless Red Sox. The final score was 10–2 in Cleveland's favor and it was the club's tenth win in a row. "Didn't throw more than three or four fast balls in the whole game and the three or four were mediocre," wrote Cobbledick. "They didn't have the zip that one looks for when Wes Ferrell cuts loose.

"One watched him through the early innings today and felt a bit sorry that a pitcher like Ferrell, gifted by nature with brilliant blistering speed should have to get by with half-speed curves and looping slow balls."[13] The Indians scored four times in the first and six more in the ninth when Wes smashed a home run "deep into the center field bleachers."

The next stop was New York where Wes beat the Yankees with a three-hitter on June 9. *Times'* writer John Kieran, for his ongoing quest to determine if it were Ferrell or Earnshaw as the league's top right-hander, interviewed Willie Kamm and Bibb Falk before the game. "It's hard to say," said Bibb. "Ferrell's had a sore arm for some time. Can't throw his fast ball and that's his big bet."

"I'd pick Ferrell," said Kamm.

"He's a lot younger," said Bibb. "He ought to pile up a great record before he gets through."

"That isn't the only reason I'd pick him," said Kamm. "You see, he's had a sore arm but he went in as a relief pitcher just the same and he stopped rallies. Then he went out and beat the Red Sox, sore arm and all. That's what I claim is a good pitcher."[14]

Red Ruffing started for New York and held Cleveland to just one hit before falling apart in the ninth. Wes retired the first seven batters before Joe Sewell doubled in the third inning. Bill Dickey singled with one down in the fifth and moved to third when Wes made a wild pickoff attempt. The lone New York tally — unearned — then came when Sewell drove him in with a single. Ferrell retired fourteen of the next sixteen batters, allowing only walks to Sewell in the eighth and Lou Gehrig in the ninth. The Indians scored four times in the ninth for a 4–1 victory. "Just as it was when Ferrell pitched the tribe to victory over the Red Sox a few days ago," said Cobbledick, "it was plain today that the boy still is suffering from that crippled shoulder that has made it impossible for him to throw a fast ball for a month or so.

"He didn't throw a fast ball today. Once when he had to make a long throw after fielding a bunt near the third base line he looped the ball fifteen feet in the air, heaving it with a stiff, painful motion.

"But his curve, and it was a beauty, was working well enough to hold such clouters as Ruth, Gehrig, Combs and Ruffing himself hitless."[15]

After the game Wes declared his arm worries were over. "It was still sore and stiff at the beginning of yesterday's game," he said, "but in the late innings it began to loosen up and by the time the game was over it felt good enough to beat any ball club in the world."

Ferrell dropped a 7–1 decision to Washington on June 12, heading to the showers after allowing eight hits and six runs in four innings. "But two of the blows were pop doubles by Joe Kuhel," observed the *Plain Dealer*, "flies that fell safe on the left field foul line just beyond the reach of Kamm, Goldman and Vosmik. They came in such spots that they alone gave the Nats four of the six runs they made off Ferrell."[16] In his two plate appearances Wes walked and doubled.

With Cleveland and Philadelphia ready for another go-between, the press was beginning to ask question why Grove and Ferrell had still not dueled. Speculation was the Grove, or Mack, wouldn't agree to it. "The great left hander is ahead of Earnshaw in the regular order of succession, but there is a feeling among the Indians the Connie won't send Grove against the Cleveland ace for fear of the effect a defeat might have on his well-known temperament."[17]

When Earnshaw beat Wes 4–2 on June 16, Cleveland's fielding support was again substandard. "Ferrell allowed seven hits in the seven innings he pitched," commented the *Plain Dealer*, "but one of them was a fly that Falk lost in the sun and another was a lucky pop by Bing Miller. But tainted as these hits were, they gave the Mackmen two runs. Another tally was the outcome of a wild throw by Falk."[18]

Wes' fast ball was back and evident for all to see on June 21 when he beat Alvin Crowder and the Nationals 3–1, allowing seven hits and two passes. With the score knotted at 1–1 in the seventh, Wes blasted a towering drive over the screen in far right center. In addition to the home run, he singled and walked in his two other plate appearances. "If any remnant of the arm trouble that has plagued Ferrell all season was present yesterday he managed to keep it well under cover," noted the *Plain Dealer*. "Certainly it didn't prevent him from throwing some of the fastest fast balls that have blazed out of the hand of any pitcher the Indians have met this summer."

The Yankees jumped on Ferrell in the opening game of a doubleheader in Cleveland on June 27. Gehrig hit a three-run shot in the first and Lyn Lary's double preceding base hits by Ruth and Gehrig plated another pair in the second. Wes then tightened, allowing just five more hits over the remaining seven innings while his teammates ran up a dozen tallies. The final was 12–5 and Wes' record was 11–4.

Willis Hudlin had a 5–1 lead in the eighth inning against the Yankees the next afternoon before Ruth jacked a three-run homer over the right field wall onto Lexington Avenue. Peck decided it was time for a change and Ferrell — who had gone down to the bullpen on his volition — came into the game. "Any time we have a tight game," the Cleveland skipper said, "and someone else is pitching Ferrell will come around and say, 'If things get tough, send me in there. I'll stop 'em!' Get that! Not I'll try to stop 'em,' but I'll stop 'em!' What makes this important is that when you send him in he does stop 'em."[19]

Wes stopped them in the eighth but the ninth inning was a disaster. "One little break in the ninth might have changed things," speculated the *Plain Dealer*. "First Ferrell seemed to have Bill Dickey, the lead-off hitter in the final inning, struck out on what looked to him and to Luke Sewell and to everybody but Umpire Hildebrand to be a perfect strike. But Hildy called it a ball and then Dickey started things with a single.

"The speedy Dusty Cooke was sent in to run for him and Myril Hoag to bat for Lefty Gomez, the second Yankee hurler. Hoag struck out, but then Combs slashed one past Eddie Morgan and into the right field corner for a double. Dick Porter retrieved the ball quickly and shot it to Morgan, who calmly held it while Cooke galloped home. A throw to the plate would have headed him off by ten feet."[20] Lary followed with a triple. Ruth walked, Gehrig reached on an infield error and Chapman singled. Wes departed, being charged with four earned runs and the loss. The final score was 9–5.

On July 1 the much anticipated matchup between Grove and Ferrell finally took place and the Philadelphia hurler came out on top. "Grove won by a score of 4–3," wrote the *Plain Dealer*, "thereby giving the lie to the rather widely credited stories that he was afraid to pitch against the Cleveland ace. But his margin of superiority wasn't great enough to settle the question of superiority — as if such a question could be settled by anything less than a long series of duels over a period of years."[21]

Philadelphia scored first in the fourth on Cochrane's infield single and Simmons' double into the right-field corner. Cleveland tied it right back up on a two-out single and a two-bagger. The Athletics scored twice in the sixth to take a 3–1 lead when Cochrane deposited a slow curve into the right-field seats; and then on a walk to Simmons, a single by Foxx and a fly ball by Dykes. The Tribe got to Grove in the seventh with three consecutive doubles to make the score 3–3. After Wes retired Simmons and Foxx in the eighth, Bing Miller laced a double off the right field screen and rookie Dibby Williams, following an intentional pass to Dykes, drove in the deciding tally with a base hit. Each hurler allowed 11 hits while Ferrell walked and struck out five and Grove passed one and fanned three. Lefty and Wes both fanned twice and singled once as a batter.

Cleveland was 36–36 and was in fourth place after the games on the Fourth of July, the traditional midpoint of the season, while Philadelphia was playing over a .700 pace at 51–20. Ferrell started off the second half of the season with a rain-shortened 5–4 loss to the Tigers on July 5. Vic Sorrell limited the Indians to six hits, among them two singles by Wes and a three-run homer in the fifth inning by Morgan.

"Wes Ferrell's ailing shoulder kept him out of action today," wrote the *Plain Dealer* on July 12, " and it is possible the he will be unable to get into either game of tomorrow's doubleheader. Roger Peckinpaugh has determined to give him a thorough rest in the hope of clearing up the trouble that has handicapped his pitching ace since the beginning of the season."

Still fiddling with his infield, Peck had just shipped Jonah Goldman off to Indianapolis in exchange for Eddie Montague. He showed up with the news that he had playing with cracked ribs and hadn't swung a bat in four days. "Through his four years at the helm of the Indians," noted the *Plain Dealer*, "Peckinpaugh has lacked the first requisite for a strong contending club — a tight infield, with a smooth second base combination. He has seen innumerable ball games kicked away by erratic infield play and has been powerless to do anything about it."

Ferrell's "thorough rest" consisted of just one more day as he beat the White Sox 10–5 on July 12. His mates scored nine times over the first three innings and Ferrell, as the *Plain Dealer* noted, "Was invincible in the early part of the game, holding the enemy to three hits and no runs. Later he either eased up or weakened and they bunched eight blows in the sixth, seventh and eighth to account for all their runs."

Wesley's next start came against Herb Pennock at Yankee Stadium on July 17 where he pitched and batted the Indians to a 2–1 victory. He allowed just three hits and struck out Joe Sewell — the game's toughest man to fan — and Babe Ruth back to back in the opening frame. The first New York safety came when Ruth deposited a fourth-inning home run into the right-field seats to erase Cleveland's 1–0 lead. A fifth-inning single by Dickey and a short flare dumped by Ruth into center in the sixth were the other two hits. Wes resolved the contest in the seventh, swinging, "with everything he had and shot one a mile a minute into the covered stands near the left field line." The game was called after a 45-minute rain delay in the ninth. "There was no denying the merits of Ferrell's moundsmanship," wrote the New York *Times*, "There was also no denying Ferrell's power with the bat, for he knocked the ball far into the left-field stands."

Ferrell lost a 3–2 game to the Red Sox in ten innings on July 21 to drop his record to 13–7. "Wes Ferrell issued one base on balls too many today," wrote Cobbledick, "and it cost him his fourteenth victory of the season.

"He looked no more like the Ferrell who held the Yankees to three hits a few days ago than Jonah Goldman looks like Babe Ruth, and yet he did make some pretty fair pinch pitching to make thirteen hits and five bases on balls count for only three runs."

The Tribe, then down 2–1, had been limited to just three hits when "a mighty triple by Ferrell off the center field fence" and a Willie Kamm single tied the score in the eighth. Wildness overcame Ferrell in the Boston tenth and he walked two batters with one down. "He had two strikes and no balls on [Otto] Miller when the batter reached for one and sent a low liner in [second baseman's] Hodapp's direction. It struck the ground four feet in front of Johnny and then, taking some weird English, twisted out of his reach and into right field, while [Al] Van Camp galloped home in front of Porter's desperate throw."[22]

Cleveland opened a five-game series with the Athletics on July 22 and round two of Ferrell versus Grove — which Lefty won 6–3 — came in the first game of a doubleheader on July 25. "He won not by outpitching the Indian ace," wrote Cobbledick, "but by having the better ball club behind him. And Ferrell lost a game that he richly deserved to win because his infield support cracked wide open in the seventh inning, allowing the A's to score three runs when, with reasonably tight play, they wouldn't have gotten a runner past first base."[23]

Ferrell passed Foxx in the second and Bishop in the third, but the only hit he allowed to that point had been an infield one. Al Simmons clanged a hot-shot off Wes' leg to begin the fourth. Foxx walked and Bing Miller dropped down a sacrifice. A ground ball to third scored Simmons and advanced Foxx to third. Dib Williams was passed intentionally and Grove singled for a 2–1 lead.

Wes was working with a 3–2 lead when things fell apart in the seventh. "[Mule] Haas started it with a single and Cochrane fouled out to Luke Sewell. Simmons also lifted a foul behind first but Morgan failed to get under it and then Al walked.

"Foxx hit to Kamm, who, instead of trying for a double play in the orthodox way, tagged Haas for the second out. Then Bing Miller got a scratch single off Ferrell's glove that filled the bases.

"And that should have been all, but Eddie Montague, after making a nice pickup of McNair's roller, threw wildly to first and Simmons crossed the plate with the tying run. McNair was credited with a hit, but by what manner of reasoning I am unable to state," wrote Cobbledick. "Montague's throw had him beaten by a full step, but it pulled Morgan off the bag. At any rate, Williams followed with a clean single and two more runners came in."

Wes' last appearance of the month was a 6–0 shutout of Walter Johnson's second-place Washington club on July 29. "Wesley Ferrell," noted the *Plain Dealer*, "spasmodically relaxed and bore down today. But, to Washington's dismay, the blond Indian ace bore down with runners in scoring position. Ferrell granted ten hits and walked five, but the fact that fifteen Senators were stranded on the bases is testimony to his effectiveness when hits meant runs."[24]

When the American League standings were published on August 2, they showed Philadelphia in first place with a 74–27 record and the Tribe in fourth place at 46–53. Grove's pitching record was 21–2 and Earnshaw and Walberg were both 16–5. Ferrell, at 14–9, was the only other junior circuit hurler with more than 11 victories. Mickey Cochrane led the American League catchers with a .336 batting average and was followed by Rick Ferrell at .320 and Bill Dickey at .316.

Wes' fifteenth win was a 9–4 victory over the Browns in a doubleheader in St. Louis on August 2. "The opener was a pretty pitching duel between Ferrell and [Sam] Gray for five innings," wrote Cobbledick. "At the end of that time the count stood at two-all, but it never was close after that for the Indians broke loose from the reservation in the sixth and scored five runs, the big blow being Ferrell's homer with two on."[25] At the plate Ferrell was perfect with a homer, a single, two walks, two runs scored and three driven in.

Detroit trounced Ferrell on August 8, counting six hits, five walks and five earned runs from him in less than four innings of a 7–1 contest. He hit a double in his lone trip to the plate. "Ferrell's case has officials of the Cleveland ball club seriously concerned last night," wrote the beat writers. "He pitched, they pointed out, like a man with a painfully sore arm. He seemed to push the ball up to the plate with a stiff, awkward motion that looked like anything but the free arm swing he uses when he is right.

"What puzzles them, though, is how a sore-armed pitcher can hurl such games as Wes has turned in in the last month against teams like New York and Washington.

"If his arm is sore they want to let him rest, so that the trouble won't be aggravated. Yet he insists he is all right, asks to be allowed to pitch, and then goes out and proves as he did yesterday that is decidedly not all right."[26]

Wes took his next turn against the Yankees on August 13 and in the first inning fanned Ruth and Gehrig when he "cut loose with stuff the like of which he has never before exceeded." The skies then opened up and the ensuing downpour cancelled the game.

"Folks had been wondering — and so had the Indian management — whether or not there really was anything ailing the great flipper of tribe's premier hurler," wrote Sam Otis in trying to explain Wes. "One day he would be so good and the next game bad, so yesterday was picked as the time to determine whether he had gone off color or not."

Round three of Grove versus Ferrell occurred on August 15 and Grove again won by a 4–3 score. "Yes, Bob took Mr. Ferrell again," wrote Cobbledick. "Took him in a battle that was something of Wes' own making, for the Indian asked to face the Mackmen on the day Grove worked. Nobody knew whether it would be yesterday or today, so only 12,000 fans turned out to witness one of the most thrilling and interesting contests ever staked in this town.

"Even Ferrell didn't know for certain until after he had carted a brand new ball to the pitching warmup slab. Then, after a dramatic lapse of a couple of minutes, out strutted the tall master workman of the Mackian mounds corps. From that moment until the final out the situation was tense, the crowd seeming to sense the keenness of the duel all the way."

Max Bishop began the contest with a single and Doc Cramer walked. They moved up on a Cochrane ground ball before Simmons was passed intentionally to fill the bases. Foxx cracked one back up the middle that Ferrell knocked down with his bare hand but couldn't make a play on. Bing Miller grounded to second, but Johnny Burnett's throw to the second-base bag sailed over shortstop Eddie Montague's head into left field. That made the score 2–0 and the bases were still loaded. Another grounder to Burnett produced an out, but Montague's relay to first was low and Simmons scored the third run.

Ferrell retired 16 of the next 17 batters and the Tribe scored a pair of runs off Grove in the sixth, but two Philadelphia singles sandwiched around a walk in the seventh made the score 4–2. Cleveland scored in the eighth inning run to account for the final score. Ferrell's record fell to 15–11 and the victory was Grove's twenty-fourth of the season and fifteenth in a row. Each pitcher allowed three earned runs. Grove gave eight hits and Ferrell six. Grove fanned four and Ferrell five. Grove passed one and Ferrell three.

Ferrell's next two starts came against Washington. He was ineffective on August 19, leaving after allowing two earned runs in less than four innings. "That old fastball of his was not in evidence." Three early hits and two runs had Wes on the ropes on August 22. "Every Nat seemed to take a lusty paste and the drives were whistling to the outskirts in a manner that boded evil," wrote the *Plain Dealer*. After the second inning, though, Ferrell regained his stride and was not seriously threatened again, allowing just three more safeties in winning his sixteenth, 5–2.

Dick Coffman of the Browns stopped Grove's winning streak at sixteen with a 1–0 shutout on August 23. Four days later he dropped an 11–1 decision to Ferrell, not lasting the second inning as Wes limited the Browns to four hits. "Excepting a tendency to wildness [he issued six passes]," reported the *Plain Dealer*, "the Indian ace was as good as had been at any time in his three-year career — as good, indeed, as he was on the day last spring when he shut out these same Browns without a hit.

"The four hits off his delivery were one clean single by Irving Burns, one two-bagger by Jim Levey that struck squarely on the chalked foul line in left field, one infield hopper by Burns that bounced off Johnny Hodapp's shins for a single, and one bounder over the box that Wes himself slowed up just enough to make it too tough for Burnett to handle."[27] Wes went two for three with the stick, driving in the first two Cleveland runs with a second-inning single.

Though Ferrell was recognized as a good hitter in his first two seasons, people were really starting to take note of his power in 1931. "Take today's game with the White Sox, for instance," wrote the *Plain Dealer* after he beat Chicago on August 31. "Wes' contribution to a 15 to 5 Cleveland victory was two home runs which drove in five runs, a single in which he later scored a run and a sacrifice which advanced an eventual run.

"Ferrell's two homers came in successive times at bat, the first in the fifth inning and the other in the sixth. His blow in the fifth was a prodigious smash into the upper left field stands more than 370 feet from home plate, and it also scored Kamm.

"In addition to these slugging attainments Mr. Ferrell did not lose sight of the fact that he was out for his eighteenth victory of the season. There is no telling what he could have done if pressed, but he was content to hold the Sox to six hits and five unearned runs." One of Chicago's runs, in fact, was counted as earned despite the fact that two errors by the Cleveland infield contributed to all of the scoring, four runs coming in the bottom of the eighth when Ferrell had a thirteen run lead. The only debit on his tally sheet was seven walks. Unable to count on his fast ball, Ferrell was relying more and more on the curve ball and it was costing him control. Walter Johnson publicly stated that he thought that Ferrell was making a mistake by not using his heater.

A 10–5 decision in St. Louis on September 5 went into the books as Ferrell's nineteenth victory. The Browns notched six hits over the first five innings—four singles plating a run in the second—but Wes led 10–1 lead going into the bottom of the sixth before St. Louis scored its second run. Four more St. Louis safeties in the eighth accounted for the final three runs.

With the season winding down, the *Plain Dealer*, on September 6, began talking about moving Wes to the outfield. "Now that Wesley Ferrell has demonstrated his ability to hit home runs on a handsome scale the boys are talking, unofficially of course, about turning him into an outfielder, even as Babe Ruth, Lefty O'Doul, Earl Webb, Bill Terry and some other notable hitters were made over.

"Yes, the age of pitching giants is coming back and Ferrell, with an impressive three-year start toward one of the greatest lifetime records in history, is in an ideal spot to reap a huge share of the glory he loves.

"Ferrell isn't what you would call a flat failure. He is in the home stretch now of what has been for him a disappointing season, yet with yesterday's game in the record only one pitcher in the majors has won more games than he and that one, Grove, is working for the greatest ball club in the world.

"Ferrell has averaged one homer for every twelve trips to the plate. So has Ruth, although Wes has a hairline edge on the Babe if you want to carry it out a couple of decimal places. Gehrig has had to carry his bat to the dish thirteen times for every circuit drive he has made, while Averill had done no better than one out of eighteen."

Wes' twentieth triumph was a 7–4 decision in Washington on September 12 and it came as the Nats were trying desperately to hold off the rushing New Yorkers for second-place. "Nine hits were all the Nationals could make off his delivery," wrote Cobbledick, "and these were scattered so effectively that a four-run lead carved out by the Indians in the first inning never was seriously threatened. Only twice, in fact, were the Nats able to put two blows together in an inning."[28]

Philadelphia's 100th victory of the year — and Earnshaw's twentieth — came at the expense of Ferrell in a 7–5 contest on September 16. "Wes Ferrell may be a great pitcher to the rest of the American league," observed the *Plain Dealer*, "but he remains just another good batter to the Athletics, just crowned American League champions for the third straight year."[29] The Tribe jumped on Earnshaw for five runs in the second inning while the only Athletics hit over the first four innings was a single by Al Simmons. Connie Mack then attacked Ferrell's professed weakness by taking out his regulars and sending in the subs. Wes prided himself on his ability to outthink hitters and hated facing unfamiliar batters. Philadelphia's newbies accounted for seven hits and seven runs in the fifth and sixth innings.

New York's ten-game winning streak was stopped on September 21 as Wes beat Red Ruffing 5–1 to drop the Yankees into a tie with Washington at 90–58. The victory allowed Cleveland to climb to a game under .500 at 74–75. New York had nine hits and left 12 runners on base but Wes was never bothered by baserunners. In fact, he reveled in it. "I rather like to have somebody on the bags," he said. "Then I know I have to bear down harder. And I don't mind facing a good pitcher. I usually get them. That means a tight ball game. I like to be in a tight ball game. If the other fellow beats me, that's his good luck. Much as I like to win, if I've really pitched a good game, I'm satisfied. That's what old Alexander used to say, and he was right."[30]

Luke Sewell also noted that Ferrell was unaffected by traffic on the base paths. While discussing pitcher George Uhle, Sewell said: "George was one of three pitchers I ever saw that I thought could pitch a ball game by themselves—in other words make their own selections at any stage of the game and go ahead and pitch without any trouble. The other two were Wes Ferrell and Alvin Crowder. Never bothered those fellows how many men might have been on base."[31]

McCarthy's men escaped a shutout in the sixth inning when two walks and a Ben Chapman single accounted for their run. "In the seventh both Ruth and Gehrig came up with two on bases," observed the *Plain Dealer*, "but Babe grounded out and Ferrell got Gehrig on strikes. Each of the Yankee sluggers was charged with four times at bat and a single by Gehrig was the only hitting they did."[32]

Ferrell ended his season with his twenty-second victory, a 7–3 contest he took from Tommy Bridges and the Tigers at home on September 26. Cleveland jumped on Bridges for five runs in the first inning, allowing Wes to coast. His only difficult inning was the fourth, when three hits and a walk plated two Detroit runs. In the bottom of the frame Wes clouted a ball that "sailed into the top seats of the concrete bleachers in left field." It was his ninth home run of the season.

* * *

Babe Ruth and Roger Maris each held the single-season home run record for approximately 40 years. Mark McGwire's total stood for just two. Wes Ferrell's mark of nine home runs by a major league pitcher in 1931 has stood for more than seven decades. His 37 career home runs also remain the standard for pitchers.[33]

* * *

The following table represents all of the Cleveland batters who had at least 75 at bats in the 35 games Ferrell started in 1931.

	Games	At bats	Runs	Hits	2B	3B	HR	RBI	Ave.
Morgan	30	105	26	47	7	3	6	20	.448
Ferrell	35	106	24	37	6	1	9	29	.349
Hodapp	29	112	19	39	3	1	1	21	.348
Averill	35	148	37	50	11	0	7	35	.338
Vosmik	33	130	17	39	9	3	5	29	.300
Burnett	22	89	14	25	5	0	0	10	.281
Kamm	25	87	13	24	5	0	0	14	.276
L. Sewell	26	104	10	26	4	0	0	15	.250

* * *

When Connie Mack passed through Greensboro early in 1931 and was asked by a local sportswriter if he thought Rick Ferrell was a good catcher,

Mack replied, "Rick Ferrell is not a good catcher — he's far better than good. Good does not explain him."[34]

Rick had watched quietly for two seasons as Wes soaked up all the attention. When *Baseball* Magazine ran an article on the catcher in its August 1931 issue, it was titled *Rick Ferrell, Brother of Wes.* "Wes is the individual star of the family. He displayed extraordinary talent at the outset of his career and he has lived up to that early promise of a 'Future Great.' As time goes on it becomes apparent that he belongs among the super-stars of all time.

"Rick of the Browns is quite overshadowed by the spectacular triumphs of Wes. But who in authority would care to predict that Rick's future won't be equally bright?

"No small measure of Wes Ferrell's success is due to his mental qualities. He is fearless, even brazen, out there on the mound. He has unconquerable spirit and cocky self-confidence that defies defeat. Rick is not lacking in these essentials. He, too, is ambitious to excel, and after an hour's chat with him one is convinced that he will. His confidence in himself is supreme — but it is quiet. There is nothing obnoxious about it. Then, too, he has unusual baseball sense, a keen alertness and good judgment. He handles pitchers well. Mentally or physically he has no defective kink in his armor."[35]

Rick came out of the gate fast in 1931, doubling twice off Waite Hoyt in the season's second game. On May 3, he went four for five with two doubles and two RBI in a 9–5 win over the White Sox. Two days later he went four for four against Cleveland.

"In his last five games previous to this week," noted *The Sporting News* on May 14, "Ferrell batted .706, with 12 hits in 17 times at bat, bringing his mark for the season up to .371. Up to the time of his third appearance at the plate in the game of May 9, he had reached first base 13 consecutive times."

Rick was hitting .347 at the end of May and .329 at the close of June. When he busted his right hand making a tag play on Boston's Urban Pickering on July 14 he was at .327. Out of action for two weeks, he managed to raise his average to .331 by August 9 before finishing the season at .306.

* * *

When the Buffalo Bisons took the field against the St. Louis Browns in West Palm Beach, Florida on March 20, 1931, it marked the professional beginning of the Ferrell Brother battery, and while Rick did the catching, it wasn't Wes doing the pitching, for he was in New Orleans with the Indians. Instead, it was 19-year-old Marvin Ferrell, whom the Browns had just

The first "professional" Ferrell Brothers battery. Marvin (left) and Rick Ferrell in the Browns 1931 spring camp (Mike McKee).

signed to a contract. George Ferrell was also there, playing left field and batting third for Buffalo.

Marvin had followed his brothers to Guilford High School and like Wes to the Oak Ridge Academy. He had spent the past few summers playing semi-pro ball in Pennsylvania and Virginia, playing first base as well as the outfield.

George Ferrell felt that Marvin would have gone further as a professional had he stuck with his natural position, which was first base. Rick thought Marvin had all of the same physical capabilities that Wes had. "He sort of wanted to play first base but I told him he was crazy, with a fast ball like he's got," said Wes of Marvin in 1929. "So he's going to be a pitcher."

Marvin and Wes resembled each other physically, standing a few inches taller than either Rick or George. While gathering photos for this book, several photos that were identified as Wes and Rick were actually of Marvin and Rick.

"Ferrell seems to have profited by his brother's coaching and being a lanky lad ... appears to have all the physical requirements to become a great pitcher," said Milwaukee manager Marty Berghammer when the Browns farmed Marvin to the American Association at the end of spring training. Marvin's famous last name hindered him, for he was overmatched in the American Association and would likely have benefited from starting in a lower classification. By the end of the season he was playing for Wichita Falls in the Texas League, where he defeated Shreveport and pitcher Thornton Lee by the score of 2–1 on September 9. With the game tied at one in the seventh inning, Lee purposely walked the number eight hitter to bring Ferrell to the plate. There was a runner on second base and two were out. As he walked to the plate, Marvin hollered out, "Yeah, they will walk a .250 hitter to get to a .500 slugger, will they?" He slammed a double to drive in the winning run.[36]

* * *

Branch Rickey was frequently in Greensboro during the 1930s to oversee and evaluate talent for the St. Louis Cardinals' farm chain. The local management told Rickey that their biggest need to start the 1931 season was a power hitter. Several days later a telegram arrived from Rickey informing them that the "Big Bertha" he promised was on the way.

"George Ferrell, well known member of the famous family of Ferrells of Guilford country having been purchased from the Buffalo Bisons of the International league, and ordered to Greensboro," wrote the Greensboro *Daily News.*

"The Cardinals, ever alert to add a star player to their extensive chain, not only wanted Ferrell to help Greensboro in the Piedmont race this season but to have on hand for the future. George is a major league prospect."[37]

George, despite spending several weeks with Buffalo at the start of the season, had another of his typical Piedmont League batting seasons, hitting .334 with 13 home runs and 84 RBI. The other big Greensboro stick belonged to Johnny Mize, who played alongside George in the Patriots' outfield. Mize hit .337 with nine homers and 64 RBI. Buffalo reclaimed George at the end of the season, arguing that St. Louis had failed to meet a deadline in finalizing his sale. "So official and technical did the document read," wrote the Greensboro *Daily News* on October 2, "that George called his attorney for consultation and it developed that he is the property of the Bisons. It's just another story of baseball technicalities."

* * *

Grantland Rice discussed the up-and-coming baseball stars who would soon be replacing Babe Ruth and the old guard in a June 1931 issue of *Collier's*. "The first nomination," he wrote, "is a 23-year-old pitcher named Wesley Ferrell. Built along the lines of Matty and Walter Johnson, Ferrell in certain particulars is a reminder of both in their earlier years. Like Matty in his younger days Ferrell has speed, a fine curve and first-class control.

"Like Walter Johnson the young Cleveland star is extremely quiet, but pleasant and courteous if you have questions to ask. If there is any talking to be done, you will have to open the conversation.

"Ferrell is a big, strong, smart, cool, serious pitcher who keeps in condition and who, before his heyday is over, may even top the winning records of Mathewson, Johnson and Alexander."

The October issue of *Baseball* Magazine also had high praise for Wes.

"The mantle of the lamented Christy Mathewson has fallen upon the shoulders of this stalwart North Carolina hurler. Where others acquire pitching finesse by years of toil and painful experience, Ferrell is a pitcher by divine right. He has everything, great speed, a sweeping curve, a tantalizing change of pace, air-tight control and the cap-stone of the pitching ace — cool self-confidence.

"Much of this great record has been made while Ferrell was not in the best of condition. In the latter half of last season he pitched with a sore arm. His arm has been sore this year. Some season when he is feeling in the flush of health, when his long right arm is unkinked and the hop of his fastball is riding high, Ferrell should make a name for himself to be remembered."

◆ 7 ◆

1932 — Peck's Bad Boy

Dazzy Vance pitched the first four innings of an exhibition game for the Dodgers in New Orleans on April 3. He fanned seven and didn't allow a hit. Wes Ferrell went the full nine, giving seven hits and six walks. He did not strike out a batter. Cleveland won the game 3–2. "Ferrell is another Christy Mathewson," raved Brooklyn manager Max Carey after the game. "That means he is one of the greatest pitchers I have ever seen. He has the same stuff that made Matty well nigh invincible, and if his arm does not go back on him he ought to develop into the best right-hander that the American League has ever produced. The secret of Ferrell's success is that he knows how and what to pitch to each hitter."[1] Coach Casey Stengel was just as impressed, remarking, "Jeez, that guy gets in my hair. He makes pitching look so easy."[2]

Wes had recovered his arm strength over the winter. "Put me down for 20 victories," he quipped at the start of training camp. "I hope to win more, but I don't want to make any extravagant promises and disappoint my friends by failing to live up to them. The sore arm that bothered me considerably last season is in excellent shape."[3] He was back to his usual cocky self. "With two out and two strikes on the batter," commented *The Sporting News* on a spring training game, "Ferrell wound up and sent the ball steaming toward the plate. As soon as it left his hand, he tossed his glove aside and started for the bench. He knew the batter wouldn't hit the ball...."[4]

The year 1932 would be a memorable one to Ferrell for several reasons. Despite bouts of arm trouble he would become both the first and last hurler in modern baseball history to reach twenty wins in each of his first four years in the show. His temper, for the first but definitely not the last time, would get him into trouble. Finally, his record looks less impressive than it really was because he had to pitch against both the Yankees and Athletics, something neither Grove nor Lefty Gomez had to do.

Wes (left) and Marvin Ferrell in Cleveland in 1932 after the Tribe had signed Marvin to a contract (Marva Ferrell Flowers).

Against the five other American League teams in 1932 Ferrell was 20–5 with a 3.00 ERA, but versus the powerful New York and Philadelphia squads he was just 3–8 with a 5.27 ERA. Grove had the same hard time with the New Yorkers as Wes did, finishing with a 5.49 ERA in 41 innings, identical to Wes' 5.48 and 42.2 numbers. "It was a tough time to be in that league," said Peckinpaugh. "We were up against two great ball clubs. It was very discouraging. You knew you were doomed the day the season opened, with those two monsters in the league."[5]

Wes opened the season with a 6–5 victory in Detroit on a frigid April 13. The Tigers jumped out to a 4–1 lead after four innings, but over the next seven rounds they managed just a single unearned run. Roy Johnson began the game with a home run off the Cleveland hurler, and a misjudged fly ball that went for a triple accounted for two more Detroit tallies in the second frame. Ferrell gave up 14 hits in the 11-inning contest and though he had but one hit in the game, "his fly to (left fielder John) Stone in the second inning would have cleared the fence with plenty to spare had anything less than a gale been blowing in. He socked one almost as hard in the fifth."[6]

Ferrell's second start was a 2–1 triumph in Chicago on April 18. He lost a shutout when third baseman Willie Kamm underestimated Smead Jolley's speed and allowed him to beat out an infield single with two down and a runner on third in the sixth inning. "Excepting that inning," wrote the Plain Dealer, "when the Sox bunched three of their hits, Ferrell had them eating out of his hand all the way. When he knew he had to pitch — and he did know it in the last three rounds when his lead was cut to a single run — he was unhittable. Only one man reached first in those innings, and he on an infield out after two were out in the eighth."[7]

Detroit had taken the first three games of a four-game set in Cleveland before Wes beat them, 8–7, on April 23, scoring the winning run himself in the bottom of the ninth. "Though he wasn't himself by any means," wrote Gordon Cobbledick, "Ferrell won and again topped the American League pitchers with three victories and no defeats. He didn't have his fast ball and his curve wasn't very deceiving, but what of it? The slump is over."[8]

With rumors afloat that his arm was bothering him, Wes put down the St. Louis squad on April 27 by the score of 7–1. "Ferrell held the Browns to five hits, three of which were bunched in the fifth inning, when they scored their only run," wrote the Plain Dealer. "Except in that session not a single member of the home team reached second base.

"Wes was as good today as he has ever been in his life, which makes it practically certain that he will work every fourth day for the rest of the season, even if it upsets the pitching order."[9] The Cleveland ace retired the side in the first inning on nine pitches. All were strikes and the first two batters went down without contact. Goose Goslin finally put wood on the ball — on the ninth pitch — and fouled out. When Rick Ferrell came to bat in the second inning, Wes waved all his outfielders in shallow before retiring his brother on a short fly.

Wes ran his record to 5–0 with an 11–1 victory over the White Sox on May 1, his teammates blowing the game open with seven runs in the eighth inning. The Chisox were limited to seven hits, all singles. "Three of them, including two infield hits," wrote Cobbledick, "were grouped in the first round to give the Sox their lone tally. Later there was another blow that never saw the grass of the outfield, so that there were only four solid hits made by the visitors....

"At no time was it necessary for Wes to bear down with all his stuff. His slow curve was his most effective weapon. It had the Sox lifting the ball harmlessly into the air or tapping equally harmlessly along the ground, and he seldom had to resort to a real fast ball."[10]

Ferrell put his perfect record up against Lefty Grove in Philadelphia on May 5 and Mack's bludgeoners routed him in the seventh inning. The final was 15–3 and all of Cleveland's offense came late in the game after Grove had an insurmountable lead. Only seven of the 12 runs Ferrell allowed were earned as the Cleveland defense, although charged with just a lone error, was something less than exemplary. Their pitcher's deportment took a similar beating. "Ferrell is too easily provoked," wrote Ed Pollack in the Philadelphia *Public Ledger*. "He has the experience, the ability, and all the necessary requisites to be of greater value to his club and himself if he would remain undisturbed when the breaks of the game turn against him.

"With perfect support behind him Ferrell could have held the rallies of the A's in the sixth and seventh. But perfect is too much to ask of any club, and the Indians are far from the best defensive team in the American League.

"When the defense cracked Ferrell sulked and gave every indication that he wanted to be relieved. It was a tough ball game and the Western star was all keyed up. Allowances should be granted under the conditions, but Wesley's shortcomings in temperament are not easily overcome, and it would be far better for the Ohio club and Ferrell himself if he would accept the breaks and ignore them.

"Grove is very much like the Cleveland ace, but the Mackmen's southpaw has improved in temperament in the past few years. Ferrell also has improved, but his exhibition yesterday was a pronounced throwback to the old days....

"In justice to Ferrell it must be recorded that had it not been for defensive weaknesses the A's would have scored only two runs in the sixth and seventh instead of nine."[11]

Willis Hudlin beat the Athletics two days later. He had a 10–5 lead before weakening in the ninth. Ferrell, who had been warming in the bullpen since the fifth, relieved and retired the side on three fly balls sandwiched around a Jimmy Foxx triple.

Wes' next assignment was a 3–0 loss to first-place Washington on May 9 in which Lloyd Brown held the Tribe to four hits. "For six innings Ferrell was just a little better than his opponent," reported the *Plain Dealer.* "In that time the Nats made just two hits, one of then a safe bunt. Only one runner had advanced as far as second base and he got there on an error. None at all saw third."[12] Carl Reynolds singled to start the Washington seventh and Joe Judge followed with another up the middle that Wes couldn't hold on to. A sacrifice and an intentional pass filled the bases before Brown rolled a base hit between first and second for the first score. Reynolds struck again with two down in the eighth when he gapped an inside-the-park home run that scored two runs.

Peckinpaugh altered his rotation after Ferrell's May 13 start was rained out in Boston, saving him instead for the Yankees in New York, where the Cleveland offense was stymied 5–0 on May 15 by Red Ruffing's four-hitter. The closest the Tribe came to scoring was Wes' third inning triple. Ferrell had limited the Yanks to just three singles over the first five innings— one off his glove — but things came apart in the sixth. Gehrig was retired after Babe Ruth drew a one-out walk but then a double, a single and finally a triple by Chapman, Dickey and Lazzeri accounted for three runs. A single, two walks, a balk and wild pitch gave New York two more runs in the next inning.

An Associated Press reporter interviewed Ferrell after the game and asked the pitcher who he felt was the best manager in the American League. "It is Joe McCarthy," replied Wes. "He's my idea of a great manager and why shouldn't I say so? Yes, we have a good manager, too. Roger Peckinpaugh knows how to get the best out of his team, but I still think McCarthy is the best in the bunch."[13]

The quotes spread quickly, giving the press a field day. Speculation began immediately that Wes was on the trading block and Alva Bradley and Billy Evans were forced into damage-control mode. "There is no more chance of Ferrell going on market," wrote Cleveland correspondent Ed Bang in *The Sporting News,* "then there is of the Yankees parting with George Herman Ruth." Some of the Cleveland players were grumbling as Wes had complained about his lack of recent offensive support. Peckinpaugh told both Wes and the team to forget the episode, but Ferrell's relationship with the fans and his teammates did not improve when he pitched poorly in his next two starts.

Forever experimenting due to worry about arm strain, the tall North Carolinian had become dependent on his off-speed stuff. "I believe Ferrell is making a serious mistake in trying to get by with the least possible use of his great fast ball," said Peckinpaugh. "He was at his best a couple of years ago when, in a jam, he would wind up and blow that hard one past the best hitters in the league.

"But all of last season and thus far in this one he has been pitching the slow curves and very little else. This was fairly successful last year for the hitters were constantly looking for that fast ball, and the slow stuff threw them off stride. Now the knowledge has gotten around the league that Wes isn't using his fast ball. It is no longer a threat. The hitters are laying for his slow curve and pounding it hard."[14]

Billy Evans traveled to St. Louis where in addition to discussing pitch selection, he advised Ferrell to stop giving interviews. "Wes," Billy told him, "You do all the pitching from now on, and we'll do all the talking. You have a great fast ball and you have been pitching nothing but slow curves. For $18,000 we are entitled to an occasional fast ball."[15]

Ferrell took the advice to heart and announced he would again be throwing heat and on May 28 beat St. Louis 3–1. "Even his warmup before the game was different," wrote Cobbledick. "He bore down on the smoke ball then, too, and when he needed it in the game it was ready. He ought to be convinced tonight that that's the way for him to pitch. Not only did he limit the Browns to seven hits scattered through as many innings, but he didn't issue a single base on balls, which was remarkable for the hurler who led the American League in free passes to first base last year."[16]

Wes picked up his eighth win working in relief versus the White Sox in the nightcap of a doubleheader on May 30. He pitched two scoreless innings but trailed by three runs coming to bat in the last of the ninth. The Tribe rallied for the victory, and Ferrell, the second batter of the inning, belted the first pitch he saw into center field to drive in a run. Following the game several Chicago players trailed Umpire George Moriarty under the stands and accused him of missing a strategic strike during the Cleveland rally. Moriarty and White Sox catcher Charlie Berry started throwing punches and while the two were down on the ground, three other White Sox players began kicking Moriarty.[17]

Wes ran his record to 9–3 with a 3–1 victory over the Tigers in Detroit on June 3. "Ferrell's game was a stirring duel between the Cleveland star and Tommy Bridges, the Tigers slim right-handed youngster, and Wes' edge was in his bat rather than his pitching arm," wrote the Plain Dealer. "He was hit freely, but always he had that little extra juice to turn on when another base knock would have meant a run — and a run in this game was more important than three or four in the nightcap." Detroit scored the first run of the game with two out in the third inning on their only free pass

Wes was built for speed, both off and on the diamond (Gwenlo Ferrell Gore).

of the day, an infield single and a clean single. "Thus Wes was facing a one-run deficit when the Indians came to bat in the fifth inning. Here also there were two out before the excitement, in the form of a single by Eddie Montague, began. Then Ferrell stepped to the plate and blasted one over the scoreboard in left center."[18]

Two days later the Tribe squandered an 8–4 lead as Detroit erupted for six runs in the eighth inning. Reliever Ferrell came into that frame with runners on first and second base and no outs, retiring the first batter on a come-backer. He then he gave up three hits and was out of the game. Mel Harder could not put out the fire and Ferrell was charged with the 10–9 loss. "Not one of the hits allowed by Ferrell was a particular robust one," said the *Plain Dealer*. "One was a perfect double play ball hit by the leaden footed Dale Alexander that, had it been handled, would have ended the inning with the Tribe still a run in front.

"But the bulky form of Umpire Bill Dinneen obscured Cissell's vision of the ball just enough so that it caromed off his glove and into center field, and there never was a chance after that."[19]

Peck's ace broke his hex against the Athletics by beating them 4–3 on June 7. "Wes Ferrell went into a huddle with his closest advisor, Wes Ferrell, shortly after noon yesterday," wrote Cobbledick. "Together they went over the whys and wherefores of his six straight defeats at the hand of the Philadelphia Athletics and together they decided to do something about it." The Athletics made 12 hits but Ferrell was tough in the clutch, and although Al Simmons hit two home runs and his mates added three doubles, all came with the bases empty. "But in spots where a long hit would have meant disaster, where even a single would have beaten him, Ferrell was quite a different pitcher."

With the game tied at two, Wes opened the Cleveland fifth with a double and scored on Dick Porter's base hit. In the seventh, with the game tied at three, Wes led off the inning by "slashing a double to the bleachers and scored the winning run when Porter doubled off the wall." With that slim edge to work with, Ferrell held Philadelphia to only a safe bunt in the last two innings. He set down Bishop, Cramer and Cochrane in order in the ninth, not allowing Simmons to come to the plate again. With the victory — his tenth of the season — Wes, along with Grove, became the top winner in either league.

Next up were the visiting Yankees who fell 6–3 to Ferrell on June 11. Babe Ruth hit a two-run shot in the first frame and New York added an unearned run in the second, but from that point on Wes allowed just two hits and fifteen consecutive New Yorkers went down in order after Bill Dickey's fourth inning double. "His fast ball fairly hummed," noted Cobbledick. "His curve broke with a snap you could almost hear and his control — after he had walked Combs in the first inning — was all but perfect." The Tribe was unable to score until Wes opened the fifth inning with a single. He laid down a key sacrifice in the eighth when Cleveland scored their final two runs.

The Ferrell-Peckinpaugh issue was reopened after the game, and it came via a compliment from the Yankees' manager. "Why, this Ferrell is another Matty!" Joe McCarthy exclaimed. "I realized last year that he was a great pitcher, but not until Saturday, when he shut us out after the second inning, did I appreciate the mental side of his skill. That young man knows how to pitch. The way he maneuvered to make each batter hit the ball where he wanted him to increased my admiration twofold."[20]

Wes delivered a pinch-hit RBI single the next afternoon, but two home runs by Ruth where too much as the Yankees lambasted the Tribe 13–5.

Ferrell put down the Red Sox 9–3 on June 15. With the game never close he pitched only "as skillfully as was necessary," allowing a run in the fifth inning and two more in the eighth. "Ferrell, in winning his twelfth victory, allowed ten hits, which doesn't begin to measure his effectiveness," wrote Cobbledick. "After the third inning, when the Indians took a 5–0 lead, he didn't exert himself enough to break a sweat, but he always had what was needed to stop the enemy when they showed signs of becoming troublesome."[21]

Only three pitchers had more than ten wins when the American League averages were published in the *Plain Dealer* on June 19. Lefty Gomez was 12–1, Grove was 12–3 and Ferrell was 12–4. Wes' next start was a 3–2 loss to Alvin Crowder and Washington on June 20, a contest that Cobbledick described as one of his most brilliant games. "He allowed only five hits, no more than two of which were hard hit balls. His control was all but perfect, for he issued only one free pass to first." The Washington second opened with a Texas Leaguer that went for a double when outfielder Joe Vosmik slipped on the wet grass. A sacrifice and an infield out scored the run. Buddy Myer hit a two-run shot in the fifth to put Washington back up 3–2, and Ferrell became so upset with himself for giving up the lead that he put away the remaining fifteen batters in order. Wes singled in the seventh and moved to third on a base hit, but that was as close as Cleveland got.

Bad weather pushed Wes' next start back to June 26 when he beat the Browns 10–5 in the first game of a doubleheader. St. Louis jumped out to a quick lead when three walks, a lone base hit and an error by the Cleveland first baseman let in four runs in the first. "Ferrell, after his first-inning wildness, was a good as usual, or maybe a bit better. He allowed only six hits and richly earned his thirteenth victory of the season." Eight batters, beginning with the last two men in the first inning, went down on strikes. "Wes Ferrell is not a strikeout pitcher," noted the *Plain Dealer*, "It is unusual for him to fan more than two or three in a game. But he was sore when the Browns scored four runs in the first inning and began to blaze 'em in."

The Yankees were securely in first place with a 48–19 record as June came to a close. The second-place Tigers were 9½ games behind and the sixth-place Browns were 13 games out. Philadelphia, Washington and Cleveland were bunched in between.

Ferrell ended June with a 7–4 victory over the Tigers. "The game," wrote the Cleveland paper, "wasn't Ferrell's best performance of the year, but, as he has often done in the past, he made up with his bat for whatever weakness there was in his pitching. He collected a double and two singles in four times at bat, batting in three runs and scored another one himself, and these four just represented the difference between victory and defeat."[22]

His fifteenth victory, which made him the league's lone top winner, came in the first game of a doubleheader on the Fourth of July in Chicago where he beat Milt Gaston 4–2. "Wes allowed the Sox seven hits, all of them bunched in the fifth, sixth, seventh and eighth innings," observed Cobbledick. "In the first four rounds, while the Indians were finding Gaston anything but an easy mark, he didn't permit a batter to reach first base. In all, he pitched five perfect innings."[23]

Washington's Carl Reynolds bowled over Bill Dickey on a play at the plate that same day. The Yankees' backstop, who had recently been hurt in a similar incident with the Red Sox, got up off the ground and slugged Reynolds, shattering his jaw. Dickey was suspended for 30 days and fined $1,000. Several weeks later, Reynolds started to choke — a life-threatening event for someone with a wired jaw — and only quick thinking by his wife, who cut the wires with a pair of manicure scissors, averted a tragedy.[24]

Wes' sixteenth win was a 6–5 decision in Washington on July 8. He allowed 13 hits, including five doubles, and walked four batters. Cobbledick thought that the Cleveland right-hander "looked like anybody but the greatest pitcher in baseball, which he unquestionably is despite occasional off days." Ferrell won, the writer postulated, because he forced himself to. "It was that heart that won the game for him today. Through most of the game he had a one-run lead to protect. He knew he didn't have his stuff. He knew he couldn't get the ball over the plate. But he bared his teeth in the Ferrell snarl and putting every ounce of energy into every pitch, pulled out jam after jam."[25] While no errors were charged to Cleveland, catcher Glenn Myatt's bad throw on an attempted steal aided in a run; another scored in the eighth inning when Joe Cronin's potentially inning-ending pop-up fell amongst the infielders for a double.

Ferrell's record for the season stood at 16–5 with a 3.37 ERA. He had been so dominant since returning to his fastball — 9–1 with a 2.50 ERA in ten starts — that speculation had begun about a thirty-win season.

Ten thousand fans at League Park, at six minutes past seven o'clock on the evening of July 10, watched Philadelphia's Eddie Rommel slip a third strike past Eddie Morgan to end the game. The final score, 18–17 in 18 innings, went in favor of the Athletics and Ferrell, working 11 innings in relief just two days after his complete game effort in Washington, was the losing pitcher.

The contest — one of the most unique in major league history — is too complex to go into detail here other than to touch on a few points. Ferrell entered the game in the seventh inning. With two down and no one on base in the ninth, and with the Tribe up by a run, Jimmy Dykes hit a slow roller to first base that should have ended the game. The play was so simple that Dykes didn't even toss aside his bat as he jogged toward first base, but the ball slipped through Eddie Morgan's legs, and Jimmy Foxx, after a pass to Simmons, doubled in two unearned runs.

The game continued on until the fatal eighteenth inning. "Ferrell," wrote Sam Otis in the *Plain Dealer*, "put Dykes and Simmons away without difficulty in the final chapter, but Foxx still had a punch left and delivered it in the form of a single to left. McNair's drive into the sunny extremities of Vosmik's territory followed, hopping high over Joe's upturned hands as he straightened up suddenly after being all set to play a first bound.

"Foxx raced all the way from first to cross the plate and McNair turned second at top speed in a bid for a triple, whereas he really should have had a single. Vosmik's fine throw to Kamm nailed Eric to end the inning but the damage had been done."[26]

Cleveland took the remaining four games in the series from Philadelphia—beating Grove twice in the process—to move into a second-place tie with the Mackmen. When Clint Brown won in New York on July 14 the Tribe was 8½ games behind McCarthy's squad and Peck had Ferrell to pitch against Gomez the next afternoon.

Wes managed to stagger through the first three innings of the 8–5 Yankees' victory, heading to the showers in the fourth. "I go out there, and I don't have anything on the ball," Wes recalled to Donald Honig forty years later. "They beat me. I'm sitting in the clubhouse after the game, and Peckinpaugh comes over and says, 'Hey, why didn't you bear down out there?'

"What the hell are you talking about?' I said. I was steamin'. 'I've been winning twenty games a year for you and pitching out of turn whenever you needed me, and you ask me why I wasn't bearing down? I always bear down. I just didn't have anything to bear down with today."[27]

Wes' seventeenth victory was a 7–0 decision in Boston on July 19. "The Cleveland ace held the troublesome Sox to four hits, one in each of the last four innings, and never permitted a runner to reach third. Only two of them, in fact advanced as far as second."[28]

Next up was Ted Lyons in Chicago on July 23. "Wes Ferrell had his eighteenth victory recorded in his own private note book today," wrote the *Plain Dealer*, "And then, in somewhat less that the time to tell it, he had nothing but his eighth defeat." The game went 12 innings. Three of the 19 hits Wes gave went to Lyons and three of the 15 hits Lyons gave went to Wes. Cleveland trailed 4–2 going into the top of the ninth but Averill hit a home run to tie the game. He hit another one in the twelfth to put the Tribe up 5–4. Wes retired the first two Chisox batters in fatal inning but then four straight singles, one of which did not leave the infield, cost Ferrell the game.

The Tribe—in second place—had the opportunity to pull to 6½ games out of first if they could beat New York on July 28, but Ferrell was pummeled again, giving 14 hits and seven runs in less than six innings as his record fell to 17–9. "Wes was in there working hard but he simply wasn't clicking in the good old fashioned Ferrell way," wrote Sam Otis.

Judge Landis was the headliner as the Athletics and Indians played the first game at Cleveland's new Municipal Stadium on July 31. Among the former Cleveland stars in attendance were Cy Young, Tris Speaker and Nap Lajoie. Lefty Grove beat Mel Harder 1–0 with Philadelphia scoring the only tally in the top of the eighth. Peck sent in Wes—whom Lefty struck out—to hit for Harder in the Cleveland half of the inning. "A long hit," said Otis, "was the only thing that could help the Indians right then and the big pitcher was the only right-handed batter on the bench from whom Manager Peckinpaugh had any license to expect such a wallop."

The next afternoon Rube Walberg topped Wes in another 1–0 contest. Ferrell allowed just two singles—both by Walberg—over the first eight innings before Mickey Cochrane led off the ninth. "The Athletics' catcher," observed the *Plain Dealer*, "picked out a ball to his liking and swung hard. Crack went his bat, splintered, but the result was a dinky single to right….

"…Al Simmons attempted to sacrifice, but his bunt was a foul pop to Willie Kamm. Ferrell started to work to Foxx and had two strikes on him when the slugging first baseman pushed a hit to right, a lazy drifter barely out of the reach of Bill Cissell and Eddie Morgan. So slow it was that Cochrane made third….

"Bearing down again, Ferrell made Eric McNair swing vainly at a couple. The infield was playing in close for a possible shut-off at the plate and McNair grazed one right through the spot Johnny Burnett had vacated. To all intents and purposes the game was over. Cochrane raced home and Foxx stopped at second. It mattered little that Miller and Dykes sent flies to Averill."[29]

Wes fired a one-hitter at the Red Sox on August 6. The final score was 3–0 and it made Ferrell's record 18–10. Dale Alexander's single in the fourth inning spoiled Wes' great performance. It was a bounder that barely eluded Ferrell's reach and then took a freak bounce over Bill Cissell's glove near the second bag and rolled into center field. "That it was a hit was beyond all doubt," reported the *Plain Dealer*, "though many of the 3,000 fans appeared to believe that Wes had turned in a no-hitter. There was no way in which it possibly could have been scored an error, for Cissell did not touch the ball at all. It was simply a mighty unlucky break."[30] The Cleveland defense played flawlessly for Ferrell. Wes walked two batters, one in the first inning and one in the fifth. Both passes came with two outs.

Wes' next start, due against Washington on August 10, was rained out. He opened a series against Detroit the next afternoon with another 3–0 shutout. Tigers' lefty Earl Whitehill held Cleveland to five hits but Wes, who allowed seven, was tougher in the clutch. His "effectiveness is attested to the fact that, saving his one slip in the sixth, he never allowed a batsman to advance further than the base to which his hit entitled him to … which is by way of proof that Ferrell had that little extra juice to turn on when it was needed."[31] Ferrell had no official at-bats in the game. He walked and sacrificed twice in three trips to the plate. The sacrifices were instrumental in the two of the three Cleveland scores. He record was 19–10.

Grove and Ferrell went at it again on August 17 and once more Lefty poisoned the Cleveland offense and Wes was trounced. The final was 11–0 and the Cleveland ace was removed in the fifth. "Ferrell, in his brief turn of duty, was nicked for nine hits, including three resounding doubles, and issued five bases on balls," said the *Plain Dealer*. "Thus ended the sensational streak in which he had scored two shutouts in a row and had allowed only one run and thirteen hits in 27 innings."

Joe Williams—writing on the same day—speculated that Cleveland and New York were about to swap Ferrell and Lefty Gomez. "The Indians, according to my information, are soured on Ferrell because he has ideas and expresses them freely. You know Ferrell well enough to know this is neither rumor nor news. Naturally, Ferrell's blast favoring McCarthy against Peckinpaugh did not set well with the Cleveland owners. They brought him into baseball court-martial. It was a laugh with him. The boy is pretty smart. But the Cleveland customers have begun to boo him. And that is something else.…

"It couldn't be strictly a money deal; it would have to be one great pitcher for another great pitcher.

"The Yankees, I am told, figure that physically Ferrell is a better pitcher than Gomez and that mechanically it is about even, anyway, and if you don't mind, I agree with them.…

"From what I hear the Yankees are under the impression that Gomez is a playboy. His romance with that Broadway gal has done him no good in the front office. On the other hand they know Ferrell is strictly a plugger. All he cares about is being a great pitcher. More than that, he wants to quit the game independently rich.…

"A close observation was placed on the young man. It was noted that he was always trying to save his arm. He refused to take orders from the catcher or the bench. He used a roundhouse, easy-throwing curve in the pinches instead of his hard fast one — and he has of the best hard fast ones in the league — or am I telling you...?

"Summed up, it makes baseball and interesting situation. Ferrell, one of the greatest pitchers in baseball, seems definitely through with Cleveland.... A trade for Gomez seems sound and logical. And yet, how can they bring him here without moving the tongues of scandal to action?"[32]

Philadelphia swept a doubleheader from the Tribe on August 19 that pushed Cleveland three games behind the A's in the race for second place. Cleveland scored all of its runs in the third inning of the 9–7 first game with Wes' contribution being a pinch-hit double that helped drive Rube Walberg from the game.

Wes' twentieth win was an 11–5 decision in Washington on August 21. Ferrell, wrote Cobbledick, "started poorly, giving up three hits and two runs in the first inning, and he finished up even more poorly, granting three hits and three runs in the ninth, but in between he hung up a string of seven horse collars and looked, altogether, like the great pitcher he is supposed to be.

"His victory today marked the fourth successive year that Wes has won twenty games. Being his first four years in the major leagues, they constitute a record that is unique in baseball history, unequalled even by the immortals of the years, two decades and more ago, when pitchers had everything in their favor."[33]

Wes was scheduled to start against Gomez in New York on August 25 but Peck held him back an extra day when Ferrell complained of a sore arm. In an interview before his recent loss to Grove, Ferrell was asked if he was as good a pitcher as he had been in 1930. "No," he replied, "I have had trouble with my pitching shoulder for two seasons. There is some sort of infection there, or nerve restriction. Some days my shoulder tightens up and I can't throw the ball as fast as when the shoulder is free."[34]

Johnny Allen beat Wes the next day, 4–2. Actually Ruth and Gehrig, who accounted for five of the eight hits and scored all four of the Yankees' runs, beat Wes. "Ferrell," said the *Plain Dealer*, "pitched a good game — perhaps the best he has shown against the Yanks this season — but the two long socks perpetrated by Messrs. Ruth and Gehrig were just a bit too much for him, what with his own mates again exhibiting that distressing inability to make runs...."[35]

While in New York, Gordon Cobbledick expanded on the Ferrell trade rumors. Dan Daniel of the *World-Telegram* wrote that the premature announcement of the deal by Joe Williams had caused McCarthy to reconsider. McCarthy stated that he was very happy with Gomez and would not consider letting him go. Connie Mack, though, was interested in trading Earnshaw and/or Walberg for Ferrell. "Connie," said the *Plain Dealer* scribe, "also has been an admirer of Ferrell ever since Wes came into the league...."

When Ferrell took his next turn on August 30 in Boston, the Tribe had just dropped eleven of sixteen games. They had lost three of four in Philadelphia, three of five in Washington, and all four games in New York. Ferrell walked the first man on four pitches. The second sent a grounder back up through the box into center field and the third hit a topper in front of the plate and was thrown out at first base. Dale Alexander and Smead Jolley singled and the Red Sox had two runs in and runners on first and third. Peck came to the mound to remove Wes but the pitcher refused to give him the ball. Just exactly what was said is unknown, but a lot of head-shaking came from both parties before Ferrell finally left. When the game restarted the Cleveland defense erred on the next two plays and Boston scored five runs in the inning. The final was 6–2 and it went into the books as Wes's thirteenth defeat.

Peck took most of the team — but not many of his pitchers, who returned to Cleveland — to Williamsport the next day for an exhibition game. There he decided to suspend Ferrell, without pay, for ten days. The reason — refusing to leave the game — was insubordination.

"Ferrell did not seem to be bearing down that day at Boston," Peckinpaugh told writer Sam Murphy. "Maybe his arm was lame. We never know when it is. The Red Sox were hitting him, and once the rival team begins to hit Ferrell, the Cleveland team goes right up in the air. The team always goes up when they expect Ferrell to do some brilliant pitching and he just shoves the ball up to the plate."

Wes also spoke with Murphy. "They are kicking me around a little lately," he said. " I suppose I got sore when the Red Sox started to beat me.... I have been trying hard to win my twenty-first game, and I suppose I did overstep the mark.

"There has been some talk about me not being able to beat the Athletics. Well, when my arm was right, and I hate to say that it has been lame for two years, I used to beat the Athletics. I met Grove when I had a lame whip....

"I tell you I can beat any team in the country when my arm is right, and I can beat a lot of them even when it is ailing. Sometimes my arm is heavy, but when you get the call to the mound you go in and pitch....

"There is a kink in my arm. I can pitch at my best when the kink is not there, but it causes me a lot of pain."[36]

Ferrell was initially philosophical about the suspension but that ended when someone on the team apparently made an additional comment about Wes not trying. "If anybody can prove I ever 'laid down,' roared Wes, "I'll be willing to pitch a whole season for nothing. I'd pay to pitch, in fact. Nobody can say I'm not in shape and haven't kept in shape. I know some games I didn't pitch well, but I was trying. My arm was sore, that's all."[37]

Wes' competitive drive was limited to the field and removed from the contest he always calmed down quickly. "Ferrell, it must be written to his credit," offered *The Sporting News*, "did not in the manner of Achilles go to his tent and sulk during the suspension. He had a long chat with President Bradley in the course of the week and promised to exercise control of his temper. He worked out daily and as soon as the club returned to Cleveland he donned his uniform to pitch to batters in pre-game practice. Then he went up in the stands as a spectator."[38]

* * *

George Ferrell spent his summer months toiling in the International and New York–Pennsylvania Leagues. Despite a home run on Opening Day, a four-hit game a week later, and a .306 average, Buffalo optioned him to Wilkes-Barre in early June.

Throughout the decade of the 1930s the American and National Leagues used different brands of baseballs; the National's usually much deader than the American's. The New York–Penn League in 1932 used the more restrictive ball. George hit .329, which was good for fourth in the league batting race. He hit five home runs and drove in 65 teammates. Johnny Mize, who played for Elmira in the same league, hit .326 with eight homers and 78 RBI.

Former New York Yankees' pitching ace Bob Shawkey managed the Scranton team, where George went from Wilkes-Barre. Scranton defeated the visiting New Yorkers 1–0 in an exhibition game in front of 6,500 customers on August 12. The game was a low-hitting affair and Ruth and Gehrig, batting third and fourth for the Bombers, managed just one hit between them. Ferrell, in the cleanup slot for Scranton, went hitless.

* * *

Rick Ferrell sent back three contracts offers to the Browns over the winter. He still did not have a signed agreement when he finally left for West Palm Beach on March 18. He began hitting the moment he arrived in camp.

"Rick Ferrell seems determined to make this his biggest year in the game," said *The Sporting News*. "He has been hitting the ball with a vengeance and catching with a finish that indicates that he is ready to dispute the claims of Mickey Cochrane and Jimmy Wilson of being the best backstop in the game. Rick's extra-base hitting was the feature of the spring work with the Browns."[39]

Shirley Povich, writing in the Washington *Post* on February 1, said "Rick Ferrell, of the Browns, is rapidly approaching the stardom as a catcher the Wesley Ferrell is enjoying as a pitcher with the Indians." Usually fifth in the St. Louis batting order behind Goose Goslin, Rick hit at a steady clip all season and was at .312 when George Earnshaw broke his hand with a pitch on June 19, putting him out of the lineup until July 10. A twenty-game hitting streak that ended on August 18 brought Ferrell's batting average to a seasonal peak of .339. Two days later the Associated Press reported Rick the American League's sixth best hitter, just behind Babe Ruth's mark of .342.

Rick finished thirteenth in the American League's MVP balloting, drawing nine votes, one more than Lefty Grove and Bill Dickey, and four more than Wes. Mickey Cochrane, inexplicably, did not receive a single vote. Dickey was the runaway winner for the catching position on *The Sporting News* All-Star team with 118 votes. Cochrane was second with 29 votes and Ferrell third with 12. Virgil Davis, Gabby Hartnett, Jimmie Wilson, Earl Grace, Al Lopez, Frank Hogan and Ernie Lombardi — in that order — rounded out the ballot.[40]

The top pitcher was Lon Warneke of the Cubs with 147 votes. Grove was second with 100 and Gomez third with 93. Wes was a distant fourth with 12 votes. Among others who received votes were Red Ruffing (8), Alvin Crowder (6), and Dizzy Dean (5).

* * *

Twenty-two thousand fans watched Wes snap Johnny Allen's ten-game winning streak with a 5–4 victory over the Yankees on September 11. He was rusty after the forced layoff and had to pitch out of several jams, the first coming when his defense erred on the opening play of the game, leading to an unearned run. Joe Vosmik made a sensational grab of a long fly by Lou Gehrig with runners on in the second inning. Ferrell had two hits in the game as a batter. The first was a smash too hot for shortstop Frank Crosetti to handle and the second was a single that drove in Cleveland's fifth run — the eventual game-winner — in the sixth. "And," commented the *Plain Dealer*, "he wound up the day in a blaze of glory by firing a third strike past the dangerous Ben Chapman with two Yankees on base and two out in the ninth."[41]

In his next start, a contest won from Washington by a similar 5–4 score, four of the runs Wes allowed were unearned. "It was Wes Ferrell," said the *Plain Dealer*, "who dominated the game in all but one inning, shutting out the aliens except in the fifth, when they staged a four-run rally that began with a freak play after two were out.

"But for the remainder of the route Ferrell was the great moundsman of old, and his 22d victory of the year was richly deserved."[42]

Wes' last appearance of the season was a 13–6 drubbing of the White Sox on September 23. It made his final record 23 wins and 13 losses. "Ferrell limited the Sox to two hits in the first five innings, and then went completely to pieces in the sixth, allowing five hits and giving three bases on balls, two of them coming with the bases filled. He stuck it out, though, staggered through the seventh, and then gave up in favor of Clint Brown."[43]

* * *

Roger Peckinpaugh understood Ferrell's compulsion to win. When Peck was brought back to manage the Tribe in 1941, it was reported that the only rift he had with a player in his first stint at the Cleveland helm had been with Wes.

"Wes Ferrell was a fine youngster," said Peck at the time. "He just hated to lose."[44]

Peckinpaugh still recalled him the same way in 1973. "Wes Ferrell? He was a fine pitcher, but he had a terrible temper. He never wanted to be taken out of a game. He would be mad, not at anybody else, but mad at himself. Because he didn't think anybody could get a base hit off him and when they did he would get mad ... he wasn't mad at a manager for taking him out of the game, but at himself. But he was a good boy...."[45]

◆ 8 ◆

1933 — First All-Stars

Neither Ferrell arrived at their respective spring camp on schedule in 1933. Payrolls were slashed throughout baseball and the brothers were unhappy with their contract offers. With the Depression at its worst, St. Louis owner Phil Ball attempted to sway public opinion by announcing that Rick had received $37,500 for his 1929 season alone, a $12,500 salary on top of his $25,000 signing bonus. The catcher — not happy with this tactic — wanted out of St. Louis.

Management was feeling the strain as well and Cleveland GM Billy Evans, the man with whom Wes argued money each spring, saw his salary cut from $30,000 to $15,000. "I think I'm worth every cent of the $18,000 I'm asking," Wes told Cleveland writer Ed McAuley in February. "In normal times a pitcher who had completed his fourth straight season of 20 or more victories would get a raise. I'm not asking that, but I don't think I should be cut. I'd like to start working with the rest of the gang in New Orleans next Wednesday, but I won't be there unless I get the same money as last year."

Just how long the brothers were willing to hold out became a moot point when tragedy struck the family. Three of the Ferrell boys— Pete, George and Marvin — had married and had their own homes. Wes and Rick, still bachelors, resided at the farm with their parents and siblings Slats and Ewell.

Marvin and his wife entertained guests on the night of March 5 and Ewell Ferrell was in attendance. Late in the evening Marvin heard a gunshot and when he went to investigate he found his brother lying on with floor with the pistol in his hand and a bullet wound to his temple. Ewell died the next morning without regaining consciousness. When asked if the shooting was an accident, Marvin replied, "I am afraid it was not. My brother was alone in the sitting room of my home, and the door was closed. My wife and several of our friends were in another part of the house, and

Wes often brooded in 1933 because of his sore arm (Gwenlo Ferrell Gore).

Ewell had been with us. He left the gathering, and a few minutes later we heard a shot in the sitting room. Upon entering the room I found my brother on the floor, apparently in a serious condition, and I brought him to Greensboro."[1] The coroner's investigation ruled that Ewell had taken his own life. The topic was rarely discussed within the family.

* * *

The Red Sox were not inactive despite a rainout of their scheduled game with the Indians on May 9. Tom Yawkey and Eddie Collins were in Cleveland for the American League spring meeting. There they traded catcher Merv Shea and a large amount of cash — usually given between $50,000 and $100,000 — to St. Louis for Rick Ferrell and pitcher Lloyd Brown. The reconstruction of the Red Sox — the acquisitions of Bill Werber and George Pipgras quickly followed — had begun.

Reaction from the Boston press was positive. "Ferrell is a great catcher," wrote Mel Webb in the *Boston Globe*. "A hard hitting one. A fellow right in his prime and possessing a true throwing arm....

"They say Rickey's a bit temperamental, like brother Wesley of the Indians, but there's plenty of argument that he's one of the outstanding catchers in league baseball today. Eddie Collins considers him so — even on a par with Mickey Cochrane — when Mickey's going at his best."[2]

Phil Ball made the trade without consulting his manager and Bill Killefer was not happy about it. "Fine job you did on me," the St. Louis skipper laughingly said to Collins when he heard of the trade. "As for Ferrell," he continued, "You may tell the world for me, I regard him as one of the best I have seen, and surely, with Bill Dickey of the Yankees, outstanding in our league. He will catch great ball for you, Eddie; and he will hit for you, and he will get all there is to get out of your pitchers."[3]

While Rick did not hit with Cochrane's authority, few questioned his prowess behind the plate. "Ferrell's catching form is near perfection," wrote *The Sporting News* in April. "There isn't a better thrower in either big league, and at bat, he's a line drive batter of the most dangerous type."[4] Yankees outfielder Ben Chapman, the American League's leading base stealer from 1931 to 1933, considered Ferrell the toughest catcher in the league to run on. "Well, everybody knows that you don't steal on the catchers, as a rule," said Chapman. "But the fellow I find the hardest to steal against is Rick Ferrell of the Browns. He gets the ball down there where the second baseman wants it."[5]

"Certainly," wrote Gene Mack, "it has been a long time since the Red Sox have had such a stylish throwing catcher as Ferrell. His pegs travel like lightening, dead to the mark and with little effort."[6]

* * *

Wes signed his contract in mid–March. "Ferrell in his letters to me," said Billy Evans, "has repeatedly said that he could and would win 25 games this year. The owners have taken him up on that....

"Here is our proposition. He must sign a $12,000 contract, but if he wins twenty games he will receive an additional $2,000. For 25 games, the number he says he can and will win, he will be paid an additional $1,000."[7]

Wes welcomed the contract, having taken to heart the season-ending innuendo in 1932 that he had not been giving his best effort, and working for the bonus would kill any suspicion of his integrity. Peckinpaugh, who lobbied unsuccessfully over the winter to have Ferrell's fine returned to him, wasn't worried that his ace was lounging around. "Wes is probably working harder each day than the rest of the squad is down here," he said just before Ferrell signed his contract.

Observing a strict diet in an effort to cure his arm woes, Ferrell arrived in camp twenty pounds lighter than his usual weight and would play the rest of his career between 175 and 180 pounds. His shoulder problems, though, had not gone away.

"My arm started to go bad two years ago," Wes told writer F. C. Lane. "At first it was a gradual process, then it seemed to become acute. A stabbing pain would strike though my shoulder every time I cut loose with a pitched ball. After a game the arm would sometimes keep me awake for hours. Various doctors have given me advice, but not one of them has cured the trouble."

Lane recognized Ferrell's reluctance to use the sore arm as an excuse and pressed him for more information.

"Pitching ball, for me the last two years has been anything but satisfactory. It has been hard work," said the hurler. "I have had to drive myself. It has been a continual fight. But I was determined to win at least twenty games each year and I have done so.

"A sore arm is the favorite alibi of the pitcher who is looking for an easy way out. It has been worked to death. Managers are suspicious of it and so are newspapers writers and so is the public. Undoubtedly many a sore arm has been faked. There is no fake about my sore arm. I know it, but how would I convince other people? No, there is only one rule in baseball. When things go wrong, you have to take it; take it and make the best of it."

When Lane prodded, Ferrell linked his temperament issues to his arm.

"It isn't only the pain, however, it's the mental unrest. It's the worry, the fear that perhaps the arm will not come around and it weighs on a pitcher. Plenty of times it has kept me awake nights....

"I have never consciously antagonized anybody. My policy is simple. Baseball is business. I give it everything I have. I have always been a strict observer of training rules. I have taken care of myself. I have given the club the best services of which I am capable. More than that I cannot do. Many ridiculous stories have been written about me by newspaper men who simply do not know the facts. I do not blame them particularly. Perhaps I should have been more liberal in discussing the facts, but I have no talent as a publicity getter. I am simply a baseball pitcher who knows his business and who does his best."

Wes also commented on his control issues.

"In some games," he said, "I've yielded a half dozen bases on balls. Every one was due to a sore arm. If my arm had been dependable, in some of those games, I would scarcely have yielded a single pass. Let a pitcher's control leave him and he is in deep water. My all round work has suffered. Even my batting has fallen off....

"Anything I pitch to a batter is the best ball for that particular time. It makes no difference what your specialty may be — fast ball, curve or change of pace, you can't depend upon that specialty alone. I like a fast ball. Every pitcher does. But I depend as much upon my curve and change of pace. Besides, my fast ball hasn't been so fast these last two years. By bearing down hard, I could show a batter, once in a while, that I still had my fast ball, but I couldn't keep the pace."[8]

Bad weather postponed Wes' first start until April 16 when he beat the Browns in St. Louis by a 7–1 score. Two hits accounted for a first inning run but Ferrell allowed just two more singles from then through the end of the sixth inning. He did not walk anyone and no additional runners advanced beyond first base. Cleveland still trailed by that run when Wes came up with a runner on second base in the top of the fifth and lined a two-bagger against the screen in front of the right field stands to tie the game. He singled past third in the seventh to drive home the game-winner. When Wes snapped off a curveball that struck out the second batter of the seventh inning, he felt a pop and then a stab of pain his shoulder. He immediately left the game.

Dr. Robert Hyland, the St. Louis club physician, examined the pitcher and said there was no cause for alarm, diagnosing a mild shoulder strain and advising two weeks of rest. Wes suffered no more discomfort after the initial pain and Hyland felt that he had just torn away some adhesions. Shirley Povich, writing in the Washington *Post*, opined that Peckinpaugh should be worried for Wes was "about half his team."

Ferrell saw no reason for panic — hadn't he pitched the last two seasons with a sore arm — and tossed batting practice three days later. His contract rewarded him for 25 wins and nothing would get in his way of his goal. "Feels fine," Wes said. "I actually believe there was an adhesion of ligaments in my shoulder. I know my arm seemed to be pulling tight on every pitch this spring. Now it even feels longer. My movement is absolutely unrestrained. I think I have remedied my ailment."[9]

He lost a 5–4 game in Chicago on April 24, allowing eight hits and four earned runs, and while his fielders were charged with just a lone error, several misplays cost Wes the game. "The most effective hitting the tribesman have done in several days," noted the *Plain Dealer*, "was nullified by their three blunders and Wes Ferrell was deprived of a shutout victory, for every one of the Sox runs was handed to them on a silver platter." Dick Porter lost fly balls in the sun in the first and fourth innings. Johnny Burnett made a wild throw in the third. Wes allowed only a scratch single to Luke Appling after the fourth inning, retiring the final twelve batters in order. "Ferrell proved that he suffered no ill effects from the accident to his shoulder ... a bit wild at the beginning of the game, he settled down at the half way mark and in the last four innings was as good as he ever has been in his career."[10]

Wes' next game was a 4–1 victory over Ted Lyons in Cleveland on April 29. "Ferrell was good enough himself to give any ball team a battle," noted Cobbledick. "His fast ball was better than it has been in two years, and his only difficulty was in controlling this delivery that has been missing from his repertory since 1930.

"Also for the first time in two years, he had something in reserve to turn on in the pinches, and the fashion in which he pitched himself out of one serious jam indicated that the great young star of 1929 is back."[11] As a batter he singled and scored the winning run in the fifth and doubled into the left-field corner in the eighth.

Next was a 7–6 decision over the Yankees on May 6 in which he gave 11 hits and three earned runs before giving way to the bullpen in the seventh inning. Ferrell had a 5–2 lead when Bill Dickey started off the sixth with a rocket that bounced off the pitcher's shin into right field. Frankie Crosetti followed with another smash up the middle that Wes knocked down but couldn't make a play on. A single, an infield error and a fly ball led to two runs.

Cleveland was in first place and another Ferrell-Grove contest was anticipated for May 12 but Connie Mack instead started Roy Mahaffey. When the top of the ninth rolled around Cleveland had a 3–2 lead and Wes—who had retired the A's in order in the sixth, seventh and eighth innings—appeared to have things wrapped up before his defense cracked wide open. Jimmy Foxx singled in front of a free pass to Mickey Cochrane and with an obvious sacrifice expected, the Cleveland corner infielders were creeping in as Ferrell delivered his pitch. "The infield procedure under these conditions is standardized," wrote the *Plain Dealer*, which opined that Tribe just didn't execute the play properly. The bunt was toward third but second baseman Johnny Burnett was late in covering first and the throw escaped him and rolled into right field. Foxx scored the tying run and runners were on second and third. The next two batters grounded weakly back to the hill; the runners holding on the first play and Wes tagging out Cochrane on the second. The next batter hit a ground ball to the Cleveland shortstop who booted it to the other side of second base. Two more singles followed and Wes was relieved. His final line was seven runs (two earned) and the loss.

Bad luck continued on Ferrell's trail in his next two starts as he dropped a 3–2 game in Washington and a 3–0 contest to Lefty Gomez on May 22. "Ferrell's defeat was his third of the year, against an equal number of victories," wrote Cobbledick after the Washington game, "making it just that much more difficult for him to reach his twenty-game total. But the kind of pitching he did today will win nine times out of ten." Shirley Povich wrote that Wes "was throwing a half-speed ball all day that sounded like a sack of mush when it collided with a bat."

Wes hurled brilliantly against New York and allowed just three over the first seven frames. "For seven innings," wrote the *Plain Dealer*, "Ferrell shut out the team that hasn't been shut out for 241 games. For seven innings he dueled on even terms with Vernon Gomez, called the gallant but goofy Castilian. And for seven innings he looked like the Ferrell of 1929 — a pitcher who conceded nothing to the best of them."

The Yanks did all their scoring in the eighth. "Babe Ruth started it by missing two swings and then dribbling a weak grounder to the right of the box. Burnett, playing directly behind the second base cushion, crossed in front of Cissell, who was stationed on the grass in right field, and fumbled the ball.

"Gehrig hit an easy grounder for what should have been the second out, but it did nothing more than force Ruth at second, after which Chapman singled and Lazzeri walked, filling the bases.

"And then Bill Dickey drove a single past Eddie Morgan that scored Gehrig and Chapman. It was a ball that Morgan could have handled had he been playing deep, as he would have been with two out. But Burnett's error had made it necessary for him to move in close in the hope of cutting off a run at the plate, and the ball went past him and into right field.

"To complete the rout of the Indians, Crosetti sent a hard grounder through Burnett's hands for a single and the third run came in."[12]

Ferrell walked six batters in the game and Dickey, who doubled his first time up, was passed twice intentionally before getting the hit that broke open the game. One of Wes' four strikeout victims in the game was Joe Sewell, the toughest man to strike out in the history of baseball. "When Ferrell fanned Joe Sewell in third," noted the New York *Times*, "it marked the first time this year that little Joe has gone down on strikes, and only the fourth time in two years. Ferrell is one of the few pitchers who have struck him out twice. He did it first two years ago."

Sewell fanned just 15 times in more than 1700 plate appearances over the last three years of his career (1931–1933) and Wes was responsible for three of them; one each season. Grove—who faced Sewell regularly from 1925 to 1933—managed just one career strikeout of Sewell and that had come back in 1926.[13]

Wes tossed a 6–0 shutout in Boston on May 27, allowing nine inconsequential hits which, as Gordon Cobbledick noted, was, "no true measure of Ferrell's effectiveness, for no more than four of their blows were clean and untainted by luck."

The 3–0 lead his mates gave him would have been enough but Wes made sure of things. "Ferrell himself fired the three run rally in the sixth that routed [Lloyd] Brown and ended the scoring for the day. With one down Kamm walked and Spencer singled him to third. Then Wes laced a long double to the bleachers in right center and both runners galloped home."[14]

His next start was a three-hit, 3–1 victory against the Browns in St. Louis on June 1. "Wesley Cheek Ferrell," wrote the *Plain Dealer*, "today gave his greatest pitching exhibition of the season and one of the finest of his career....

"Ferrell held the Browns to three hits, all of them singles and only one a clean drive, and would have shut them out but for the mysterious attack of wildness that seized him every time [Debs] Garms, the young St. Louis outfielder, stepped to the plate.

"Garms walked four times, and it was his last pass in the eighth inning that led to the Browns' only run, being followed by a scratchy hit and an infield out."[15]

Wes was ineffective in protecting a 3–1 lead in his next start on June 5 when the Tigers jumped on him for five hits and three runs in the top of the fifth. He had two hits while in the game and led off the bottom of that frame—in which the Tribe scored three runs to go back ahead—with a base hit before being lifted for a runner.

Roger Peckinpaugh was fired as the Tribe's manager on June 9 and his successor, Walter Johnson—arguably the greatest right-hander in history — decided to watch one game from the stands before talking the helm. The contest was a 5–2 victory over the Browns in which Wes started slowly — allowing eight hits and both runs in the first four innings — but finished by retiring thirteen of the last fourteen batters. Ferrell and Earl Averill — the Tribe's big stick — both homered in the game; the first of the season for each. Averill's home run was a line drive down the right-field line in the first inning that accounted for Cleveland's first two runs. Wes' shot — "a taller and longer sock into the seats in left" — came in the third and accounted for the club's third and fourth runs.

Intensity was always present in Wes' eyes (Gwenlo Ferrell Gore).

A much-anticipated duel between Wes and Schoolboy Rowe was delayed twice by rain and when the teams finally met in Cleveland on May 17, it was Tommy Bridges instead who toed the rubber for the Tigers. Wes allowed seven hits—four coming in the fourth when Detroit scored both their runs— in taking the 3–2 decision in ten innings.

"Ferrell," wrote Cobbledick, "contributed something more than a classy bit of pitching to his cause, for he also hit the longest home run ever made in the stadium by any player on any club — a sock that a Ruth or Foxx would have been proud to include in his collection.

"It was the first hit of the game on either side, coming in the third inning with the bases empty. It traveled to the remotest corner of the covered stands in left field, landing a half dozen rows from the front.

"After the game General Manager Billy Evans of the Cleveland club was curious enough to order an accurate measurement of the distance from home plate to the spot where the ball struck the seats. It was found to be just 450 feet."[16] The home run tied Wes with four teammates for the team lead, though he was the only one to hit both of his at spacious Municipal Stadium.

Ferrell's eighth victory was an 11–1 drubbing of Philadelphia on June 21. Wes gave but six hits while Earnshaw and Walberg did the hurling for the

Mackmen. Cleveland's record after the game was 33–28 and they sat five games behind the front-running Yankees in third place. The next day, after Oral Hildebrand beat his club, Connie Mack had nothing but praise for Johnson's mound staff. "The Cleveland pitching staff will not go bad," said the Philadelphia manager, "and that will keep the race hot, too. What fine young pitchers those are! And have you noticed how much alike Ferrell and Hildebrand are in their splendid form...."[17]

Washington swept a doubleheader from the Indians on June 25 to move a game and a half in front of New York and Ferrell, in dropping the first game 9–0, allowed nine hits and six earned runs in less than five innings. "Wes," reported the *Plain Dealer*, "ran afoul of faulty play in the very first inning, when Bill Cissell gummed up Cronin's pop to short center, the ball dropping for a double to score Goslin from first base. It should have been an easy out to retire the side.

"Again in the second Ferrell nailed the first two batters. This time Knickerbocker fumbled Luke Sewell's drive and the catcher went around on singles by Whitehill and Myer. Another tally after the side should have been down!

"The heaviest blow was yet to fall, however. Myer started the fifth with a hit to left and was forced on Manush's grounder to Cissell. Goslin walked, but Ferrell fanned Cronin for the second out, only to fill the bases by passing Schulte.

"Right there came the explosion. Joe Kuhel sent one toward right that Morgan should have handled. Eddie failed to get to the ball and two runners went across the plate.

"Bluege singled to left to score Schulte, but Vosmik's throw to check Kuhel at third struck the runner and he also tallied while Ossie moved up to second, from where he counted when Sewell banged a hit off Ferrell's shins into center. Wes thereupon surrendered to Howard Craghead...."[18]

* * *

Ferrell, Grove, Gomez, Alvin Crowder and Hildebrand were the selected pitchers when the American League's first All-Star team was announced on June 26. Fan voting had been going on for several months and the tally printed in the *Plain Dealer* on June 25 listed Grove with 327,242 votes, Gomez with 253,000 and Wes with 193,120. Next in line was Hildebrand with 86, 232. Grove's pitching record at the time was 9–4 while Wes and Gomez were both 8–5. Ferrell's ERA was 2.60, Grove's 3.23 and Gomez's 3.51.

* * *

Johnson brought Wes back on two days rest to face Washington on June 28 when the Nats pounded out a 15–2 victory for their sixteenth win in eighteen games. Buddy Myer opened the game with a routine grounder that second baseman Bill Cissell booted. Four hits and a walk followed and Ferrell was gone from the game without having retired a batter.

Johnny Allen and the Yankees beat Wes by a 4–2 score at Municipal Stadium on July 1. Ferrell got off to a shaky start by walking Dixie Walker in front of singles by Sewell and Ruth. Gehrig plated a run with a fielder's choice and Ben Chapman drove in another with a fly ball. Luckily for Wes, a base-running blunder by Gehrig ended the inning. From then until the ninth New York managed just a safe bunt in the second, a single in the third, a walk by Bill Dickey in the fifth and a double by Gehrig in the sixth. With the game knotted at 2–2, Wes opened the ninth by walking Gehrig on four straight pitches. Tony Lazzeri shot a triple over the right fielder's head for the game-winner and Dickey followed with a fly ball for an insurance run.

* * *

Grove didn't have his stuff on May 6 when the Browns knocked him out in the fourth inning. Rick Ferrell homered and had two of the seven hits Lefty allowed. In his first game for the Red Sox on May 11, Rick had two hits off Mel Harder and scored the club's only run in a 4–1 loss. In his second game on May 14, Rick had three hits off Tommy Bridges and drove in the winning run in the ninth inning.

When the Red Sox took four out of five games from the first-place Yankees in mid–June, Rick had eight hits in 14 at bats. He went three for four with a home run and four RBI as the Sox knocked out Lefty Gomez in a 13–5 rout on June 14. The next afternoon, in an 8–5 win over Johnny Allen, he went two for two with a double and two RBI before leaving the game after taking a foul tip off his hand. Eight hits in 13 at bats, including three doubles, was Rick's contribution as the Red Sox pounded Earnshaw and Walberg and took two of three games in Philadelphia on July 4 and 5.

Always the consummate but never colorful performer, Rick finished a distant third behind Dickey and Cochrane in the popular voting for the All-Star team; those backstops drawing 297,382 and 174,530 votes respectively by June 25 while Boston's new receiver had but 29,431. He did, however, have the respect of his peers. He also was swinging a hot bat — 33 hits in 81 at bats in June for a .407 average.

J. G. Taylor Spink, in his column in *The Sporting News* on June 8, said he expected the American League's catchers to be Cochrane and Ferrell.

"The Sox," wrote the Boston *Globe* in early July, "did not begin to climb the moment Ferrell arrived, but it did not take long. The pitchers were going whichways, and Ferrell slowly began to straighten them out. He played great ball himself, holding to his remarkable fielding and gradually began to hit.

"Now Rick is well up at the top of the American League pile of backstops. He had proven to be the most valuable of the Sox recently acquired assets, and he has been the fulcrum to stand the pressure of the uplifting lever."[19]

The following table is the offensive production of Dickey, Cochrane and Ferrell through the end of June. The Philly and Boston backstops had been charged with just one error each and while Dickey had made four.[20]

	At bats	Runs	Hits	2B	3B	HR	RBI	BB	Ave
Dickey	226	23	70	11	4	7	45	21	.310
Ferrell	219	27	66	9	1	3	30	30	.301
Cochrane	174	43	48	9	3	7	26	51	.276

Rick started and caught the entire All-Star game. He hit the ball the opposite way all four times; two fly balls to right field, a sacrifice that moved Joe Cronin up to second in the sixth inning when the score was 3–2 in favor of the American League (Cronin scored for the 4–2 final) and a ground-out to the second baseman.

The Sporting News reported that Cochrane — who did not appear in any games between July 2 and July 10 — had suffered a rib injury a week before the game. Dickey may have suffered a hand injury in batting practice though he was available for duty and back in the New York lineup the next afternoon.[21] When asked after the game why he had not made changes, Mack replied, "I didn't shake the team up because it's against all my instincts to disturb a winning combination. Nothing made me feel more badly than the fact I didn't use Foxx, Lazzeri, Dickey and pitchers Hildebrand and Ferrell."[22]

Rick usually referred to the inaugural All-Star tilt as his greatest game, saying in 1944, "I didn't do any hitting that afternoon. But I guess I caught a pretty good game. They didn't hit our pitchers very much." In 1993 he said, "Every time I came back to the bench, Mr. Mack would tell me to sit beside him. I thought he was a very old man at that time and that he'd be half asleep before the game was very far along. But he was the most energetic manager I'd ever seen. He'd sit there and ask me about the pitchers. He'd want to know if he had good stuff. He'd tell me what he was planning for the next inning and he'd ask me what I thought."[23]

Dickey — listed on 80 ballots — was named the catcher on *The Sporting News'* 1933 All-Star team at the end of the season.[24] Mickey Cochrane finished second with 25, Virgil Davis third with 21 and Ferrell fourth with 18 tallies. Seven other catchers, including Gabby Hartnett with two votes, rounded out the nominations.

Dickey and Ferrell finished in a tie for the twelfth spot in the BBWAA American League MVP balloting with nine votes. Cochrane received five.

* * *

Wes began the second half of the season by dropping a 6–2 decision in the opener of a doubleheader in Washington on July 8. "The first game, "noted the *Plain Dealer,* "should have gone into the records as a tight pitching duel between Wes Ferrell and Alvin Crowder. Ferrell pitched a good game — much better than the score indicates — and with the smarter support that Crowder received might have won.

"But he didn't get it. Here are the details: With one out in the fifth Ossie Bluege singled, bringing Luke Sewell to bat. Now Sewell, a right-handed batter, hits to left field three times out of four. Against a slow ball pitcher such as Ferrell has lately become, he is almost a dead cinch to hit to left.

"But when Bluege started for second on the hit and run it was Bill Cissell, the shortstop, who dashed over to cover second base. Sewell cracked a sharp grounder — a perfect double play grounder — straight through the spot vacated by Cissell and two runs followed.

"The three made by the Nats in the seventh sewed it up, and in that inning the side would also have been retired scoreless but for Hale's muff in right field."[25]

Ferrell walked two batters and did not record a strikeout. He had fanned just nine batters in his last ten starts. His fastball was gone. Walter Johnson's pitching staff — the same one Connie Mack a few weeks earlier declared would remain true — had collapsed. Mel Harder was nursing a sore elbow. Willis Hudlin was walking with a cane after suffering a spike wound. Clint Brown had just been released from a two-week hospitalization. Johnson tried using Hildebrand as both a reliever and a starter and he came up lame. The Cleveland pitching staff began questioning Johnson's decisions and on August 1 Hildebrand clashed with his manager, refusing to leave a game in which the manager tried relieving him. While the scenario was familiar to the Ferrell-Peckinpaugh incident of 1932, the fine to Hildebrand was just $100. He was suspended for several days before apologizing to Johnson.

The Cleveland writers, throughout the turmoil that saw the Tribe sink to sixth place with a record of 39–45, noticed that the silent Ferrell was working less frequently. In his next start, in Philadelphia on July 14, Wes took a 2–0 lead late into the game. "Ferrell and the Tribe looked like a cinch as the last of the eighth got under way," wrote the *Plain Dealer*, "and they still looked like a cinch as Wes disposed of Roger Cramer and Mickey Cochrane, the first two batters in the semi-final period.

"But Ferrell was jealously guarding his shutout. Refusing to give Jimmy Foxx a home run ball to swing at, he walked him. Then Ed Coleman, who had been helpless all afternoon, bounced a single through the infield.

"And then old Uncle Tom [Bing Miller], cutting at the first ball pitched, lined it over Joe Vosmik's head and into the stands. It barely cleared the barrier but it couldn't have been more effective if it had sailed cleanly over the roof atop the second deck."[26] The final score was 3–2 and Ferrell, with his record at 8–9, had lost five straight decisions.

He was unimpressive — as a hurler, anyway — in his next assignment, an 8–7 loss in Boston on July 19. "Ferrell proved a better hitter than pitcher," went the *Plain Dealer*'s recap of the game, "for he slammed a home run over the left field wall, started another rally with a single, drew a pass and scored three runs. But he couldn't hold the biggest lead the Indians have given a pitcher in several weeks—chiefly due to the fact that his brother, Rick, catcher for the Sox, drove one over the wall in the fourth with two mates on base."[27]

Wes' home run came in top of the fourth and put the Tribe up 5–0. He made a big tactical blunder, however, for when he crossed the plate he flashed his brother a big grin. Rick's home run in the bottom of the same inning cut the lead to 5–3. Rick "highbrowed" his sibling with a very slow trot around the bases. "Wes," noted the Boston *Globe*, "did not regard this as a brotherly act, for, when a new ball was tossed out to him, he kicked it all over the diamond."

The Yankees took both games of a doubleheader from the Indians in New York on July 23. Ferrell and Hildebrand, each going five innings, were the losers by identical scores of 8–1. Wes was trailing 2–0 when things fell apart. "Ferrell got them without trouble in the third and fourth, but they broke loose with a six-run attack in the fifth. Only three hits were needed to produce twice as many runs, for there was a base on balls, a hit batsman and a fielder's choice that failed to retire a man. These things came along, with Dickey's scratch single and Sewell's double, before Gehrig slammed a homer into the right field bleachers."[28]

Johnson held Wes off for ten days before starting him in St. Louis on August 2 where the Browns jumped out with four runs in the first inning.

"That show of power failed to dismay Manager Walter Johnson," wrote the *Plain Dealer*, "for he had no relief pitcher in the bull pen. And Ferrell's work in the next four innings justified his confidence. It wasn't until the sixth that the Browns scored again, and it took a pair of scratch safeties in the mud to bring about their two runs then."

Wes' one-out walk in the third inning was the start of a Cleveland five-run outburst. He made the score 6–4 in the fourth when he hit a solo shot "far into the stands in left center." Rain then halted the game for close to an hour and sloppy field conditions contributed to the Brownie tallies in the sixth. Two doubles in the eighth knocked Wes from the game before the Tribe broke the game open in the ninth. Ferrell was not involved in the decision.

"His once great arm is shot," wrote Stuart Bell in the Cleveland *Press* on August 4. "Unless some miracle happens to the Ferrell pitching arm, it would appear the halcyon hurling days of this blond giant is over." Bell suggested it was time to try Wes in the outfield. Ferrell was in a quandary, not wanting "his desire to play the outfield interpreted as a confession of failure in the box. The same young man who complained of a sore arm almost steadily through his four highly successful seasons, refuses point blank to blame his 1933 record on any physical ailment."

Johnson was as reluctant as Wes. "Sure, Wes and I have talked about it," said his manager. "But I haven't given up on him as a pitcher. I've been watching him closely for some time and I think he would make good as an outfielder. He has always been a dangerous batter. Day after day service would make him still better in that respect.

"But as badly as we need a hard hitting outfielder, I won't make him [Ferrell] one until I'm convinced that he can't win as a pitcher. And I'm not yet ready to make that admission."[29]

Johnson sat Ferrell down for twelve more days before he dropped an 8–7 contest to Grove on August 15. The Tribe made nine hits off the Philadelphia left-hander, including three doubles, a triple and a home run. The Athletics' defense committed four errors. "Two of the greatest pitchers the American league has ever seen hooked up in one of their frequent duels at the stadium yesterday," wrote Cobbledick, "and it turned out to be a contest to see which one could allow the greater number of runs."

Wes, conversely, had finally beaten Grove. "Ferrell put most of his bad pitches into the first three innings, when the Mackmen scored five of their runs. After that he was considerably better than his opponent, but after that was too late."[30]

Wes' 100th career victory — his first in almost two months — came in the second game of a doubleheader with Boston on August 20. He allowed two runs in both the first and fifth innings but settled down to retire thirteen of the last fourteen batters; a ninth-inning walk being the only baserunner after the fifth. Rick Ferrell had three of the Red Sox's seven hits and the final was 9–4. The game was most entertaining for the crowd as Boston manager Marty McManus threw a punch at Cleveland coach Ed Gharrity and pitcher Bob Kline also provided a big laugh. "Kline burned up in the sixth inning when Umpire Red Ormsby called a second strike on him," wrote Cobbledick. "He stepped out of the box to tell Mr. Ormsby what he thought about it. While he was arguing, Ferrell pitched. Kline dashed to the plate, and still on the run, took a vicious swing for the third strike. After that he was too mad to pitch, and the Indians drove him from the box in the same inning."[31]

Wes beat first-place Washington 5–4 in 11 innings on August 26 and in the process halted Heinie Manush's 33-game hitting streak. The batting Ferrell belted his fifth home run of the year into the left-field stands in the sixth inning to break a 2–2 tie. "Still fighting for a place on the pitching staff whose foremost member he was for four years," wrote the *Plain Dealer*, "Ferrell pitched the full distance to win his tenth victory of the campaign and second in two starts. And he pitched it as he has pitched only one or two games since the season began.

"In seven of the eleven innings he turned the Nationals back without a hit, and it was only the five blows they bunched in the seventh that enabled the visitors to accumulate the respectable total of ten.

"That was Ferrell's only bad inning, and the only one that threatened to beat him until Burnett came through in the ninth with the tying blow. Thereafter the Nationals didn't get a man to first base."

Johnny Allen and Herb Pennock of the Yankees surrendered successive pinch-hits to Wes on August 24 and 25. He scored the winning run in a 6–4 Cleveland win following his blow off Pennock.

It took the sore-armed ace an inning to get loose on September 3 but the result was a 14–3 victory in Chicago in which his stick contribution was a single, a home run and three RBI. "While this was all going on Wes Ferrell was coasting along to his eleventh victory of the year," noted Cobbledick. "After a wobbly first inning in which the Sox got five hits and three runs, Ferrell pitched brilliant shutout ball, allowing only seven blows in the last eight rounds."[32]

Cleveland had climbed into third-place with a 19–11 record in August but they were unable to hold off the Athletics, who swept them in a four-game series in Philadelphia in early September, Ferrell being routed by the Mackmen on September 8 to leave his pitching record at 11 wins and 12 losses. "Wes Ferrell," wrote Cobbledick," was one step nearer the outfield tonight and the Indians were a notch closer to fourth place.

"For Ferrell collapsed in two big innings this afternoon and the Athletics made it three straight over the Redskins, 9 to 2, cutting their third-place lead to two games.

"The erstwhile pitching ace also drove another spike in his claim to an outfield trial by hammering his seventh home run of the season into the upper deck of the left-field stands in the fifth after Roy Spencer had walked, thus accounting for the only runs made by the Indians."[33]

Wes' round-tripper left him one shy of the team lead; Earl Averill and Odell Hale each had eight though that point in the season. Averill had 548 at-bats, Hale 296 and Ferrell just 92! Municipal Stadium was not an easy place to hit home runs. Adjusting to the field had caused havoc with Averill's ability to hit the ball out of the park. Though he was the club's leader with 11 home runs in 1933 (two were inside-the-park), Averill hit just five over-the-fence homers at Municipal Stadium and four on the road. All ten of Hale's home runs came on the road and one of Joe Vosmik three home runs at Municipal was inside-the-park. Ferrell hit three home runs at home and four on the road. Even the great Babe Ruth, though slowing down, never managed a four-bagger at Municipal Stadium in two and a half seasons as a visiting player. "Babe Ruth has given up trying to hit a home run in the stadium," noted *The Sporting News* at the end of the season. "In the Yankees' games in Cleveland he shortened his grip and attempted to poke his hits through the infield."[34]

All of this emphasizes Ferrell's ability to hit the long ball. "On the basis of home runs per time at bat," said the *Plain Dealer* on September 8, "Wes Ferrell is second only to Jimmy Foxx among four-base manufacturers of both leagues."

The next afternoon — September 9 — Ferrell debuted in left field, filling in for Vosmik, who had suffered a broken hand a few days earlier. He did not pitch again in 1933, playing his final 13 games in the outfield. The results were a mixed bag.

He batted fifth in the lineup and singled in his first time at-bat, scoring the team's first run in a 5–3 loss that saw Philadelphia move within a single game of the Tribe for third place. "Wesley Ferrell, who as lately as a year ago ranked with the greatest pitchers of baseball history, is enthusiastic over his switch to the outfield," wrote Cobbledick after the game.

"I don't want to pitch any more," said Wes. "I've lost interest in pitching. I think my future lies in being in the game every day. I can hit the ball, you know, and I can go and get it in the outfield."

Cobbledick agreed that Wes — at least as a pitcher — was a good hitter but asked him what he expected if he had to produce on a regular basis.

"I'd be a better hitter than I am now," Wes declared. "It's all a matter of timing. When you're in there only every fourth day — or every tenth day, as I've been most of this season — it's hard to perfect the timing of your swing. That comes with steady work and practice. I'd hit .300 — with plenty to spare. I'd outhit anybody in our outfield now. And I'd hit a lot of home runs, maybe 30."

Wes also expressed confidence in his fielding, declaring that he could outrun half of the fly-chasers in the league, and that his arm was strong enough to make the long throws back to the infield. "I haven't been fooling around in the outfield. I've been working there. I'm a good judge of a fly ball. I can go back and I can come in fast. I know what I can do. If I didn't I wouldn't be sucker enough to ask for the change."[35]

Wes' noble experiment blew up in his face the next afternoon when he failed to catch a routine fly ball that led to four runs in a 7–3 loss to Washington. "Ferrell took a half dozen steps to his left, stationed himself under the ball and then, as Averill jogged across from center field, became confused and stepped aside, apparently thinking that Earl intended to make the catch."

Monte Pearson and Alvin Crowder were locked in a 1–1 duel on September 12 when Wes stepped to the plate in the seventh with two runners on. He singled in both runners for the 3–1 final. Cleveland was idle until dropping a doubleheader in New York on September 17 by 3–2 and 6–1 scores. Ferrell scored two of the three Cleveland runs, one in each game. Trailing 2–1 in the opener, Wes started the seventh inning with a double to center field and scored on the ensuing play to tie the game.

Ferrell had a double and two singles when Oral Hildebrand tossed a two-hitter in Fenway Park on September 18 but it was likely that the Cleveland pitcher was not happy with Wes for both Boston hits were flares to left field. "Had a real outfielder, instead of Wes Ferrell, been in left field, the Sox' two fungo base hits would have been gobbled up easily," wrote the Boston *Globe*." Gordon Cobbledick felt the same way. "A faster and more experienced outfielder, skilled in the art of playing the hitters, probably would have caught both balls and Hildebrand's name would have been added to the list of pitching immortals who have shut the door in the faces of the enemy for nine full innings."[36]

The next afternoon the Tribe lost a 4–3 decision to the Red Sox. Cleveland had runners on first and second with one down in the fourth inning and Wes was at bat when he tried ducking out of the way of a wild pitch. The ball struck his bat and dropped into fair territory in front of the plate.

Rick Ferrell pounced on the ball and threw to third base to start a 2–5–3 double play, Wes being the final out at first base. The pitcher-turned-outfielder shot his brother a hard stare as they passed but Rick just laughed at Wes. Boston had a 4–1 lead in the ninth before the Tribe managed to put a couple of runners on with two outs. Wes "rammed one to the bleachers in right center" to drive home two runs.

* * *

George and Marvin Ferrell played for Bob Shawkey at Scranton in the New York–Pennsylvania League in 1933. George hit .301 with 85 RBI. Marvin had a 4–8 pitching record before moving to the outfield where he hit .285.

"Marvin Ferrell," noted *The Sporting News* in early June, "showed some of the hurling ability of his big brother, Wesley of the Cleveland Indians, May 30, against Wilkes-Barre, when he shut out the Barons, 4–0." In addition to his three-hitter against Wilkes-Barre, Marvin also tossed a five-hit, 2–1 win against Elmira on June 6.

George played left field and filled in at third base when needed. When Marvin was knocked from the hill by Harrisburg on August 8, George came in from left field as relief pitcher. Marvin handed George the ball and trotted out to take his brother's spot in the outfield. By the end of the season George and Marvin were playing alongside each other in the outfield, batting fifth and sixth in the lineup.

♦ 9 ♦

1934 — Brother
Battery in Boston

The Red Sox opened the season with an AP poll of 97 sportswriters picking them to finish third behind Washington and New York.[1] New manager Bucky Harris was enthusiastic, saying "This club may not win the pennant, but I don't see how we can be kept out of the money." Rick Ferrell signed his contract in January with little fanfare as Eddie Collins offered him a raise of several thousand dollars.

Wes' salary issues were much more complicated, and both he and Earl Averill returned unsigned contracts to Cleveland on March 1. "It's funny the Cleveland club should have so many 'temperamental' stars in its ranks," said Rick Ferrell sarcastically. "You don't see the other clubs in the circuit having trouble."[2]

Cleveland planned to shave $75,000 off their 1933 payroll of $275,000 and their offer to Wes called for a base salary of $5,000 with a bonus of $500 for each victory over ten, $600 for wins 15–20 and $700 to $800 for each win beyond 20.[3] The Sporting News opined that Ferrell's value had deteriorated to virtually nothing from an estimated $200,000 that the wealthy teams like the Yankees, Cubs or Giants would have paid for him at the start of the 1931 season.[4] While expecting a cut based on his 1933 season, Wes was confident he would bounce back. He also wanted out of Cleveland.

Billy Evans had tried to trade Wes over the winter but there were no takers; for while Walter Johnson believed Ferrell's arm was sound, the feeling around baseball was that his fastball was gone. On March 4, Wes asked the Indians to name a price for his contract, thinking he would go the free-agent route and sell his services to a bidder of his own choice. The Indians responded with a figure of $25,000 and a two-week window to decide. The offer was withdrawn when Wes failed to act by March 21.[5] "I've

Wes (left) and Rick: The Brother Battery in Boston (Gwenlo Ferrell Gore).

got enough money to run me for 30 years and keep the old Packard moving, too," said Wes, "But frankly, I don't understand this baseball business. You go out and win ball games, and they cut your salary. If you should happen to have a bad season, I expect they would want you to pay for the right to pitch. I have been informed the Cleveland club asked waivers on me, but Washington and Chicago in the American League and Brooklyn in the National League refused to waive. These waivers were nothing more than feelers. If the Cleveland club was willing to let me go for the waiver price, then why did they offer to release me for 25 grand?"[6]

In an effort to counter flak he was receiving from the Cleveland press, owner Alva Bradley released a detailed account of the money Wes had received while in the employ of the Indians. Beginning in 1927 and including bonuses and fines, the Indians had paid the pitcher a total of $64,954.76.[7]

When reports began circulating in April that Cleveland GM Billy Evans was coming to the Ferrell farm to iron out contract problems, a local sportswriter for the Greensboro *Daily News* decided to drive out to interview Wes. There he found George and Wes sitting on the running board of Wes' Packard, waiting for Marvin to arrive so they could begin their workout. "How about you and I going on a nice long trip, fishing and playing golf," Wes told the writer. "You forget about the newspaper business and I'll forget about baseball. If things get too tough I can pitch semi-pro ball for $200 or $300 per game, and then we can move on to the next fishing spot or golf course."[8] Wes denied having heard from the Cleveland management, and reiterated his plans to hold out until he was paid what he felt he was worth; a contract of at least $15,000. The pitcher expected that if they couldn't sign him, the Indians would make a deal for him sooner or later. When Marvin arrived, Wes joked about fining him $1,500 for being late. The writer watched Wes throw and declared him free of arm problems.

An AP story on April 12 quoted Walter Johnson as saying Wes had just talked himself out of being the greatest pitcher in baseball. "Ferrell was a great pitcher, and still is for that matter, but he just talks too much for his own good," said Johnson, citing a rift between Wes and the Cleveland front office over the incentive clause in the 1933 contract.[9] "There's one thing I wish would be straightened out, and that is that Ferrell did not lie down on the job last year," said the Big Train. "He likes to win like all of us, even more so than some of us, and wanted to pitch his regular turn last year, but with his arm in bad condition, and there is no doubt in my mind he did have a bad arm, he could not take his regular turn. This he thought came from the front office, but I was the one who believed it would be hurting him and the club for him to pitch with his arm like this." Johnson went on to say that Wes was an ideal player, "never drinking or getting out of condition. I hate to see a fellow like that out of baseball."

When no agreement was reached, Ferrell was automatically placed on the ineligible list ten days after the season began. "If Cleveland keeps me out of baseball this year," he said, "I'll never pitch another game for them."[10]

Ferrell kept in shape with daily work at War Memorial Stadium in Greensboro, throwing batting practice to Piedmont League teams. On May 13, he pitched and lost a 3–2 game to a team from Bassett, Virginia, while pitching for the semipro Reidsville Lucky Strikes. The next day, W. G. Bramham, the minor league commissioner, issued a warning to all Piedmont and Bi-State League teams that Ferrell was on Organized Baseball's ineligible list and that any player appearing in a game with or against him would face sanctions.[11] The Bassett team arrived in Reidsville for a rematch on May 19 where a large crowd watched a pitcher named Lefty Jenkins best

Wes for a second time. The final score was 5–2 and a batter named Drewery hit a three-run homer off Wes in the first inning.

Years later Wes described the game to author Donald Honig. Some of his facts were clouded by the passage of time, but Wes' humility and sense of humor were clear. "They came from miles around, some of them in horse and buggies. Come to see the great Wes Ferrell pitch. The first guy comes up. Wearing overalls and tennis shoes and a faded little cap. And smoking a cigarette! I get two strikes on him. He steps out and flips away the cigarette. Oh, I'm thinking, what a smooth way to earn $100. I wind up and give him my high hard one ... and he hits it over the center-field fence. The great Wes Ferrell never pitched harder in his life, and those guys killed me. Line drives all over the place. I finished out the game in the outfield. Never been so embarrassed in my life."[12]

* * *

Meanwhile the Red Sox had gotten off to a mediocre start as Bucky Harris' pitching staff immediately collapsed. Herb Pennock and Rube Walberg, 40 and 37 years old respectively, were no longer the workhorses they had once been. George Pipgras was lost after undergoing surgery to remove a growth from his elbow in June. Grove, though, was the major catastrophe.

Lefty had had injuries in the past, most notably his susceptibility to blisters on his throwing hand, but now he was suffering from something different. His arm was sore from the moment spring camp opened, and though he tried to downplay the problem, it did not improve. Eddie Collins drove Lefty to the Athletics' Fort Myers training site to see Mack's trainer, Doc Ebbling. He, like his Boston counterpart, could not find a problem and advised Lefty to pitch through the pain. Harris said the whole thing was a mystery to him. Grove underwent the gamut of known baseball remedies; having teeth removed in Atlanta in April and later having a tonsillectomy, but nothing helped.

Lefty's first appearance of the season came against the Browns on May 5. He worked to five batters—allowing a walk, triple, single, double and another walk—before heaving his glove up in the air and storming off the mound. Nine days later he tossed almost seven innings of three-hit relief, and when he beat the Indians on May 23 it appeared he was over the hump.

Cold weather forced the cancellation of the Indians–Red Sox game in Cleveland on May 24, giving Tom Yawkey and Harris time to sit down with Alva Bradley and Billy Evans to discuss the trade that brought Wes to Boston. There does not appear to be any doubt that the Ferrells had planned a reunion in Boston. When the Red Sox stopped in Greensboro for an exhibition game on April 10, Rick Ferrell convinced Harris to let Wes throw batting practice to the team. Eddie Collins phoned while Harris and Yawkey were in Cleveland finalizing the trade, saying that he had run into George Ferrell on the Piedmont circuit and George told him that his brother's arm was in fine shape.

The trade — Ferrell and Dick Porter in exchange for Bob Weiland, Bob Seeds and $25,000 — was announced on May 25 and Wes was notified on a Greensboro golf course. "I am ready to step out there and pitch," he said. "Naturally, I am tickled over the deal. Who wouldn't be? With my brother, the best catcher in baseball, to handle my slants, I am sure of winning a lot of games for the Red Sox."[13]

The timing was right, for Grove's arm immediately gave out and Wes stepped in to take the reins at the team's ace, catching up with the club in Detroit in time to witness the Tigers— powered by two Hank Greenberg homers— shell Lefty on May 28 for 12 hits and eight runs in less than six innings of work.

Wes was working hard on the sidelines getting ready for action when Grove dropped a 2–1 decision in the opener of a pair in Washington on June 2. The Red Sox managed just five hits and averted a shutout on a Rick Ferrell double and an ensuing single in the fifth inning. Boston broke the second game open with six runs in the top of the ninth and Wes, who delivered a pinch-hit single, stayed in to pitch the last inning. He caused his new teammates some apprehension by allowing three hits and three runs before retiring the side. Rick was aghast, for the fastball that Wes had shown him over the winter was nowhere to be found.

The Red Sox opened a series with first-place New York at Fenway Park on June 5 and were leading 5–1 going into the fourth when Harris lifted his starter — who had walked seven batters— and replaced him with Ferrell. Wes arrived on the hill with one down, one run already in and the bases loaded. The first two batters he had to face were Ruth and Gehrig. Ruth flied to center to make the score 5–3 and Gehrig grounded out to end the inning. The Yankees then went down in the fifth, sixth, seventh and eighth innings without a hit. Earle Combs led off the ninth with an infield hit, only to be erased on a double play. Ruth singled but Wes— earning his first Boston win with 5⅔ innings of two-hit relief— got Gehrig on a grounder to end the game. Boston *Globe* writer James O'Leary said that Ferrell "had the Yankees guessing at all stages with his change of pace and sharp-breaking curve."[14]

Boston split a doubleheader with the Yankees the next afternoon, knocking them out of first place with a 7–4 win in the nightcap. The Bombers had pummeled Grove for 13 hits and seven earned runs in just four innings in the opener. A week later on June 13, Grove allowed 13 hits and eight earned runs run in less than five innings of relief work, but was the winning pitcher as Boston triumphed 15–13 over Detroit.

Wes allowed eight hits and three walks as he pushed the Red Sox to .500 with a 4–3 win over Washington on June 10. All of the Nats' scoring came in the second and third innings, after which — according to the *Globe* — they "were hamstrung and hogtied by Ferrell's blazing curve." Wes crashed a double off the left-center wall to start the eighth and "bashed a long fly to deep center to win the game" when he arrived at the plate in the ninth with the bases loaded.

The Cleveland-turned-Boston ace was the 3–2 victor over George Blaeholder and the Browns on June 16. "Ferrell," noted the *Post*, "was not quite as stingy with his hits as in days gone by, had nevertheless showed flashes of a former greatness and an ability to bear down just when the opposition threatened seriously."[15] Wes was able to survive several stormy situations and the game was knotted at two going into the ninth inning when Rick Ferrell scored the winning run after opening the frame with a single.

The pitching Ferrell received credit for a 14–9 win over the White Sox in Boston on June 20, in which he allowed all nine runs (five earned). Chicago scored four times in the seventh — aided by an infield hit and errors by the Boston shortstop and right fielder — to erase a 9–5 lead, but the Red Sox scored five times immediately thereafter.

Mel Harder was next when Wes started opposite his old team on June 24. It was a tight contest with the Tribe holding a 2–1 edge after eight innings, but Ferrell, who was very anxious to top his old team, apparently spent it all in fanning Hal Trosky, Odell Hale and Bob Seeds in that frame, for Cleveland erupted for four runs in the ninth on four hits and an error to account for the 6–2 final.

Wes was unimpressive in his next two starts. He was lifted for a pinch-hitter in the sixth inning on July 1 against the Athletics after allowing a run in the second inning and four more in the fourth. The Red Sox scored five early runs on the Fourth of July but New York came back with two runs in both the third and fourth innings. After Babe Ruth doubled to lead off the fifth, and Gehrig reached when an infielder muffed his easy pop-up, and Chapman singled to fill the bases, Ferrell was relieved. He received no-decisions in both contests.

Though the game was played in Boston, the holiday hero was the Bambino, and his every move brought a cheer from the crowd. The fading superstar attempted to fool the Ferrells with a third-inning steal of second base. When Rick threw him out the crowd roared their disapproval.

Donald Honig asked Wes what it was like pitching to Ruth. "Like looking into a lion's jaw, that's what," replied the pitcher. "Hell, man, you're pitching to a legend! And you knew, too, that if he hits a home run, he's gonna get the cheers, and if he strikes out, he's still gonna get the cheers. You were nothing out there when Ruth came up.

"You look around, and your infielders are way back and your outfielders have just about left town, they're so far back. And here you are, 60 feet away from him. You got great encouragement for your infielders, too. The first baseman says pitch outside; the third baseman says pitch him inside. They're worried about having their legs cut off. 'Take it easy, boys,' I told them. 'I'm closer to him than you are, and I'm not worryin'.' The hell I wasn't. Ruth could swivel your head with a line drive."[16]

Lefty Grove tossed two innings against New York on July 3 and then did not reappear on the field for three weeks. The third-place Red Sox were within easy range of the Yankees for the top spot in the league, and the Boston *Globe* opined "everyone in the American League will freely admit that if Grove was Grove the Red Sox would today be setting the pace in the American League." Joe Williams of the New York *World-Telegram* agreed. "To put it briefly," he penned, "Lefty, in shape, would have had the Red Sox on top at this moment...."

Williams then switched to Wes. "So the Indians figured they could give up Ferrell and still have plenty of pitching strength, and, besides, there was no way to tell whether Ferrell would come back with a recovered arm or not. Well, it turns out the Indians' pitching is not very strong this year and could use a man like Ferrell — I mean a Ferrell who was both recovered and contented.

"It would be somewhat ironic, wouldn't it, if it should develop that the Indians' failure to deal with Ferrell in the spring cost them the championship? I happen to know that Walter Johnson, the manager, didn't exactly relish the idea of letting him go.

"Ferrell is still a great pitcher,' Johnson told me at the baseball writers' dinner last winter. 'He would make the Yankees a sure pennant winner, and he'd help any club that can pay him what he thinks he's worth.'

"Johnson spoke not only from close critical observation but from actual clinical experience. He had warmed up with Ferrell just before the season closed, and the pitcher had shown him most of his old time stuff.

"This being so, you find yourself wondering why the Indians didn't give the temperamental young man a decent contract and go along with him for another season anyway. You don't pick up pitchers like Ferrell every day. Or even every year, either, for that matter."[17]

The Ferrells were Tom Yawkey's first successes (reprinted courtesy of *The Boston Globe*).

* * *

The catching Ferrell was also drawing raves. "A great all round player" was how James O'Leary of the *Globe* described him after he had a perfect day at the plate with a walk and three singles on July 5. Rick, who had been around the .300 mark right along, hit .410 in July and peaked for the season at .348 on July 26. A bad August and September would drop him below .300 but Rick was still going strong at midseason when he finished fourth in the popular vote for the second All-Star squad as reported by the Associated Press on July 2.[18] Dickey led the fan voting with 102,000 tallies and Cochrane was a distant second with 19,000 votes. Ferrell and Rollie Hemsley drew just over 6,000. A week earlier, though, the BBWAA released a poll of their members and the American League catchers' race was much closer. Dickey still won with 147 votes, but Cochrane and Ferrell finished with 124 and 96 votes respectively.[19]

* * *

Wes Ferrell's last start before the All-Star Game came against Philadelphia on July 6. Boston won 18–6 and it wasn't much of a contest. Each Ferrell made three hits. Wes gave up one run in the first inning, three more — all unearned — in the fifth, and finally two in the top of the ninth when the game was out of reach. He held the Athletics' big boppers— Bob Johnson and Jimmy Foxx — to a combined one for eight and the newspaper recap of the game said that Wes, whom they felt never had to overextend himself, appeared close to his old form.

The Athletics took a 10–7 lead into the ninth inning the next afternoon and the Boston fans were heading for the exits when Eddie Morgan began the home ninth with a single. Roy Johnson followed with a double and Carl Reynolds drove them both in with a single to make the score 10–9. Connie Mack changed pitchers at that point and brought in Roy Mahaffey. "Every spare player in the Athletic lineup was out in front of the dugout yelling to their mates to stand firm," observed the Boston *Post.* Dick Porter drew a walk, and pitcher Rube Walberg, due next, was called back to the bench. "Then out of the Boston dugout trotted Wes Ferrell, with long bat in hand." He connected on the first pitch, "a smashing hit that bounded off the high wall like a bullet."

"The ball went so far and so fast that many spectators figured it would clear the wall entirely. But it didn't. Cramer, running far back, made a desperate leap in the air, but didn't come anywhere near connecting." Both runners scored and the Red Sox were 11–10 winners.

Wes kept the Browns off the board until the ninth inning in his next starting assignment, a 7–2 victory in 104-degree heat at St. Louis on July

13. He opened the scoring in the third with a tremendous home run off Dick Coffman. The ball "landed in the top row of the left-field bleachers just to the east of the score board."[20] He deposited another Coffman pitch into the left-field seats in the fifth and this time two teammates, including Rick, who opened the inning with a double off the left-field fence, rode home on the blast. The score was 4–0 and Wes had knocked in all four runs.

"Opposing batsmen," wrote James Gould in the St. Louis *Post-Dispatch*, "say 'he don't throw nuthin' and he ain't got nuthin',' but, like 'old man river,' Wesley Ferrell, supposedly a 'broken-armed' pitcher, and certainly one without his old 'fast ball,' appears to 'just keep rollin' along' and adding victories to his 1934 list.

"What makes him win, if he's shy his fast ball? Well, a good guess would be a combination of excellent control and uncanny knowledge of what a batter does and does not like....

"Wes, the pitcher, allowed only six scattered hits in the first eight innings and, hitting two home runs—both regular wallops—drove in twice as many runs as the Browns' whole team scored.

"Rick, catching in his usual faultless fashion, hit a single and double and walked once in four times up, besides handling his brother's service in high-class style.

"The two Ferrells, therefore, made almost half as many hits as the Browns, scored three runs and batted in four. A fair afternoon's work for any battery, brothers or not."[21]

Wes topped the White Sox 6–2 on July 17 to run his record to 7–1, allowing six hits—three to Al Simmons—while walking three and fanning five. Rick Ferrell had two singles and two walks in his four trips to the plate while the Chisox managed just three safeties through the first seven frames. "Wes Ferrell's brilliant casting proved altogether too much for the hapless White Sox this afternoon," wrote the *Globe*.

Cleveland leapfrogged over Boston into third place with a 5–3 victory on July 20 but the Red Sox continued the game with Wes' 7–6 triumph the next afternoon. He was not particularly effective, allowing a triple and three doubles among the 13 hits he surrendered, and trailed until his mates scored four times in the eighth inning. Rick Ferrell doubled in the tying run and scored the winning run before turning things over to his brother. "Once in front," observed the *Globe*, "Ferrell did not seem like the same hurler. He put his fast ball on exhibition for the first time during the fray."

Rick had a big series—nine hits in 16 at bats—as Boston split a four-game series with the league-leading Tigers in Detroit beginning on July

23, and when *The Sporting News'* issue of August 2 published the league averages, Rick was sandwiched between Lou Gehrig and Jimmy Foxx as the sixth-best hitter in the league. Wes and Elden Auker squared off on July 25 and neither starter lasted two innings. Detroit's seven hits knocking Ferrell out in the second inning, though Boston won 9–7.

Wes pushed his record to 9–1 with an 8–0 whitewash of Washington on July 30. The standings on July 31 showed the Yankees in first place with a 59–36 record. Detroit was second at 60–37 and the Red Sox were fourth at 52–47.

Ferrell was in and out of trouble against Washington on August 4 but fine fielding allowed him to take a 4–3 edge into the ninth before the Nats tied it up. Wes recorded two outs in the tenth but after a double and an intentional pass, Dave Harris hit a Texas Leaguer that a Boston outfielder overran for an error. Two runs scored and Harris ended up on third. An ensuing popup was dropped by the Boston second baseman — another error — and Harris scored. The final was 7–5.

The Red Sox jumped out to a 10–1 lead when they beat the Athletics 11–9 in Philadelphia on August 8. Rick Ferrell plated two runs in the second with a triple and Wes drove him home. Rick led off the third inning with a double and Wes once again banged him in. A 10–1 lead so early in the game looked like an easy win, but a bases-loaded homer by Jimmy Foxx and a two-run shot by Ed Coleman drove Wes from the hill in the third inning. The *Globe* reported that Wes "left in high rage, kicking up the grass and hurling the ball away in disgust."[22] Lefty Grove relieved Ferrell and allowed two runs over the final six innings to pick up the win. "Sometimes Wesley was too much of a competitor," wrote Bill Werber, the Bosox third baseman and friend to the Ferrell Brothers. "Harris finally walked to the mound to get the ball. Wesley just turned his back and walked out toward shortstop. When Harris finally managed to corral him and get him into the dugout, Ferrell struck himself in the jaw with his fist and slammed his head into the concrete wall. Bucky had to pin his arms to his side to keep him from doing further damage."[23]

Grove apparently discussed the same incident at the 1944 All-Star game in Pittsburgh, but with slightly different details. "Wes was one of the greatest pitchers and one of the greatest competitors I have ever seen," began Lefty ... "I'll never forget one day when Ferrell was knocked off the mound. He was boiling with rage when he came into the dugout. He sat there smacking himself on the chin with his clenched fist. Then it happened. All of a sudden, his eyes glazed and he slid off the bench to the floor — cold as a herring. He had knocked himself out."[24]

Lefty Gomez' nineteenth victory opened a four-game set for the Yan-

kees at Fenway Park on August 10 and Rick Ferrell made three safeties as
the Goofy One beat the Sox 10–3. The next afternoon the teams locked up
in a duel that went 13 innings. Babe Ruth broke a scoreless tie with a homer
deep into the right-field bleachers in the eighth inning but Boston tied the
score in the ninth. Tony Lazzeri put New York back ahead by a 2–1 score
with a shot over the left-field wall in the top of the thirteenth but Boston
tied the score on a double, an error and two walks. The first pass by Yankees' pitcher Jimmie DeShong was intentional, the second one fatal. "For
at this point," wrote the New York *Times*, "Wesley Ferrell stepped up as a
pinch-hitter for Ostermueller and without very much ado slammed a single to centre to break up the game."[25]

Werber also had a take on Wes in these situations. "Ferrell wanted
the ball, and if he was not pitching, he wanted to pinch-hit. In the late
innings of a close ball game, Wesley could sense when a pinch-hitter might
be needed almost before the manager. He would go to the bat rack, select
his bat, and walk to and fro in front of manager Bucky Harris, waving his
bat."[26]

New York and Boston split a doubleheader on August 12. Official
attendance was given as 46,766 for each game as big crowds turned out
for what was expected to be Babe Ruth's final Boston appearance. What
the New Yorkers got in the first game was too much Wes Ferrell. The Yankees scored twice in the first after Frankie Crosetti began things with a double off the left-field wall. Wes fielded an ensuing bunt and threw wildly
past first base into right field. Ruth and Gehrig followed with singles but
Ferrell tightened up, retiring Dickey on a fly ball and punching out Ben
Chapman and George Selkirk. The game was tied at three when Wes began
the eighth with a double, his second hit of the day. Pitcher Johnny Murphy fielded a bunt but threw too late to third base as Wes slid in safely
under the tag. Babe Ruth then misplayed a liner into a triple. The final
was 6–4 as the Yankees tallied one more in the ninth.

Lefty Grove tossed his first complete-game victory in more than two
months when he beat the Browns 7–3 on August 14. The game was deadlocked until the seventh when Rick Ferrell — who had earlier tripled and
scored a run — led off the frame with a double and advanced on a single.
The next batter hit a hot shot to shortstop and Rick got caught coming
down the third-base line, but when the Browns failed to back up the play
properly he was able to slide safely back into third. Grove almost killed
the rally by hitting into a bases-loaded double play but the next three batters hit safely.

The *Globe* reported that Wes looked like a million dollars in tossing
a two-hit shutout against the Browns on August 17. He walked but one

batter and the two hits he allowed — both singles—came in the fourth and fifth innings.

The visiting Tigers took out of three from Boston who made four errors as Grove dropped the first contest 8–6.Detroit had won 14 consecutive games to break open the pennant race and Wes was expected to oppose Schoolboy Rowe, who was gunning for his fifteenth consecutive victory, in the series' finale. Ostermueller started instead and Rowe beat the Red Sox 8–4 to extend Detroit's lead over New York to 5½ games.

The next afternoon, August 22, Wes topped the White Sox at Fenway Park. The contest went ten innings and was one of his most celebrated victories. He allowed seven hits, fanned five and passed one. Al Simmons had his hitting streak snapped at sixteen games. The final score was 3–2. Chicago scored an unearned run in the third inning when Evar Swanson, one of the era's fastest players, singled with two down and stole second base. He came home when Roy Johnson muffed a fly ball. Base hits by Luke Appling and Jimmie Dykes plated another run in the fourth.

The Chicago pitcher, Les Tietje, also tossed a nice game, allowing ten hits; two to Rick and three to Wes. The Boston pitcher came to the plate with one down and the bases empty in the eighth, trailing by a run. On a two and two count, he tied the game by lofting a towering shot that dropped out of sight behind the left-field wall.

The game remained knotted until the last of the tenth inning when Wes, again with the bases empty, but this time with two outs, homered once more to win the game. "It was a most dramatic climax to a great ball game," wrote the *Globe*, "in which one man, and he the pitcher, was the whole show, both on defense and offense."

"It was a mighty blow that decided the extra inning contest. After the impact with the bat, and the ball shot into the air, Simmons and Haas, the White Sox outfielders, started for the dressing room before the ball passed over their heads. Neither took a backward step, because they knew the moment the ball was hit that it was going to clear all barriers and land somewhere on the farther side of Lansdowne Street."[27]

"There was an outburst of applause," continued the paper, "When he did his stunt in the eighth, but it was only a murmur compared with that which started after the ball began its flight, and continued for some time after he had made the circuit of the bases. It was kept up, in fact, until the fans were physically all in from hugging and pounding their neighbors."[28] Ferrell started 23 games for the Red Sox in 1934 and his team supported him with nine home runs. Max Bishop, Moose Solters, Carl Reynolds, Roy Johnson and Bill Werber each hit one. Wes hit the other four.

Ferrell dropped the first game of a doubleheader to the Indians on

Wes in top form while with Boston (Gwenlo Ferrell Gore).

August 26 by a 3–2 score. Five of Cleveland's 11 hits and all of their scoring came in the first as Earl Averill and Hal Trosky came up with back-to-
back singles with one down. Averill was retreating toward third after
watching a routine fly ball being gathered in for the second out but he
scored when the Boston center fielder unleashed a wild throw back to the
infield. A sharp single followed and Trosky, who initially was holding at
third, tallied when the ball skipped past the left fielder. All three Cleveland runs were ruled earned even though Boston was charged with two

errors. The Red Sox scored twice in the fourth inning with a Rick Ferrell double leading to the first run. Oral Hildebrand then walked Wes with runners on second and third and retired the next batter for the third out. Again in the sixth, Wes approached the plate with two down and two runners in scoring position. This time Hildebrand struck him out; Ferrell swinging so hard that he fell down.

Ferrell's next start came on his normal day in the rotation but not in an official game. Both the Braves and the Red Sox used their regulars in an exhibition game on August 31 to raise money for the Boston welfare fund and Wes hurled for the Red Sox.

* * *

Rick Ferrell plated the winning run of a 2–1 contest in Philadelphia on September 2 with a deep fly to center field in the ninth inning. When the American League batting averages were published on September 3 they showed the three catchers—Dickey, Cochrane and Ferrell—running dead even. With all three having similar playing time, Dickey was hitting .324, Cochrane .323 and Ferrell .319. The Boston backstop had been the leading hitter of the three—based strictly on average—for most of the year, peaking at nearly .350 late in July only to tail off over the last two months of the season. In an era when teams played on hot summer days and 20–25 doubleheaders were not unusual, Ferrell had several seasons where his batting average tanked in the latter part of the year. Likely there was a fatigue factor involved.

Rick does appear to have been worked harder than Cochrane or Dickey in 1934, catching in 24 of Boston's 26 doubleheaders, starting both ends 12 times and catching every inning eight times. Cochrane caught in all 20 of Detroit's doubleheaders, but started both games just six times and caught every inning only thrice. Dickey—who missed significant time at the end of the season with a broken hand—appeared in both ends of 13 of New York's 21 doubleheaders. He started both games five times and caught every inning five times.

* * *

Wes' next pitching assignment was a 6–3 triumph in the opener of a Labor Day doubleheader in Washington on September 3, in which he limited the Nats to four hits and no runs over the first seven innings. An error, an infield hit and two clean singles accounted for two runs off Ferrell in the eighth. Joe Cronin, who beat out the infield hit, suffered a fractured right wrist when he collided with Wes, who was covering first base. Cronin did not play again that year and lingering effects from the injury would haunt him — and his Red Sox teammates—for several seasons.

Wes dropped a 5–1 game in Cleveland on September 8. He allowed 14 hits and was in constant trouble throughout the game.

The Red Sox split a tightly played four-game set which opened in Detroit on September 9. Hank Greenberg's timely batting won the first two games before Rick Ferrell got his turn in the third game with a tenth-inning double off Schoolboy Rowe that made Lefty Grove a 4–3 winner in relief. Tommy Bridges dropped the finale 1–0, allowing just four hits. The Red Sox strung three of them in the fourth inning, including one by Rick, for the game's lone score.

Milt Gaston beat Wes 1–0 in Chicago on September 14. The six hits he allowed was one more than Ferrell gave. The first two Chicago batters of the game were retired before Al Simmons walked and moved to third on a single by Zeke Bonura. Working carefully but not intentionally to Luke Appling, Wes put him on with four balls. Another walk scored the only run of the contest.

Neither Ferrell brother was around at the end of Wes' next assignment, a contest in St. Louis on September 18 which Bobo Newsom lost 2–1 after holding the Red Sox without a hit until the tenth inning. The siblings had been tossed in the second after Newsom fanned Wes on three pitches. The third one was a called strike and umpire Lou Kolls gave the Boston hurler the thumb as soon as he turned to argue. When Rick started from the dugout in support of his brother, he was tossed as well. "I had two strikes on Wes," recalled Newsom in 1945 — although he remembered the umpire incorrectly — "And decided I might sneak a fast ball past him if I could cut the corner of the plate with it. Wes knew Hornsby's rule and he didn't even swing at the ball. Umpire Bill McGowan called 'strike three,' and then things started to happen.

"Wes jumped at McGowan. 'That wasn't a strike,' he yelled. 'He's not allowed to throw a strike on a two-and-no count because Hornsby will fine him.' Rick Ferrell joined in the argument and McGowan threw them both out of the game. Later on, they were fined for the rumpus they caused, and I was fined for throwing the strike, despite the fact that I got him out."[29] The next day, the American League president dished out $100 fines to each brother. Wes was suspended for five games and Rick three.

Wes made his last start of the season against Washington at home on September 25. He pitched a gem — scattering five hits, fanning four and passing no one. The only thing he lacked was run support. Bob Burke started for Washington and matched goose eggs with Wes for eight innings. With runners on first and third in the last of the ninth, Rick Ferrell cracked a single over second base to make his brother a 1–0 winner.

* * *

While Wes and Rick were drawing raves in Boston, George Ferrell was tearing up the Red Sox minor league system after he and Marvin Ferrell signed with the Columbia, South Carolina, Sandlappers in late April. Columbia was Boston's affiliate in the Piedmont League. Always the consummate professional, George sought advice from such hitters as Paul Waner, Jimmy Foxx and Rogers Hornsby — his idol. He also altered his batting stance on the advice of Joe Jackson.

"Joe Jackson," George told his son years later. "He was outlawed in baseball, but lived in Greenville, South Carolina, and he showed me a lot. I was playing for Columbia for an exhibition game and he brought his team there but he couldn't play. They say he was illiterate, but he was no illiterate when he picked up that damn bat, I tell you that! He walked up to that plate, and he was not illiterate there, either. He was smart as a whip."

George had another typical year and by late June was leading the Piedmont with a .408 average. He pounded three home runs off Greensboro pitcher John Chambers on May 18 and belted a homer in support of Marvin's complete game victory against Richmond on May 31. The Columbia franchise was transferred to Asheville, North Carolina, in early June but the change in venue did not bother George's hitting. When Boston moved him up to their Reading team in the New York–Pennsylvania League in July, the Boston *Globe* quipped, "If George continues to slap the apple in the manner in which he has in the Piedmont League, the Ferrell family may play one-third of the team on given days at Fenway Park next summer."[30]

George Ferrell hit .300 during his month-long stay in Reading. On August 17, stepping off of the field after driving home the game winning run, George was informed that he had been traded to Williamsport

George S. Ferrell with one of his favorite dogs. Rick raised show dogs and George, hunting dogs. Both of them endorsed dog food products (George W. Ferrell).

for Joe Cicero. Cicero played for the Red Sox as a teenager and 15 years later at the end of World War Two reappeared in the majors for Connie Mack, but his biggest claim to fame was that his cousin was Hollywood legend Clark Gable.[31] George was not happy with the news and requested to go back to Asheville. That request was honored and he finished out the year as the second leading hitter in the Piedmont League. He was named as the center fielder on the League's post-season all-star team.

* * *

The Red Sox also had their eye on the family's 20-year-old cousin, Beverly "Red" Ferrell, who had been playing semipro ball in Durham, North Carolina. Bev had been recruited by Duke and Wake Forest as a football player after a stellar career at Durham's Central High but baseball was his love. His father — Grover Cleveland Ferrell — was Lonnie Ferrell's younger brother, and Bev had drawn the interest of both the Yankees and Red Sox before joining George and Marvin in Asheville where he worked out while negotiating a contract. Eventually, with family counseling, he signed with the Baltimore Orioles of the International League, who offered him a $1,000 bonus.

* * *

The Ferrells headed home after the season ended where four of them — Wes, Rick, George and Bev — played in a series of October exhibition games in Greensboro, Durham and Asheville.

The leading pitchers in the American League were Lefty Gomez and Schoolboy Rowe who were 26–5 and 24–8 respectively. Wes finished at 14–5. Though neither Ferrell received a vote in the prestigious *The Sporting News* MVP ballot, Wes— despite missing almost a third of the season —finished eighth in the BBWAA's American League MVP voting.

Peer evaluations of 154 American League players were revealed in a poll at the end of September. Lou Gehrig (134 votes) outpolled Jimmy Foxx (17) and Hank Greenberg (3) at first base while Mickey Cochrane led the catchers with 107 votes. Bill Dickey and Rick Ferrell drew 34 and 11 nods respectively. Gomez and Rowe topped the pitchers with 153 and 132 votes. Mel Harder was named on 14 ballots while Red Ruffing and Wes Ferrell drew two votes apiece.

◆ 10 ◆

1935 — The Best Player in Baseball

In a performance that he referred to as his most memorable game, Wes Ferrell began the 1935 season with a brilliant 1–0, two-hit shutout at Yankee Stadium on April 16. "An opening day is always tougher than the rest," said Wes when given the nod by new manager Joe Cronin. "Not only yourself, but the whole ball club is nervous and doesn't play its best ball. I'll have it especially tough if I have to start against the Yankees, because I'll have to beat Gomez.

"But I don't mind it a bit. I'm not particularly pleased with my showing this Spring, but when the regular season gets underway, I'll bear down just a little harder and probably will get results."[1]

"It's twenty games for me in the winning column this year or no count. My arm never felt better. There isn't even a twinge of pain left in my right shoulder, which gave me so much trouble my last three years with Cleveland."[2]

Ferrell had spent the spring working on his control and it showed, for he neither walked nor struck out a single batter. "The Yankees," wrote Mel Webb in the *Globe*, "could not fathom that delivery, only once they swung and missed but in this fastest of starting ball games, Ferrell had almost innumerable strikes called for him. His control was marvelous."

Lefty Gomez turned in a fine effort as well, and the only run of the game came in the sixth inning when Bill Werber doubled and moved to third on a bad pickoff attempt. Roy Johnson fanned but was able to take off for first when catcher Bill Dickey didn't handle the third strike cleanly. Forgetting about Werber, the New York catcher started to chase Johnson toward first base. He threw to Gehrig, who made the play at first but his return throw to the plate was wild; not that it mattered as Dickey was not in a position to take the throw, and Werber scored.

Wes Ferrell (left) and Lefty Gomez before their opening day duel in 1935 (Gwenlo Ferrell Gore).

"Ferrell still pitches as Matty did — with no exaggerated motion, no fuss and no effort, but with plenty on the ball," wrote Frank Graham. "It was not precisely pleasant to sit by and see him take a decision over Vernon Gomez and throw the Yankees for a loss, but it was interesting for anyone who has an appreciation of the fine art of pitching. His smoothness, his control and the ease in which he turned back all the Yankee hitters, save Selkirk in the fourth inning and Gehrig in the seventh, compelled your admiration....

"A pitcher can be so good that he simply cannot lose, not even in a close fought contest such as that of yesterday, and Ferrell was that good."[3] Sixty thousand fans had been expected at Yankee Stadium but cold weather held the crowd to around 30,000. "Rick Ferrell," continued Graham on the other half of the brother battery, "is about as good a catcher as you would wish to see on any afternoon, hot or cold."

"Wes had everything against those Yankees," said Rick, "He was faster than he had been in three years, and, as you know, his control was perfect. He could put that ball anywhere he wanted to." Lou Gehrig chipped in his two cents, saying "He looked like the Ferrell of four years ago. He wouldn't give anybody a fat ball to hit at. And how many times was he behind the hitter all afternoon?"[4]

Ferrell's second start of the season came in Washington on April 22 where he accounted for four of his team's 11 hits in a 4–2 victory. Earl Whitehill matched Ferrell until the fifth when a two-out double by Wes and a subsequent single plated the first run of the game. Boston scored twice in the sixth when Rick Ferrell drew a two-out walk in front of a couple of base hits. "The Sox got a little shameful that they were letting Wes do all the work, so they got a pair of runs in the sixth without him," said the Boston *Post*.

Protecting a 3–2 lead, the Boston pitcher tallied an insurance run in the top of the ninth when he smashed a triple — the longest hit of the game — to "extreme center field." Wes couldn't close it out in the ninth, retiring the first batter but becoming visibly upset when his left fielder dropped a routine fly on the next play. He walked a batter and went 3–0 to the following hitter before a great play by Max Bishop on a grounder headed up the middle accounted for the second out. Walberg replaced Ferrell for the last out.

Eddie Collins and Tom Yawkey's biggest rebuilding decision to date had brought Joe Cronin over from Washington to replace Bucky Harris as the Red Sox manager following the 1934 season. Cronin was under a lot of pressure, for not only was he expected to produce a contending team, he was also anticipated as the team's hitting and fielding leader. The broken wrist he had suffered the previous season was still giving him trouble, and had been aggravated by a bad sprain in spring training.

Lefty Grove dropped his second start of the season. 10–5 to Washington, at home on April 26. Only two of the runs were earned, for his infield — lead by Cronin's three miscues — made five errors. The Boston *Post* said that "Cronin looked like a guy with an iron glove trying to catch a tennis ball."

Wes took his next turn on April 28 and the *Post* said he pitched a beautiful game. His "masterly control and an assortment of pitches were, in the main, completely mystifying the Senators." Ferrell allowed five hits through eight innings and took a 3–1 lead into the ninth, but two errors by Cronin on routine grounders led to four unearned runs and a 5–3 loss. The Washington ninth consisted of a Cronin error, a single back through the box, a sacrifice bunt, another error by Cronin, a clean play by Cronin that produced an out, a hit-and-run single through the vacated shortstop hole, a single between first and second and a single to right.

"Temperamental Wes was rightfully pretty sore by this time," wrote the *Globe*. He was stomping around the mound and Cronin, no doubt feeling pretty down, had to rush in and steady Wes who looked like he was about to walk off the field. Joe calmed him down and Wes retired the final batter on a fly ball. "Cronin himself has had a terrible time of it," noted the *Globe*. "Under the big pressure he has lost, for the time being, his easy going manner in the short field, and his nonchalance."

Grove was scheduled to start in Philadelphia on May 1, but cold weather caused Cronin to use Fritz Ostermueller instead. Boston scored two runs in each of the last three frames for an 8–6 victory. A Rick Ferrell walk and successive pinch-hit singles by Bing Miller and Wes Ferrell produced the Boston runs in the eighth inning. Rick singled in the ninth and scored the final run after catcher Jimmy Foxx threw wildly on his attempted steal of second base. Joe Cronin had two special weapons in 1935; the pitching of Wes and Grove, and the pinch-hitting of Wes and Bing Miller, who combined for 22 substitute hits and 17 RBI.

Ferrell's second loss of the season was a 5–2 decision in Detroit on May 4 in which he allowed 11 hits. "It was too cold a day for a fellow like Ferrell to pitch effectively," commented the *Post*. "He had everything he has had in other games in which he has worked as witness the seven strikeouts he got during the seven innings he worked.

"In the fifth, the worst inning Wes had, in which the Tigers punched out three hits which were good for two runs; he also had three strikeouts, disposing of Greenberg, Goslin and Owen, a trio of pretty fair batters, by the whiff route."[5] Boston was down 5–1 when Wes led off the top of the eighth with a line drive that hit the third-base bag. The pinch-runner sent in for Wes scored the second Boston run. The club's first score had come in the fifth when Wes drew a bases-loaded walk.

Cronin lost more than just a game in the standings when the Indians beat the Red Sox on May 8. Grove — making his first start in almost two weeks— had yet to find his fastball but was effective "breaking a semi-speed ball over the outside corner." In the seventh inning he suffered a split finger on his glove hand when stopping a line drive. He would not pitch again for another two weeks.

Wes had been hit with a line drive in batting practice on May 6 but he was ready for his turn against the front-running White Sox in Chicago on May 9. The Windy City boys had come out of the gate fast and were 10–0 at home, with half of those wins coming against Detroit and New York. Wes and the Sox trounced them by a 10–1 score. Rick Ferrell doubled in the fourth inning and both he and Wes hit safely in the seventh when the Red Sox scored three times. Wes singled again in the eighth.

"The Ravaging rampage of the remarkable and ruthless White Sox, who have swept through the American League with reckless abandon, was drawn to a quick and peaceful conclusion today when they ran into Boston's Red Sox," wrote the *Post*. "With Wes Ferrell pitching as only Wes Ferrell can, the White Sox reverted to form."[6]

The Boston writers felt Wes was in beautiful form. He allowed eight hits and Chicago scored its lone run in the ninth inning when the score was 10–0. "True, he gave five bases on balls during the game," wrote Jack Malany in the *Post*, "but not once was it because of lack of control. He wasn't giving the hitters anything good to hit, and if they refused to bite, and accordingly got a free passage, that was all right with Wes." Even the Chicago writers tipped their hats; Warren Brown writing, "The 'W' is for Wesley, more familiarly, Wes. But the 'W' might well be for Work, since in all the league which this stout-hearted Boston Red Sox right-hander graces there is none who toils harder than the man who just put an end to the remarkable home stand of our Chicago White Sox last Thursday."

"Wes Ferrell is One-Man Club" was the Boston *Globe*'s headline four days later after he tossed a five-hitter in St. Louis, winning 2–1. The Browns loaded the sacks in the first inning on a hit and two walks but Wes pitched his way out of the jam, allowing just two more runners until St. Louis scored in the eighth. Wes accounted for the game winner in the seventh when he hit "a mighty clout into the distant pavilion, down toward the center field bleachers."[7]

The White Sox were still in first place when Wes beat Sam Jones in a 13-inning, 2–1 pitcher's duel at Fenway Park on May 17. Boston scored once in the sixth inning and Wes took a two-hit shutout into the ninth before Zeke Bonura tied it up with a home run into the center-field bleachers. Babe Dahlgren began the Boston thirteenth with a double and Wes—intending to sacrifice—dropped down a perfect bunt that went for this third hit of the game. Moments later Dahlgren scored the winning run.

Grove allowed four hits and two runs in a 4–1 loss to Cleveland on May 20. The Indians scored an unearned run in the second inning when Lefty fielded a come-backer to the mound and threw high to first base. Rick Ferrell hit a home run over the fence in left-center in the sixth inning that made the score 2–1, but that was as close as Boston came.

Wes had the last laugh against his old team with a 12–5 victory on May 22 that knocked the Indians out of second place. Joe Vosmik lined Ferrell's third pitch of the game into the right-field seats for a two-run homer and, noted the *Globe*, "No lesser personages than Manager Walter Johnson and Coach Steve O'Neill led the verbal barrage against Ferrell from the Cleveland bench as Vosmik trotted around the bases."[8] Things got worse in the second inning when a single and two doubles accounted for two more runs. Cronin walked to the hill to talk it over with Wes, and when the big right-hander got back to work he retired the next three batters to get out of the inning and allowed just four more safeties the rest of the way. Indians' hurler Monte Pearson had held the Boston bats in check through the first four innings, giving up just singles by Wes and Mel Almada before the Red Sox exploded for six runs in the fifth inning and six more in the eighth. Wes contributed a walk and a single in those rallies and Joe Cronin crashed his first Fenway homer of the season in the eighth.

The fast-moving Detroit Tigers and Schoolboy Rowe beat the Red Sox 5–3 on May 23 to move past Boston into the first division. A foul tip off Rowe's bat in the ninth caught Rick Ferrell's thumb, putting him out of action for a week. Twice during the game Rick hit line drives toward right field only to see both balls speared by Hank Greenberg. After being retired the second time, the Boston backstop, in a classic display of Ferrell temperament — and there should be no doubt that anyone in the family ever took losing lightly — "heaved his bat at the ball as Greenberg started to toss it around the horn."[9]

Grove, struggling over the last four innings with an open blister on the middle finger of his pitching hand, won his second game of the season the next afternoon in an 8–4 decision. The Detroit sticks found Lefty for 14 hits, hit 15 balls to the outfield, drew two walks, didn't strike out once and left ten runners on base. Grove didn't like to pitch in cold spring weather — Jimmy Foxx often joked about Lefty's assortment of early season "ailments" — and this was just his first complete game while Ferrell already had six. "He had felt fine all Spring," said the *Globe* of Lefty, "and has in his heart great confidence that there's still to be shown a lot of zip in that old soup bone — this perhaps, as soon as the weather really gets good and warm. However, his 'fast one' of old times is still delaying its appearance."[10]

Tommy Bridges, though running into trouble in the ninth, beat Boston on May 25 by a 3–2 score. A pinch-hit single by Wes got the tying run as far as second base before Bridges closed out the game.

Ferrell opened a series with the Browns at Fenway Park the next day and Cronin began things by booting a ground ball. Sammy West followed with a double and Jack Burns sent a single to center that Boston outfielder Mel Almada erred on, allowing two runs to score. A walk, a sacrifice bunt and a single accounted for two more runs. A walk, another sacrifice and then a single drove Wes from the game in the second inning; his final line being five hits and four earned runs. Boston came back to win the game 8–7.

Joe Cronin, feeling that second baseman Max Bishop was past his prime, traded Moose Solters to the Browns on May 26 for Oscar Melillo. Solters had been an uninspiring player in Boston, but with the change of uniforms—and some batting advice from Rogers Hornsby—he started to hit with a vengeance, especially against the Red Sox. When the Browns beat Boston on May 27, Solters tripled in a run in his first at-bat. The next afternoon he had three hits and drove in the winning run against Ferrell in the ninth inning. Starter Grove had pitched ineffectively, giving 11 hits— including three doubles, three triples and a home run—in less than eight innings. Johnny Welch relieved Grove, and Bing Miller delivered a pinch-hit double hitting for Welch that tied the game in the home eighth inning. Wes came into pitch the top of the ninth but a double and subsequent single by Solters won the game, 6–5, for St. Louis.

Philadelphia opened a three-game series at Fenway Park on May 29 in which the Red Sox took the first game 10–9. It was a strange contest in which Boston scored eight times in the seventh inning. Wes drew a walk and scored as a pinch-hitter during the big rally.

He was the headliner in the following day's doubleheader. "The Sox," wrote the *Globe*, "particularly the courageous, indefatigable Mr. Ferrell, missed satisfying their royal rooters by the veritable eyelash." Wes started and won the first game. He lost the second one in relief only after his clutch ninth-inning double took the contest into extra frames. The opener was tied at two when Philadelphia broke through for two unearned runs in the sixth inning due to "Ferrell's wildness and uncertain fielding by Cronin, Werber and Reynolds." Wes allowed six hits and passed three but none came after the sixth inning. The Red Sox broke the game open in the eighth on two doubles, a sacrifice, a dropped fly ball, an intentional pass, a single, a long outfield fly by Rick Ferrell and singles by Wes and Mel Almada. The final was 7–4.

The Red Sox trailed 8–7 going into the bottom of the ninth in the nightcap and things looked bleak with a runner on first and two down. Rick Ferrell, who replaced Moe Berg behind the plate when Wes came in to pitch the top of the ninth, drew a walk to keep things going. That brought his brother to the plate in the money spot and Wes lashed a double toward the left-field corner. The tying run came home and only a brilliant backhanded lunge and stop by Bob Johnson prevented Rick from tallying the winning score. "These ears never have heard at Fenway Park such a din of approbation as that which greeted Wes," wrote the *Globe's* Gerry Moore, "Thousands who were on their way to the exits returned to their seats...."[11] Wes set the down the Athletics in order in the ninth and tenth innings, and including the first game had pitched five perfect frames.

Despite running out of gas and allowing five runs in the eleventh inning, Cronin left him in to finish the game. Joe was dependent on Wes and Lefty no matter what the situation. It was better to lose with your aces, he felt, than with your second-stringers. "The reward for his Herculean efforts for Ferrell," noted the *Globe*, "was one win and one defeat ... it is only hoped that his efforts did not leave him ineffective for the near future."

Ferrell's next start was a 3–2 duel he took from Bump Hadley in Washington on June 4. Washington scored a run in the fourth and Boston tied it up in the fifth on two singles sandwiched around a walk to Wes. The Boston ace was protecting 3–1 lead when the first batter of the ninth reached him for a triple. He met the emergency by retiring the side on a short fly ball and two ground balls. "Ferrell may not have his fast ball of old," wrote the *Globe*, "but he knows where to heave the pill. Seven of the Nationals popped to the infield and seven more sent up harmless flies in the outfield. Not many were meeting Ferrell's offerings solidly."[12]

Grove — declaring his arm finally ready — opened June with a six-hit shutout of the Yankees. From then until the end of the season he would go 18–9 and Wes 18–10, giving Cronin as formidable a one-two pitching punch as any manager in the major leagues. Washington snapped its eight-game losing streak by beating Lefty 5–4 in 10 innings on June 5. He pitched well before his control went to pieces in the tenth. With one down and two on, Grove hit a batter to fill the bases and then walked in the winning run.

The Yankees dropped a 2–1 game at Fenway Park on June 7. Boston scored both of its runs in the fourth inning on hits from Cronin, Reynolds, Rick Ferrell and Babe Dahlgren. Rick scored the winning run.

Wes started the next afternoon and couldn't get out of the second inning. He retired the first three Bombers, but a walk to Gehrig to start the next frame and then four straight singles by Lazzeri, Dickey, Selkirk and Crosetti, plated two runs and left the bases loaded. Johnny Allen hit a come-backer to Wes who threw to Rick for the force at the plate, but Dahlgren erred on Rick's relay to first and another run came in. A double by Earle Combs knocked Wes from the hill. The final was 12–6 in favor of New York.

With Chicago, Cleveland, Washington, Detroit and Boston all jockeying for second place, the Red Sox took a pair from the Tigers at Navin Field on June 11. Grove won the first game 3–1 and Ferrell the second 5–2. Both pitchers allowed five hits. "Those two temperamental pitching veterans, Robert Moses Grove and Wesley Cheek Ferrell," wrote the *Post*, "looked like the Grove and Ferrell of four years ago ... the fast ball that Ferrell has been looking for all season was his this afternoon. He had plenty of speed, as did Grove in the first game, and, until the ninth, Ferrell also had very good control."[13] Boston scored a run off Alvin Crowder in the first inning of the nightcap and two more the next frame when Rick Ferrell rode home on his brother's two-run shot over the left-field wall. Wes allowed just two hits and had a 5–0 lead after seven innings. A walk, an error by shortstop Dib Williams—who was subbing for Cronin—on a potential double-play ball, and a single led to a Detroit run in the eighth. A walk, a single, and a double off of Dahlgren's shins plated a second run in the ninth.

A 10–8 win over Detroit three days later made it three out of five in the series. Detroit scored four times in the seventh to wipe out a 7–4 Boston lead but the Red Sox finished the scoring with two runs in the eighth and one in the ninth. George Hockette started for Boston and neither he nor reliever Hank Johnson pitched well. Grove came into the game in the bottom of the eighth after his club had taken a 9–8 lead, and pitched the last two innings. "The official scorer named Grove the winning pitcher," wrote *The Sporting News*, "although Boston was ahead when he went to the box. It was pointed out that Grove was the only Boston pitcher able to curb the Detroit attack and that he was entitled to the victory."[14]

Ferrell's former mates jumped on him for six runs in the opening frame of a 9–7 game on June 15 that saw the Boston hurler's record fall to 9–6. The Red Sox batters, piling up 17 hits, came back to score five times in the sixth inning and take a 7–6 lead. "With a victory in his grasp Ferrell, who usually improves as the game progresses," wrote the *Globe*, "served a home run ball to Hale and a double and costly error by Dahlgren tossed the contest back to the Indians." Ancient Bing Miller was the hitting star for Boston, driving home four runs on two doubles and a pair of singles. Rick and Wes each had two hits and drove in a run.

Cleveland made it four straight by swamping the Red Sox 11–2 score on June 17. Oral Hildebrand pitched a six-hitter for the Indians and Rick Ferrell, going three for three, was the only batter who did any damage. Rick doubled and scored the first run in the second inning, then drove in the other run in the third.

Wes' next assignment came in St. Louis on June 19, and he became the first American League pitcher to win ten games. He gave up three home runs—two by Solters—and the game was tied at five before a triple, two doubles—one by Rick Ferrell—and a single netted Boston three runs in the eighth inning of the 8–5 final. Wes had four singles to bring his batting average to .472 (25 for 53) for the season, and his hitting was more of a feature in the game than his pitching.

"That Ferrell will win 25 games or more this season is now the expectation," wrote the *Globe* the next day, "This Spring he cautiously got himself in shape and spent much more time reaching for control than he did to getting a lot of 'smoke' on the ball. He has shown an ability to bear down when he has to do so, and sensibly has saved his arm all he could."[15]

After Grove ran his record to 6–5 with a rain-shortened, six inning three-hit shutout of the Browns on June 21, the Red Sox traveled to Chicago where Wes dropped a 4–2 game to Ted Lyons two days later. The White Sox jumped on Ferrell for four hits and three runs in the second inning and three more hits and another run in the third. Wes settled down and held Chicago scoreless the rest of the way but his mates could do little with Lyons, who allowed more hits than Wes but kept them scattered until late. The Red Sox pitcher had two singles as a batter; driving home the club's first run in the seventh inning and scoring the second in the ninth.

The next afternoon the Red Sox closed out their 16-game western swing with a 6–4 loss to the White Sox. Grove took the loss in relief, and two errors by Joe Cronin played a big role. Lefty took over for starter Gordon Rhodes in the seventh inning with the score knotted at four and Chicago scored right away on a double, a ground out, an easy hopper that skipped past Cronin, and two more singles.

Ferrell's next start came in Philadelphia on June 27 where Mack's big sticks— Foxx, Johnson and Pinky Higgins— did a number on him. Johnny Marcum held Boston to four hits and a pair of runs while his teammates scored 14 times. Marcum started the fireworks himself when he drove a Ferrell fastball over the fence in the third inning. Higgins hit a ball "completely over the left field roof" in the fourth inning and then a two run shot "soaring into the center field upstairs section" the next inning. Johnson also homered and Wes was gone after allowing nine hits and seven earned runs in less than five innings.

* * *

Eddie Mooers owned the Richmond Colts. He was an old International League infielder and had close connections to the Philadelphia Athletics, Boston Red Sox and New York Giants. He hired Eddie Rommel to manage in 1935 and purchased George Ferrell's contract from Williamsport in March. Ferrell, whom Mooers described as "one of the finest minor league baseball players now performing on anyone's lot," quickly became a crowd favorite for hitting timely home runs over the left-field wall into the James River.

George homered in each end of a doubleheader on May 3 against Norfolk and drove in eight runs. He blasted two home runs and drove home seven teammates in a May 26 game with Charlotte. On August 22,

Ferrell hit two homers and had six RBI in a 14–1 win over Portsmouth. "George, how about a couple of homers tonight?" kidded a sportswriter before the game. "He filled that request, perfectly," wrote the Richmond *Times-Dispatch* the next day, "and did the fans, and the press box, like it!"[16] George promised another home run to the writers on August 24 and crashed a "terrific clout" into the James off future Brooklyn Dodgers' pitching ace Kirby Higbe. Jim Bagby, Jr., Charlie Wagner, Clyde Barfoot, Jim Lyle, Jake Mooty and Higbe — all pitchers who performed in the majors — were victims of Ferrell's long blasts.

George S. Ferrell: Most Valuable Player in the Piedmont League (George W. Ferrell).

On July 31, a Wilmington hurler named Cozad was leading Richmond late in the game. He was pitched an intimidating game, allowing just three hits while plunking six batters. Ferrell, upon becoming the seventh victim in the eighth inning, paid a trip to the mound to deliver Mr. Cozad his comeuppance and both players where ejected. Two weeks later when Richmond returned to Wilmington, Ferrell and Rommel were arrested, George charged with assaulting Cozad and Rommel for aiding Ferrell to evade the charges by skipping town. Both were acquitted in court.

Despite rumors that the Red Sox were bringing him to Boston, Ferrell remained in Richmond for the entire season where he was named the Piedmont League's Most Valuable Player. He hit .377 –winning the batting crown — and hit 25 homers and drove home 110 runners. He was the only unanimous selection to the League's All-Star team.

* * *

Cousin Beverly Ferrell played for the Thomasville Orioles in the Georgia-Florida League. At the beginning of July he hit a ball that sailed close to 450 feet on the fly, clearing the 399-foot left field wall of the Thomasville Stadium. It was the first time a ball had cleared the fence in ten years. Legend had it that the only other man ever to clear that fence — despite numer-

GREAT RACE FOR PITCHING PAIRS

August 7, 1935. Wes and Lefty lead the field of teammate pitching pairs in the majors (reprinted courtesy of *The Boston Globe*).

ous exhibition games being played there by major league squads—was Shoeless Joe Jackson.[17]

* * *

Lefty Grove's thirteenth victory was a 5–4 decision in eleven innings over the Athletics on August 3. He showed plenty of his old-time smoke in hurling superb ball, highlighted especially in the tenth when he pitched out of a jam that saw the Mackmen put runners on second and third with no outs. His dark side, though, emerged after two fielding miscues. "Twice," noted the *Post* the next day, "Lefty Grove failed to run out ground hits yesterday, and in the first stanza he lost a base hit because of that failure. It looked as though Lefty became a bit peeved because of Bill Werber's bad throw."

Grove trailed 3–1 going into the bottom of the eighth but after two singles, a sacrifice, a fielder's choice and an intentional pass to Rick Ferrell, Wes singled in the tying run with a pinch-hit. Jimmy Foxx led off the Philadelphia eleventh with a double, scoring to put his club in front 4–3, but the Red Sox came up with two runs in the bottom of the inning to make Grove the winner.

The Red Sox split a doubleheader with the Athletics in front of the 40,800 fans in Fenway Park on August 4 with Wes annexing his eighteenth triumph with a 10-inning, 7–6 win in the first game. "Destiny's child, Wes Ferrell," wrote the *Globe*, "who seemed fated to be robbed of the verdict when his support tottered in the eighth, appropriately carried across the winning run." Ferrell took a 5–2 lead into the eighth inning but errors by Cronin and Werber helped Philadelphia tie the game. Things looked bleak when Pinky Higgins blasted a home run in the ninth to send his club up by a run but with two down in the Boston ninth a walk to Cronin, a single by Rick Ferrell—"always ready to assist brother Wes"—and a single by Dib Williams knotted things at six. Wes started off the Boston tenth with a single to left and scored the winning run three batters later when Roy Johnson singled into right field.

The standings and statistics in the *Globe* the next day showed the Red Sox at 51–46 and Ferrell the majors' top winner at 18–9.[18] Dizzy Dean was next at 17–7, followed by Hal Schumacher (15–5), Tommy Bridges (15–7) and Carl Hubbell who was 14–7.

New York—in town for a four-game series that opened on August 5— pounded six Boston hurlers in a 10–2 abbreviated game that was halted after five innings due to heavy rain. The fifth inning was farcical. "With another downpour imminent," noted *The Sporting News*, "the Yanks endeavored to make three outs, but the Sox endeavored just as much not to retire them. During this period the Yanks stole four bases."[19] The *Globe* used a photograph of Rick Ferrell purposely juggling the ball at home plate, and Myril Hoag, who stole both second and home in the inning, waiting just short of the plate for Rick to tag him out. "Ferrell finally had his way and they gave Hoag a stolen base, of all things!"[20] Both managers— Cronin and McCarthy — were fined $100 for their stalling tactics.

Two days later Grove and Ferrell went against Johnny Broaca and Lefty Gomez in a mid-week doubleheader that drew 33,000 fans to Fenway. Cronin made a throwing error to open the third inning of game one, a frame in which the Yanks drew first blood. New York had a 5–3 lead when Wes popped out as a pinch-hitter for Grove to start off the bottom of the ninth. Boston was down to their final out when Cronin lined a three-run homer over the left field was that made Grove — now 14–7 — a 6–5 winner.

Ferrell went looking for his nineteenth win in the nightcap but came up short. The *Globe* reported he looked tired — he was starting on two days of rest — but might have gotten by passably except for George Selkirk, who drove home runs with two-out hits in both the first and fifth innings. Wes left the game after the sixth, trailing 5–1. The final was a 6–4 Gomez victory.

With the Tigers pulling away from the pack, the Red Sox, who along with Cleveland and Chicago were chasing the Yanks for second place, faced off against Washington in a doubleheader at Fenway Park on August 11 and Cronin again sent his two aces to the mound.

Lefty dropped the first game 4–2. Boston fielding miscues in the third inning accounted for three unearned runs, and a passed ball by Rick Ferrell led to another tally in the sixth. The Red Sox managed to fill the bases in both the first and eighth innings but could not score. Wes— pinch-hitting in the eighth with the bases crammed — scorched a liner right at the shortstop, who converted it into a double play. Boston's two runs came in the third on a walk, a double and then Rick's line single up the middle. When Cronin made Boston's third error the fans were all over him with a chorus of boos. "Babe Dahlgren (who was bought for $5,000)," wrote Jimmy Powers of the New York *Daily News*, "has saved Joe Cronin (bought for $250,000) 30 errors on wild pegs."[21] Needless to say, Lefty was in a black mood.

Wes took the nightcap 5–4, causing the *Globe* to write, "For the greater part of the second game it looked as if the unprecedented experience of Grove and Wes Ferrell losing on the same day was to be met." Wes had better luck than Lefty. Buddy Myer and Heinie Manush, with three hits apiece, did most of the damage for Washington who took a 4–3 lead into the bottom of the eighth inning. With runners on second and third and one down, Wes, who had two singles as a batter in the game, hit a ground ball to third base but on the ensuing throw to the plate Bill Werber hit the Washington catcher hard enough to dislodge the ball. Mel Almada followed with a double off the left-field wall for a Boston lead and "Wes thereupon put on steam and retired the Senators in the ninth on four batters."

The Boston hurler started a classy double play in the second inning after Manush slashed a one-out triple. Cecil Travis hit a come-backer to Wes, who feinted to third to keep Manush from starting too soon. Then Heinie — waiting as Ferrell wheeled as if to throw to first — broke for the plate. Wes didn't even look at first, instead making a complete pivot, trapping and tagging Manush between third and the plate and firing to second where Melillo slapped a tag on the advancing Travis.

After Werber, Cronin and Dusty Cooke hit solo home runs in a 3–1 Grove victory in Chicago on August 15, Boston, with a 57–49 record, was five games behind the second-place Yanks.

Wes lost 4–3 in 14 innings to Vern Kennedy the next afternoon in a game the *Globe* referred to as "one of the hardest-fought and most dramatic games famous old Comisky Park has ever seen." Rain threatened all afternoon and Cronin was hoping for a postponement that would allow him to set up his rotation with Wes opening the next two series in St. Louis and Detroit. Chicago's Rip Radcliff began the game with a single off Oscar Melillo's shins and rode home on a Jimmie Dykes double. Jackie Hayes singled off Wes' glove in the second and scored on a two-out double by Kennedy. Rick Ferrell one-hopped the left field wall in the third inning to drive in Boston's first score. Chicago scored a run to go up 3–1 in the fifth but Wes induced consecutive foul pop-ups with the bases loaded to extract himself from the jam. Boston got one back — though they should have gotten more — in the sixth when Cronin doubled in a run with a one-out gapper to right-center. Joe attempted to stretch it into a triple and was thrown out, thus negating Rick Ferrell's ensuing single. Boston tied the game the next inning when Melillo led off with a triple and scored on Wes' slow topper down the third-base line.

The game continued to the fourteenth inning; the Red Sox could not cash in on scoring opportunities in the ninth and tenth. Luke Sewell opened the fatal frame with a liner to left that Roy Johnson tried to shoestring; the ball ricocheted off his shins enabling Sewell to land on second. Kennedy sacrificed Sewell up a base, and Cronin and the Ferrells went into a conference on the mound. Radcliff was passed intentionally and Cronin called another confab. Wes worked the count full before Tony Piet, with both the infield and outfield in, ripped a clean single for the ball game.

Most of the Red Sox players were in a foul mood on the train to St. Louis but Wes tried laughing it off, telling the *Globe's* writer, "I lost 10 pounds in that game, but that isn't bothering me half as much as losing my batting eye. Why, I didn't get a single hit."[22] The writer, Gerry Moore, said, "It was bad enough to lose the decision with Wes in the driver's seat, but it was the type of game that took every bit of energy and nerve power that a pitcher has. Now it is a question of whether Wes will be ready to take his turn in the scheduled finale of the [next] series."

Grove and Ferrell started a doubleheader on August 20. Lefty won his game 7–3, staging "a slight display of temperament" when outfielder Dusty Cooke erred on consecutive plays in the fourth inning that allowed St. Louis to cut Boston's lead to 4–2.

The second game was an 8–5 Brownies victory in which Wes allowed 15 hits. He was fine early but three straight hits after two were down in the fourth, one a Moose Solters double, plated two runs. Solters tagged Wes again in the next inning for a three-run homer, but Boston fought back in the seventh — an inning that Rick Ferrell opened with a double — when singles by Wes and Mel Almada produced three runs. Solters singled off Wes' glove to start the St. Louis eighth. The next batter hit a double-play ball but Dahlgren fumbled the relay at first and drew an error. A Texas Leaguer over shortstop and a come-backer off Wes' shins that bounded into right field plated one run and left runners on first and second. A soft liner just out of the reach of Dahlgren and a popup into shallow left that Cronin caught, but inexplicably held while the runner scampered home, made the score 8–3. Boston made some noise before going down in the ninth — Dahlgren, Wes and Cooke started the inning with consecutive singles — but it was too little too late.

Cronin's squad dropped a doubleheader to the Tigers on August 21 and Rick Ferrell was pretty beaten up. He had taken a foul tip off his shoulder in St. Louis, and now, in Detroit, he was clipped twice more, once on the left arm and once on the thigh. "The blows did not cause Rick to forget his gallantry, however. Chasing a Fox foul in the fifth, he bowled over a woman sitting in the first tier of boxes and then gained an ovation from the throng by showing a great solicitude for his victim."[23]

Boston beat Detroit the next afternoon but the victory was costly. Wes pinch-hit in the fourth and drew four straight wide ones from Tommy Bridges. In an ensuing pick-off attempt at first, Hank Greenberg fell on Ferrell and severely sprained the pitcher's ankle. It was expected that he would miss ten days.

"Rick Ferrell was the whole works offensively in the opener," noted the *Globe* after the Sox swept a doubleheader in Cleveland on August 25.

The backstop had four hits, drove in four of the club's runs and scored the other. Cleveland had taken a 4–3 lead into the last inning but Rick banged in the tying and winning runs with a single up the middle. The catching Ferrell's batting average after the game was .308, down slightly from his midseason peak of .318 on July 21.

Cleveland returned the favor on August 28, taking a pair behind the fine hurling of Thornton Lee, who beat Grove 2–0, and Mel Harder, who won the nightcap. The Red Sox gave Grove no support, mustering but four hits off Lee. Rick Ferrell, suffering an "attack of lumbago," caught both games with his back tightly wrapped. Cronin used three pitchers in the second game and almost started Wes, who was back on his feet.

A 6–2 win in Philadelphia on August 29 went into the books as Ferrell's twentieth win of the year; the fifth such season of his career. Pitching with a wrapped ankle, Wes beat Mack's ace, Johnny Marcum, for the second time that year. The Athletics managed eight hits, including one in the seventh the *Globe* felt was really an error by Cronin. The hit which scored Philadelphia's second run was off Wes' glove. "Ferrell has pitched games which have been more impressive," said the *Globe*, "But he's back in winning stride again, having discarded the crutches and getting foothold with the leg which awhile ago threatened to handicap him for the balance of the year. Now, Wes says he's going to shoot hard at the 25-victory mark — the target which he set up for himself in the Spring."[24]

Wes credited his quick recovery to a bottle of homemade horse liniment. "When Dad heard about my accident, the first thing he did was to get a bottle and mail it to me in Cleveland. I took off the bandages, tape, and other folderol, gave my ankle a good drenching with it and you saw how quickly I threw away those crutches. Why, I can even dance better than Rick now. And that's saying something."

With Ferrell now back in form, Cronin predicted the Red Sox would outplay Cleveland and Chicago for third place. Immediately after making that statement Fritz Ostermueller went down for the third time that season. Early in the year "Ostey" had taken a line drive off the kneecap and missed several weeks. A Hank Greenberg smash caught him in the face and he missed several more weeks. Finally, a week after a drive hit him on the thigh, he found himself unable to walk and X-rays detected a fractured leg.

Wes was bombed in the first game of a doubleheader with Washington on September 2, leaving in a 6–0 hole after failing to retire a batter in the third inning. Reliever Jack Wilson pitched a great game, crowning his effort with a home run in the eleventh inning to win the game. A loss in the nightcap dropped Boston's record to .500, leaving them in fifth place,

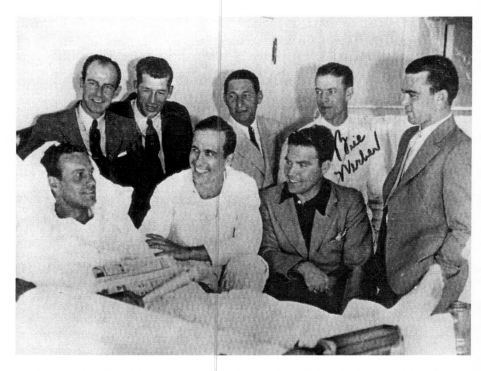

Wes is visited by his teammates after he was hospitalized with an ankle injury. Identifiable in the photograph are (back row from left) Rick Ferrell, Lefty Grove, Al Schacht and Bill Werber (Gwenlo Ferrell Gore).

just behind Cleveland and Chicago. Rick Ferrell went three for five in the doubleheader, and his ninth-inning sacrifice in the second game helped Boston to pull even and take the contest into extra innings.

Cronin sent his aces against the Indians on September 5. "Wes Ferrell and Lefty Grove," wrote the *Globe*, "once again staged their Damon and Pythias act, which fast is becoming a gag among the other American League clubs."[25]

Grove dropped his fourth straight with an 8–1 loss in the opener but Ferrell dominated the second contest, winning 6–1 and not allowing a ball to be hit beyond the infield for six innings. Cleveland put some pressure on Wes in the eighth when four consecutive singles left the bases loaded, with Earl Averill and Joe Vosmik advancing to the plate with one down and one run in. "However," wrote the *Globe*, "Wes put on the heat, fanned Averill and forced Vosmik to ground to Manager Joe Cronin for a force-out." Rick Ferrell scored the first Boston run in the second inning when he hit a ball over the left-field wall that bounced off an amplifier and back onto the field. It was ruled a double. "Wes Ferrell, as usual, fielded brilliantly, handling four difficult chances in the first four innings."

Wes faced the White Sox in the opening tilt of a doubleheader at Fenway Park on September 8 and won 6–2. "When big Wes Ferrell is at best, the path to victory for the Red Sox is always clear and well defined," wrote the Boston *Post*. "And as Boston's great right-hander, even after only two days layoff, was complete master of the situation yesterday, he gave the Boston team the start which resulted in a great double triumph of the Chicago White Sox."[26] The contest was scoreless until Boston broke it open with five runs in the sixth inning. Rick Ferrell's bases-loaded single drove in the first two runs and Wes delivered the coup de grace with a double high off the wall in left-center that plated two more.

Ferrell's twenty-third win was a 13–4 laugher against the Browns on September 13. Lyn Lary opened the game for St. Louis with a double and scored when Rick Ferrell — who hadn't played since a foul tip ripped off the nail on his right thumb on September 10 — threw the ball into left field on an ensuing steal. The Red Sox started their scoring in the fourth when two walks, three singles— one by Wes— and a double plated four runs.

Grove notched his eighteenth victory two days later with a 9–5 decision. Lary again opened the game with a hit but Lefty retired the next two batters. Three straight walks, a single and then a fly ball lost in the sun that went for a triple followed, and Grove was down 5–0. He was still trailing by that margin when Cronin popped out to start the home sixth. Three singles— one by Rick Ferrell —followed and eventually a run was in and two were out when Grove was due to hit. "Boston's No. 1 hero, Wes Ferrell," wrote the *Globe*, "went to bat for his pal, Grove, in the midst of this rally and singled off the scoreboard to knock in a run." The Red Sox scored six times that inning and Grove, trailing 5–1 when Wes hit for him, was the winning pitcher.

Detroit was next, opening a four-game series at Fenway on September 16. The individual heroes in each of those games were Bridges, Wes, Wes, and Lefty. But for an ill-timed gust of wind it would have been Wes, Wes, Wes, and Lefty.

Tommy Bridges chalked up his twentieth win in the first game but he was lucky to get it. "In the eighth with the sacks crammed and two out," observed the *Globe*, "Wes Ferrell pinch hit for Melillo, and lifted a towering drive that looked certain to clear the left-field wall. But the stiff northeast breeze held it back and 'Goose' Goslin was able to camp under it for the final out, a few feet shy of the barrier, much to Ferrell's obvious disgust."[27]

Ferrell won his twenty-fourth game the next afternoon by a 5–4 score.

"He was as good," opined the *Globe*, "in fact he was better, in the ninth inning then he was at any other stage of the game, and he disposed of Gehringer, Greenberg and Goslin, the three G men, in the order of their coming to bat, striking out the last named as clean as a whistle." Detroit loaded the bases in the second on a single, a walk, and Wes' own error on a mishandled bunt. He worked out of the jam, allowing just a single run on two grounders and a strikeout. Hank Greenberg hit a two-run homer in the third for a 3–2 Detroit lead but Rick Ferrell knocked in the tying run the same inning.

Wes retired the first two batters in the seventh before juggling Greenberg's easy grounder; his wild throw past first base allowing Detroit's big first baseman to advance to second. Oscar Melillo fumbled an ensuing grounder just long enough to allow the batter to beat the throw at first, and Babe Dahlgen's relay throw to Rick Ferrell at the plate was both too wide and too late to catch Greenberg, who hadn't stopped at third. Boston plated the tying and winning runs in the bottom of the seventh on two doubles and two singles—one by Rick Ferrell. Elden Auker, the Detroit starter, "was particular not to give Wes Ferrell a good ball to hit, and passed him the first two times he was at bat."

Walberg and Schoolboy Rowe dueled the next afternoon into the last of the ninth with the score knotted at three. After the Boston leadoff man singled and made second on an outfield bobble, Rick Ferrell dropped down a sacrifice that Rowe couldn't handle and Boston had runners on first and third. Pinch-hitter Bing Miller was passed intentionally, bringing pinch-hitter Wes Ferrell to the dish with no outs and the sacks full. Though there was no room for Wes, Rowe wasn't intimidated—firing his first two pitches in high and tight. "It was Wesley Ferrell again as a Red Sox game winner," said the *Globe*, "The North Carolinian stepped into the Wednesday ball game as a pinch hitter, after winning the Tuesday one as a pitcher. The bases were filled in the ninth, and then another safe sock by Wesley, a blow to handcuff Owen, and to bring home the bacon."

Mel Webb, writing in the *Globe* the day after Ferrell won the game from Rowe said, "We wonder how, when the season's all over, it is going to be easy to pick anyone other than Wes Ferrell as the season's most valuable ball player — to any club."[28]

Forty-nine thousand fans jammed their way into Fenway to see a doubleheader with the Yankees on September 22. Ten thousand more were turned away and much of the overflow crowd was placed in roped-off areas in front of the bleachers. Several times during the game the infuriated bleacher populace unleashed barrages of refuse down on the crowd whom they felt were obstructing their view. One fan was hit in the eye by a bottle and required medical treatment. Another suffered a black eye when hit by a ground-rule double. Mel Almada spiked a fan while attempting to catch a fly and suffered a stomach wound himself when he crashed into one of the stakes used to rope off the crowd.

Wes lost the first game by a 6–4 score, and though five of the New York runs went into the books as earned, it's doubtful that any of them were merited as the Boston outfield had a horrible day. "Ferrell's support in the first inning was very bad," commented the New York *Times*. "With two out and Chapman on via a pass, Gehrig hit an easy fly to short right, whereupon Cooke dropped his glove, stumbled and the fly went for a single. Then Roy Johnson lost Selkirk's fly in the sun for a two-bagger. The inning netted three runs, and Cronin's error cost another run in the third." The ball Johnson lost in the first inning actually hit him on the top of the head. Mel Almada lost a fifth-inning fly in the sun that went for a triple and another run.

A special events contest was held between the games of the doubleheader. "Rick Ferrell, who won the accuracy throwing contest for catchers, prevented a clean sweep by the Yankees of the five events contested. Rick threw a ball from home plate into a barrel at second base. None of the other catchers succeeded in doing this, although Joe Glenn of the Yankees tossed it in on the bounce."[29]

Wes' final appearance of the season, his twenty-fifth victory, was a 7–2 decision taken from Philadelphia on September 25. "Wes turned in a neat performance, limiting the powerful array of visiting sluggers to five hits, two of which came in the ninth inning." The victory assured Boston a first division finish and $400 bonus money for each Red Sox player. "As often is the case when Brother Wes is doing the flinging, Rick Ferrell was the No. 1 batter, driving across two runs in each of the three-run clusters that the Sox broke off in the first and seventh innings."[30]

* * *

The year 1935 was the best of Wes Ferrell's career, and an argument can be made that he was the best player in baseball. He finished second in the BBWAA's American League MVP race; his 62 votes trailing only Greenberg's 80. Other players with more than 20 points/votes were Joe Vosmik (39), Buddy Myer (36), Lou Gehrig (29), Charlie Gehringer (26) and Mickey Cochrane (24). Greenberg also won *The Sporting News'* MVP Award and Wes finished fifth. Rick Ferrell was in a three-way tie for tenth. The top six pitchers receiving votes for *The Sporting News* All-Star team were Dean (201 votes), Hubbell (100), Ferrell (52), Grove (31), Bridges (18) and Rowe (11).[31]

J. G. Taylor Spink highlighted the stars of 1935 in his *The Sporting*

News column on October 3. "The man with a smirk for fate..." is how he described Ferrell. "Hard-to-handle Wesley.... A really great pitcher, with the perfect pitching psychology.... Make 'em hit at the bad ones, is his policy, his secret of success...."

Spink also commented on Dizzy Dean. "The greatest pitcher in baseball.... The most colorful hurler the game has seen in years.... A right-handed Rube Waddell.... Dizzy by name but as crazy as a fox...Full of homely philosophy, right up from the soil.... He is finding out puh-lenty about fame and fortune and appreciation...."

The contrast between Ferrell and Dean is interesting. Both had come from rural America, bursting upon the scene with unbridled talent, and both pitched beyond the limit of their physical endurance, causing their arms to burn out before the age of 30. Cincinnati scribe Tom Swope, writing about Dean in *The Sporting News* early in 1931, observed that the major league managers who had seen the Dizzy One considered him the "the most promising young pitcher to come into the majors since the advent of Wesley Ferrell."[32]

By most currently accepted statistical evaluations, Dean and Ferrell had similar peak value with the edge going to Wes for sustaining his career longer. Yet Dean, and for that matter Lefty Gomez as well, are in the Hall of Fame while Ferrell remains outside the sanctum. Why is that? Dean and Gomez were fortunate enough to play in New York and St. Louis; on great teams that provided them with World Series and more media exposure, but were they really better pitchers than Ferrell? They, like Wes, had their peccadilloes. Dean was not especially liked by his teammates. Gomez had, while an active player, an alcohol problem that put a strain on his marriage.[33] Both, though, understood the role of the media and were adept at playing the clown, — thus "Dizzy" and "Goofy"— something they clearly were not. Wes wasn't capable of that, wearing his competitive heart on his sleeve for all to see, and incorrectly is remembered historically as a hothead and a troublemaker.

F. C. Lane penned an article in the September 1935 issue of *Baseball Magazine* titled *That Contradictory Character — Wes Ferrell*. "A strange bundle of contradictions is Wesley Ferrell of the Boston Red Sox," he wrote. "With a rigid regard for training rules and an almost ascetic outlook upon life, Ferrell has suffered, far more than most players, from lack of condition. A young man of blameless character and of the highest principles, he has been embroiled with two major league managers— Roger Peckinpaugh and Walter Johnson. With a determination to succeed in his chosen vocation that amounts to almost a passion, he has been branded as something of a troublemaker...."

The Ferrell family watching Wes and Rick in action. From right are Pete Ferrell, Alice Ferrell and Rufus Ferrell (the other two are unidentified). The photograph was likely taken at Griffith Stadium in 1935 (George W. Ferrell).

"Perhaps a certain fault in temperament is his. Ferrell is of a stern, uncompromising breed. When he thinks he is right, he will not yield an inch. Stubborn, some managers have thought him, and to that, a thoughtless public has added the epithet, swell-headed. Inflexibility of purpose may seem quite like stubbornness, and an unwavering faith in one's ability may well pass for egotism.

"Ferrell's faith in himself has never wavered. He knows he is a great pitcher and he is quite as simple and straight forward in expressing that opinion, as he would in discussing the weather. To him it is but simple frankness and honesty, the recognition of a fact which is quite foreign from boasting. And isn't Ferrell right?"

John Kieran, writing in the New York *Times* in August, noted that Wes would never be confused with a diplomat. "He isn't a mixer or a boon companion of all and sundry. He doesn't bother to cultivate friendship or even acquaintances. He does his work, goes about his business and likes to be left alone....

"Joe Cronin and Tom Yawkey say underneath everything he is a great fellow. Maybe he is. Two years of trying to find out left this observer badly baffled. To an investigator with a friendly turn of mind, he was decidedly

Dizzy Dean (left) and Wes. The two best right-handed pitchers in baseball during the 1930s (Gwenlo Ferrell Gore).

THEY ARE THE RED SOX "IT" BOYS
By Gene Mack

WES FERRELL

Because—this tall, blond and handsome Wes has "out-Merri-welled" the tall, dark and handsome character made famous by Burt L. Standish. When big Wes trudges to the plate in the role of pinch-hitter, with his cap set rakishly on his head, well — if any other Red Sox player in history ever aroused such enthusiasm we can't think of his name just now. Wes, for a guy that is supposed to be highly temperamental, has the perfect mental equipment for a pinch-hitter. Completely relaxed and an easy swing that drives a ball a mile.

His hitting has somewhat overshadowed his pitching which happens to be about the best in the American League. Wes has the heart and the head and if he once had a bad arm you'd never know it now.

BOB GROVE

Because—after having their enthusiasm bottled up for an entire year, the Red Sox followers are making up for it now when long Bob really "turns it on."

There's nothing like a "fire" ball pitcher to set a baseball audience "pop-eyed." The futile "swish" of the other fellow's bats after the ball has smacked into the catcher's mitt is sweet music to the fans. Everybody turns to everybody else and says, "Ya can't even see it." A St Louis paper commented on the fact that Grove coached at first base when he wasn't pitching. He wasn't suppose to show that much interest, but Lefty has this Red Sox team at heart, and the whole town is with him in his glorious "comeback."

JOE CRONIN

Because he was so anxious to make good in this man's town he tried too hard and had the misfortune to put on a fielding show at times that was something below his brilliant Washington form, but Joe Cronin had the courage to stick out that jaw and come fighting through in the face of defeat and make his knockers like it.

Joe is of the old school; he had a badly infected foot, but cut the shoe off at the affected part and gamely continued to play. A lot of the moderns would have taken a vacation.

For years the Red Sox searched for a player who could hit that left-field wall. Joe Cronin fills that bill, and then some. Better still, he hits that wall when it means something.

RICK FERRELL

•Because—although he is the stylist among catchers and moves around in a "ho-hum" sort of way, the fans would rather see Rick coming up there to bat in the pinch than any player on the club. Behind that mask of effortless play is a fighting heart that never quits.

In outward appearance, Rick Ferrell doesn't look to have the stamina of a George Gibson or Oscar Stanage, but he's in there day in and day out, always going at top speed. When it comes to tagging men at the plate, he's in a class by himself.

Like Charley Gehringer, he makes things look too darn easy.

August 9, 1935 — Tom Yawkey's stars (reprinted courtesy of *The Boston Globe*).

cool, merging on the chilly. But leaving that aside, which probably is where it belongs, he stands out as the greatest pitcher-hitter combination in baseball history, a remarkable figure in a diamond setting."[34]

* * *

The following table represents the offensive production for all of the Boston Red Sox players who had at least 75 at bats in the 38 games Wes Ferrell started in 1935.

	Games	At bats	Runs	Hits	2B	3B	HR	RBI	Ave
W. Ferrell	38	119	22	42	2	1	6	23	.353
Johnson	34	143	23	48	9	3	0	23	.336
Cronin	35	142	22	45	16	2	6	28	.317
R. Ferrell	37	138	13	42	11	2	0	17	.304

	Games	At bats	Runs	Hits	2B	3B	HR	RBI	Ave
Melillo	24	90	15	27	2	2	0	9	.300
Almada	36	153	25	44	8	0	0	17	.288
Dahlgren	38	133	21	37	5	1	0	12	.278
Werber	32	124	23	34	9	1	3	15	.274
Cooke	24	82	12	22	2	1	2	9	.268

◆ 11 ◆

1936 — The Blow-Up
in Boston

Big things were expected of the Red Sox after off-season deals had brought Jimmy Foxx, Roger Cramer, Eric McNair, Heinie Manush and Johnny Marcum — a 17-game winner in 1935 — to Boston. Tom Yawkey had spent nearly $1.25 million on players since purchasing the club, and farm director Billy Evans — Wes' former GM while with the Indians — was building a minor league system that was anticipated to soon rival that of the St. Louis Cardinals. Detroit was predicted for another flag with the Red Sox second and the Yankees third.

Yawkey's purchases at the height of the Depression had been the talk of baseball, but there were hints that all was not well within the Boston ranks, and several managers predicted headaches for Cronin in 1936. The team was being referred to as the "Prima Donnas" and the "Millionaires." Wes' contract called for $15,000 with a $1,000 bonus if the team finished first or second.

Cronin was talking pennant and focusing on the offense. He left instruction of the young pitchers to the Ferrell Brothers, Grove and Herb Pennock. "Every day both Wes Ferrell and Lefty Grove," wrote *The Sporting News*, "are down in the bullpen giving advice to young hurlers and correcting faults in the rookies."[1] When Manny Salvo, a nervous young pitcher from the Pacific Coast League, arrived in camp, Wes went out of his way to make him feel comfortable. "If that's prima donna stuff, give me some more of it," said Cronin after observing Wes.[2]

Grove had come into camp in good spirits. "I've never seen a pitcher," said the usually taciturn Rick Ferrell, "who has been forced to change his style and met with the success Mose has." Bing Miller added, "A pitcher doesn't really get smart until he hurts his arm; Lefty here has always gotten by on a great fast ball. He didn't have to worry about a good curve ball

EVERYONE LAYS FOR THE LITTLE RICH BOY

April 3, 1936 — The Boston Millionaires (reprinted courtesy of *The Boston Globe*).

and change of pace. But when he saw his speed slipping a little, he began to pull the string on that fast one. He learned to pitch to the corners; to give them that slow curve and fork-ball when they weren't looking for it."[3]

The infield was a chief concern. Cronin intended to play first base himself but that was before Foxx arrived. Initial plans called for Foxx at first, McNair at second, Cronin at short and Bill Werber at third. Oscar Melillo was still available and when Werber held out in the spring, Cronin gave Johnny Kroner a look as well. Eventually the Boston skipper settled on an opening day lineup that featured Melillo at second base, McNair at third and Werber in right field. All bets were off when Cronin broke his right thumb in two places in the season's second game.

Wes' pitching and hard work were also drawing raves. Rick declared him capable of delivering a greater variety of stuff to the plate than any pitcher he ever saw. "A remarkable fellow, apparently, is Wes Ferrell, who couldn't pitch his way out of a cellophane wrapper, if he relied on his fast ball," wrote Shirley Povich. "He learned the art of pitching after he lost the burning fastball that was his greatest asset when he broke in ... the new Ferrell gets by, and very nicely, too, thank you, on control alone. His

Rick (left), George and Wes Ferrell in Richmond, Virginia, where the Red Sox played the Colts in an exhibition game before the start of the 1936 season (George W. Ferrell).

ability to pitch to a spot, to pull strings on the hitters, is serving him even better than did his fast ball."[4]

Wes fanned ten — including all three pinch-hitters sent against him — as he opened the season with a 9–4 victory over the Athletics at Fenway Park on April 14. He allowed ten hits and six walks, but, as reported by the *Globe*, "was his usual iron-nerved, inscrutable self in the pinches." Two errors apiece by Cronin and McNair lead to two unearned runs, and Rick Ferrell "caught his customary smooth game, dropped a neat hit-and-run double into right field during the fourth inning explosion, drew a walk and scored a run."[5]

Grove's first start was rained out the next day, and it was so cold on April 16 that Cronin opted for another starter instead. Boston won 10–4 and Cronin's thumb was broken in a fielding collision. Joe and Rick Ferrell decided to start Grove at Yankee Stadium on April 17, despite it being another frigid day, and Lefty was magnificent in holding New York to two hits in an 8–0 whitewash. "It was a funny situation," declared Rick, "Lefty hadn't pitched since a week ago Tuesday. He worked out one day in the Harvard cage after our return to Boston and caught a slight cold. Joe and I had our fingers crossed when Lefty started working, but once he began we felt confident he had all his stuff."[6] Rick had two hits in the game, one a line shot into the left-field stands.

Wes tossed a five-hitter on April 19, taking a 2–1 decision in Philadelphia. Rick, who already had two singles in the game, drew a leadoff walk in the top of the seventh when Boston was trailing 1–0. An infield single and then a sacrifice by Wes moved the runners into scoring position. A single and a fly ball followed, and Wes— once presented with the lead — "waltzed through the final three frames and pitched to but 10 Athletics."

Boston's two-man pitching tandem continued with Grove's three-hit, 8–1 win over Washington on April 21. The game was halted in the seventh inning due to rain and Washington's lone run —coming on an error by McNair — was unearned.

Wes dropped a 9–1 game in Philadelphia on April 23, giving eight hits and nine runs in four innings. "Coupled with Wes' collapse," commented the *Globe*, "was the sloppy field play of the Sox. Three errors were committed by the Boston club, each of which aided the Mackmen in piling up their nine-run total. Ferrell might not have done so badly if his support had been up to par, as only a third of the Philadelphia runs were earned."[7] The lackadaisical fielding of the Sox was already evident to the writers. Werber and McNair ran into each other on an easy grounder that went for a hit, and Foxx fell asleep on a Philadelphia double steal. Even Wes threw away a ball in the fourth inning when Philadelphia scored five runs.

Grove took a 7–2 victory from the Yankees on April 25. Only a two-run homer by center fielder Myril Hoag — Joe DiMaggio had yet to make his debut — deprived him of a shutout. Boston scored six early runs the next afternoon but the Yankees roared right back to an eventual 12–9 victory. Cronin employed three pitchers before Wes entered the game and allowed single runs in each of the last two frames. There was a collision at the plate in the sixth inning when George Selkirk tried scoring on a grounder to first base; bowling over the catching Ferrell in an attempt to jar loose the ball. "Rick, who can be as fiery as any of the high-strung Hose on occasion," noted the *Globe*, "lost little time in delivering a few epithets to Selkirk when they got up and only the act of Umpire Bill McGowan's in stepping between the antagonists prevented further activity on their parts."

Rick went three for three in an 11–8 win over the visiting White Sox on April 28. Boston was in danger of squandering a late lead when someone in the crowd noticed Grove loosening up in the bullpen. When Joe heard the fans hollering for Lefty—who apparently had started warming on his own volition—he called time and sprinted to the pen. "Do you think you're ready to pitch to the batter, Mose?" he asked. Grove retired all five batters he faced to close out the game.

Wes had a 6–3 lead but left the game after putting on the first two batters in the seventh inning the next afternoon. The contest was knotted in the ninth when Rick Ferrell smashed a drive past ChiSox third baseman Jimmie Dykes to account for the game-winner. Talking with writers, "Cronin admitted afterwards that Wes Ferrell's arm has been stiff and commended Wes on his action in asking to be relieved." The Boston manager also discussed his other pitching woes. Marcum had come down with a sore arm and though it was still April, Joe said he was contemplating using Wes and Lefty out of the pen in addition to their starting duties.

Grove began May by shutting out Cleveland. Rick Ferrell, continuing his torrid hitting, was listed as the league's leading hitter with a .439 mark when the averages were posted on May 2.

Over 30,000 fans showed up at rainy Fenway on May 3 to see Wes blank Tommy Bridges and the defending World Champion Tigers on two hits. Ferrell's pregame warmups were halted three times by rain, and Boston coach and funnyman Al Schacht drew a laugh by holding an umbrella over Wes' head. Ferrell faced just 31 batters, and Goose Goslin accounted for both safeties; bouncing a base hit up the middle that Wes got leather on in the second inning and then a line single in the seventh. Detroit's only free pass came in the ninth inning. "As often happens when Wes is pitching," declared the *Globe*, "brother Rick Ferrell drove home Boston's first run, and what could have been the deciding marker, by bouncing a solid smash on top of the left-field wall and over into Lansdowne Street for a home run as leadoff batter in the second inning."[8] Wes banged in the second run and then "the dandy little catcher clouted a solid

FERRELLS PULL THE BIG BROTHER ACT WITH "CATS"

double to left center and scored a run in the fifth that just about sealed the game...."

Two days after Grove shut out Detroit on May 5, the Red Sox were atop the standings with a 14–6 record.

Jimmy Foxx's seventh and eighth home runs of the season contributed to eight early runs against St. Louis on May 7. Wes allowed 11 hits—though two were balls his outfielders lost in the sun — and when the Browns scored three times in the fourth, he "put on his usual display of disgust with himself and life in general by banging his glove on the ground and kicking up the turf during his walk to the dugout." That brought a chorus of boos from the Fenway fans which continued over the next few innings and later, during another trip to the dugout, "Wes made the mistake of performing that popular disdaining motion of putting his fingers to his nose and pointing them in the direction of the fans."

Ferrell finished the game a 9–6 winner and didn't think much of the incident, saying after the game the riding from the fans was a lot of fun. "This byplay hardly means anything," agreed the *Globe*, "as the same fans who were hollering for Ferrell's scalp yesterday will be the same ones who will cheer him to the echo later in the season when he delivers one of his inimitable pinch-hits or low-hit mound performances."

Unfortunately the incident was reported around the country. "But, unknown to most fans," wrote Hy Hurwitz, "Wes is of a peculiar nature. He raised the rumpus at himself. The reason for his acting up was he had permitted the Browns to score. Nothing bothers Ferrell so much as allowing an opponent to tally against him. When the Browns registered their sixth inning tally, Wes was just kicking himself for making this possible.

"When he strolled to the bench he was telling himself he must be pretty tough when the Browns could score twice in the same game when he was pitching. He exploded. He has shown a lack of control over his feelings in the past and no doubt will do it again. It is a complex which Ferrell cannot shake.

"However, he had no right to raise his thumb to his nose. It was a pantomime no ball player should indulge in, especially in front of a home crowd. The Ferrell display will cost him some of the popularity he has acquired since donning a Boston uniform some two years ago. Then, again, maybe some of the crowd has lost its popularity with the hard-working Ferrell."[9]

Rick Ferrell went three for four with a home run and three RBI in a

Opposite: May 4, 1936— Wes shuts out the Detroit Tigers on just two hits (reprinted courtesy of *The Boston Globe*).

12–9 loss as Boston began a road trip by dropping two of three in Washington. Grove had his first bad outing of the season, losing the third game 4–0. He asked Cronin to relieve him in the fourth inning after he had been touched for seven hits and four earned runs.

The next stop was Pittsburgh for an exhibition game, where Wes voiced his dissatisfaction with the layover, for he was scheduled to open the next series in Detroit, and the side trip meant two successive nights on the sleeper train. While in Pittsburgh, Cronin expressed his hope that Fritz Ostermueller would be ready to step up and deliver. Joe began his pep talk to the lefthander with, "Now, you can't expect to pitch like Grove and Ferrell...."[10]

It rained for most of the day on May 12, and Mickey Cochrane pushed for a postponement so he could use Schoolie Rowe against Wes the next afternoon. The showers broke just before game time, and the 5–0 contest was decided when the Tigers scored three runs in the first inning. "Wes yielded eight hits, but two runs were all the Tigers actually deserved," said the *Globe*. "The rain-soaked infield, on which almost a ton of dirt had to be dumped to make it fit for play after the rain, and erratic fielding gave the champions their other runs."[11] *The Sporting News* reported that, "Detroit quickly jumped into the lead by shellacking Ferrell for four hits and three runs in the initial frame." The Boston scribes described the course of action as a single to left, a single through the vacated shortstop hole on a hit-and-run, a roller toward second that took a crazy hop in the mud — dribbling into center field for two bases— a routine grounder to shortstop which was fumbled for an error, and a clean single.

The Boston writers accompanying the Red Sox were not impressed with Cronin's moves when the club dropped a 7–2 contest in Cleveland on May 15. When the situation called for an obvious intentional pass, Cronin's only command to Rick Ferrell was to "be careful." Joe also pulled Oscar Melillo in the middle of an at-bat and replaced him with Wes. "In the first place," opined the *Globe*, "there is Melillo's spirit to be thought of. In the second place, Wes Ferrell would have a terrific time trying to get a long hit in League Park here with a 415-foot left field expanse and a 290-foot right field stretch. Mel Almada was the logical man if anybody."

Ferrell dropped a 10–3 contest in Cleveland on May 16; allowing 12 hits in five-plus innings and causing the Boston *Post* to comment, "Once again the great Wes Ferrell failed to fool the hitters with his assortment of slow twisters and teasers." The next afternoon the Red Sox won 8–7 in Chicago when Rick Ferrell blasted a ninth-inning home run a half dozen rows up in the left-field seats.

Lefty Grove's 2–0 whitewash in Chicago on May 18 was his fourth shutout of the season. He strained his arm in the fourth inning. "Mose so informed Manager Joe Cronin at the end of the inning" reported the *Globe*, "and Cronin immediately dispatched Ostermueller and Wilson to the bullpen where they kept warmed up for the rest of the afternoon just in case Grove needed help. Cronin contacted Lefty at the end of every inning to ask him if he wanted assistance."[12] Grove's record after the game was 7–1 and his ERA was 0.83. On May 23, he was involved in a collision at first base. He sustained a cut which required a suture, and a dislocated a finger on his throwing hand.[13] In his next twelve starts he would go 4–5 with an ERA of 4.83.

Wes was unable to make it past the second inning in St. Louis on May 20. It was his third straight winless start. "The failure of Wes Ferrell to turn in a least one victory has, of course, been the biggest single disappointment of the road trip," wrote the *Globe*. "It has bothered Wes himself. He paced up and down the hotel lobby last night like a caged lion and this morning Manager Cronin was toying with the idea of sending Wes back against the Browns today to relieve his tension."[14]

Ferrell did start that day—May 21—and beat St. Louis 6–2, allowing seven hits and single runs in the sixth and eighth innings. "Every member of the Fenway Hose virtually played his heart out to assist Big Wes his fifth victory and thereby restore his waning confidence in himself," reported the *Globe*. Though practically a teetotaler, Wes was so happy that he drank a beer on the train ride back to Boston.

The Red Sox pulled to a half-game behind the first-place Yankees after Wes opened a big series against them with a 5–4 decision at Fenway Park on May 26. Rick Ferrell was out of the lineup with a twisted ankle. "Ferrell not only unfurled one of his patented pitching performances in allowing the Yankees 10 hits in chalking up his sixth win of the season," noted the *Globe*, "he also drove home the first Boston run with a sharp single to center in the third."[15]

"He was particularly effective in the pinches," noted the New York *Times*.

Wes led 5–2 with two down in the ninth before three consecutive singles left him facing Joe DiMaggio with the sacks juiced. Wes had retired the rookie in his four previous trips to the plate, but this time DiMaggio drove in two runs with a single to right. Next up—with the tying run on third and the go-ahead on first—was Lou Gehrig, who had also been held hitless thus far on the day. The count went full before he lifted a lazy fly to end the game.

Bad luck did in Wes in his next start, a 6–4 loss in Philadelphia on May 30. "Wes lost the first game as the after-the-game sum-up showed," wrote Jack Malaney in the *Post*, "because Eric McNair couldn't find the ball in the sun and two runs came in. Later on a run down could have had one man but tried to get two and lost both also let two more runs score when one or even both might have been prevented." Herman Fink was the winning pitcher for Philadelphia. "Wes, with the same break in luck and backing that Fink got, would have broken the jinx this A's park has over him and won his game. Only in the second and third innings was he really touched up and he would have emerged from those sessions with only one run each inning being scored on him had McNair not lost that ball in the sun."[16]

Ferrell's next foe was Johnny Allen and the Indians on June 3. Neither the Fenway fans nor the Red Sox bats had made much noise by the time the home club came up in the seventh on the downside of a 2–1 score. Suddenly, the somberness was broken by the trumpet strains of "Tessie" floating across the field. During Wes' recent victory over the Yankees, a bleacher fan had begun to play the old Red Sox Royal Rooters' fight song on his horn. Now the Beantown batters responded with a five-run eruption and "appropriately, and like old times," reported the *Globe*, "it was Handsome Wes in person, who, in the process of attaining his seventh victory of the season, delivered the ringing single to center field that sent the Sox out ahead and on their way to triumph." The final was 6–2 and neither of the Cleveland runs were earned as the Sox infield made two errors—one by Cronin and one by John Kroner.

"Although a couple of times Wes patentedly was in jitterish spots," continued the recap, "half of the 10 hits off of him were of the scratch variety."[17] Wes was also determined to make amends for his nose-thumbing performance the previous month, saying "I wanted to make the fans forget about my last game here, and beating Cleveland isn't exactly damaging to my appetite or humor." Allen, feeling no pain, arrived back at the Cleveland hotel at two in the morning and proceeded to rip up both the lobby and his room, punching several hotel employees in the process.[18]

Ferrell's next start, against the White Sox and Ted Lyons on June 7, opened with Rip Radcliff smashing a liner off the pitcher's left knee. The contest had to be halted until Wes could walk it off. When play resumed he was found for ten earned runs in seven innings and a 13–5 loss. Cronin's second-inning error accounted for two unearned runs, and when Wes came out of the game in the eighth, "the high-tension star kicked over a water bucket in his disgust with himself."

Detroit was in town next and Grove, working on his normal three days of rest, opened the four-game series with a 6–3 victory on June 8. Wes, coming back after two days, won 4–3 on June 10. "Wes' famous 'nuthin' ball' was in the hands of the master once again," noted the *Globe*. "The big fellow had his control back and except in a couple of instances the bristling Tigers were completely befuddled.

"Everlasting tribute to Wes' ability to get the goats of opposing batters with his unorthodox stuff was given in the eighth when Charley Gehringer, one of the greatest natural batters of all time, obviously gave up all attempts to meet Wes' delivery squarely and half-heartedly tried to push a safe hit past third baseman Werber, only to have the ball go right at busy Billy.

"Another example of Wes' almost hypnotic powers came in the sixth inning when Goose Goslin took successive molasses-slow pitches right through the heart of the plate for second and third strikes. The venerable Goose couldn't have looked sillier."[19]

Brother Rick of Those Two Great Ferrell Boys

RICK IS A MASTER AT TAGGING BASE RUNNERS— HERE HE IS PREPARING TO TANGLE WITH SELKIRK OF THE YANKS

RICK FERRELL

THE POETRY OF MOTION

PICTURE BOOK HITTER WITH A REAL PUNCH

May 5, 1936 — Rick Ferrell, an artist behind the dish and with the stick (reprinted courtesy of *The Boston Globe*).

* * *

Boston was 2½ games behind the Yankees after a 7–5 victory over St. Louis on June 11 that came courtesy of the catching Ferrell's bat. "Rick's sixth home run of the season, over the left-field wall, with nobody on base, in the fourth inning," reported the *Globe*, "followed by his line two-bagger against the same barrier with the bases full in the very next chapter accounted for four runs that wiped out a 4–2 lead fashioned by the Brownies."[20]

Rick's career home run total of 28 in slightly over 6,000 at-bats gives the false impression that he was not a powerful hitter. Though not a big man, Ferrell was ahead of his time in experimenting with weight training, and had powerful chest and back muscles. He was capable of hitting Fenway's left-field wall with singles and doubles that potentially could have been home runs in other parks. He also had a significant on-base percentage and was considered by both the writers of the day and his peers as a good man to have at the plate in a tough situation.

"I played in a lot of big parks and didn't go for home runs," Rick said in 1981. "I was a line-drive hitter and I just went up there looking for base hits and a good batting average. You have to analyze yourself and see what you can do well and that's what I did best."[21]

* * *

Cronin was able to reset his rotation around his aces after rain and scheduling issues kept the Red Sox idle until June 16, and Grove began Boston's second western trip by dropping a 4–2 contest in Chicago. He allowed eight hits and four earned runs in five innings and the only offense the Sox could muster were two solo home runs by Foxx. Rick Ferrell opened the sixth inning with a triple but died on third. Wes captured his ninth win — making him the league's top winner along with Grove and Monte Pearson — with a 9–4 decision over Ted Lyons the next afternoon. Foxx hit a three-run shot in the first and Wes hit his first round-tripper of the season; a towering shot that hit high up on the center-field bleacher wall. The ball caromed back over the center fielder's head and Wes circled the bases before it could be retrieved.

St. Louis knocked out Grove in the third inning on June 20, enabling Wes to become the first American League hurler to reach ten victories when he shut out the Browns on two hits in the first game of a doubleheader the next afternoon. "Wes Ferrell's performance was a thing of beauty," wrote Gerry Moore in the *Globe*. "Both hits were scratch affairs, one by Beau Bell in the second inning and one by Tommy Carey in the fifth; both came with one out and no Brownie reached third."[22] Just 29 St.

Louis batters trudged to the plate in the contest, and the final 12 went down in order.

The Red Sox lost an opportunity to gain ground on New York when they dropped the nightcap. Desperately looking for a relief pitcher in the middle of the game, Joe turned to Wes, who told him he could give him an inning but three would be too much for his arm. "Incidentally," observed the *Globe*. "Grove was all dressed in civilians and sitting in a box with owner Tom Yawkey when this came about. We asked Manager Cronin if Lefty wouldn't have been helpful in such a spot." Cronin's answer was, "It's too dangerous on your resources for the drive down the stretch."

On June 22, Joe announced a revision of his pitching rotation in anticipation of a big showdown with the Yankees at the end of the month. Grove hadn't pitched well of late and was in a terrible mood, not talking to anyone on the team. Cronin said that Lefty, who worked less than three innings in his last assignment, would start on two days rest versus Detroit and then be used only in relief against the Indians. Thus, figured Cronin, he would thus be rested and ready to open the New York series on June 30. "The other major shift in the pitching plans," wrote the *Globe*, "will find Ace Ferrell pitching every third day during the coming wars. This plan suits the handsome North Carolinian. He expressed the self-same desire on the eve of his great performance yesterday. 'Ah feel great,' said Wes. 'Ah'm certainly ready to go every third day and win, too. Ah'm real cocky now.'"[23]

* * *

Boston dropped the first game in Detroit 8–7, and after the contest reporters were openly second-guessing the manager's decisions. Cronin pulled starter Johnny Marcum almost immediately after he had completed a string of retiring 12 batters in a row. Then Joe, at a crucial time late in the game, failed to turn what looked like a routine double play. Cronin was under intense pressure and much of it was self-induced. His wife reported that he was unable to sleep or eat properly. Joe said that if he were ever the owner of a team, he would never employ a player-manager, for the dual stress was too much on a man.

"The boy manager has been having very little luck with his 'famous' hunch moves lately," wrote the *Globe*. "Manager Cronin is fast driving himself to the breaking point in trying to handle the entire burden of defensive strategy as well as directing his pitchers and take care of a thousand and one other details in the life of a manager."

Cronin was losing the respect of his veteran players. Neither Grove nor Wes Ferrell had any faith in his ability to play shortstop and they resented him making pitch selections from the field, a problem that plagued Joe for much of his Boston career. He couldn't stop himself even though "Herb Pennock advised him that his pitchers and catchers were burning up over the slur to their intelligence."

"He was nervous as hell," wrote Elden Auker in his biography. Auker was with the Red Sox for just one season — 1939 — before telling Tom Yawkey that he would not play again for Cronin. "He was always kicking the dirt out there at shortstop. After the pitch, he would run onto the mound, grab the resin bag, throw it down, and say something like, 'Keep the ball down. Make him hit a curveball. Make him hit the fastball.' He was always on the mound and it just drove us pitchers crazy.

"Cronin did this to all the pitchers except Lefty Grove. When Cronin would start to walk toward the mound, Lefty would start to the dugout. Lefty wouldn't talk to him when he came to the mound, so he stayed away from Lefty."[24]

The Sporting News soon reported that "Joe Cronin saves Bob Grove the embarrassment of waiving him off the mound when he loses his stuff by allowing Mose to walk out of the box on his own volition."[25] Whether Cronin was really concerned about embarrassing Grove — or himself — is open for interpretation, but a bad habit was being established; one that would bite the team later in the season.

Oscar Melillo told Cronin, "Joe, you're so busy giving signals that half the time you don't see the batter hit the ball." When Cronin became so distraught about his poor fielding that he started dropping to one knee to field routine grounders, Melillo said, "For Pete's sake, Joe, if you're going to miss 'em, you might as well stand up and miss 'em like a big leaguer."[26] When Jimmy Foxx was asked in 1944 why Connie Mack won pennants with star players while Cronin had not, Foxx replied, "One manager knew what he was doing, the other didn't. Cronin didn't." Foxx later refuted the quote, "But on or off the record," wrote long-time Boston writer Harold Kaese, "Foxx, dozens of players, managers and experts have accused Cronin of mishandling hurlers."[27]

* * *

The offensive support Boston provided Grove in his 7–6 victory over the Tigers on June 23 seemed to go a long way in easing his anger. Lefty had often voiced his resentment to the press that his teammates were not scoring runs for him; something, at least to that point in the season, that wasn't true. Boston had scored 71 runs in Grove's fifteen starts, or 4.7 runs per contest. For Ferrell they had tallied 87 in seventeen starts or 5.1 runs per contest, and with Wes— likely, with the exception of Foxx, the best hitter on the team — a lot of his support came from his own bat.

* * *

The following table represents the offensive production of all the Boston batters who had at least 75 at bats in the games Wes Ferrell started in 1936.

	Games	At bats	Runs	Hits	2B	3B	HR	RBI	Ave
Foxx	38	146	31	59	8	2	12	36	.404
R. Ferrell	34	115	19	38	9	1	1	13	.330
W. Ferrell	38	116	20	36	6	1	5	21	.310
Cramer	38	162	22	50	6	0	0	14	.309
Manush	21	79	12	24	4	0	0	12	.304
Cooke	26	87	17	25	5	0	1	6	.287
McNair	32	124	18	34	4	1	0	12	.274
Werber	36	130	16	34	6	1	3	24	.262
Cronin	22	88	6	20	4	1	0	13	.227

* * *

The next afternoon the score was again 7–6 but this time in Detroit's favor. The Red Sox were 5½ games behind New York and falling fast. Wes was working in his two-day rest pattern and, at least early, was locked in another duel with Tommy Bridges. He allowed a run in the second inning, four in the sixth and finally single runs in the seventh and eighth. Detroit's four-run surge came primarily via a bunt, a walk, a dink single and a double. Wes had a perfect day as a batter with a walk, a sacrifice, two hits, two runs scored and two driven in. He blasted his second homer of the season in the eighth, but Marv Owen's shot in the bottom of the inning was the deciding blow.

The Red Sox moved to Cleveland for four games where Ostermueller, Marcum, Ferrell and finally Ostermueller again were scheduled to start. Boston won the first game but dropped the next three. Grove got the call to preserve a 5–3 lead with a runner on first and no outs in the sixth inning of the second game. The first batter dumped a 0–2 pitch into right field and the second bounced one up the middle that second baseman Booby McNair made a nifty play on. Cronin, though, dropped the relay at second, McNair got the error, and Cleveland went on to take a 6–5 lead by the time Grove got out of the inning. Boston came up with a rally in the ninth — Wes drawing a walk while batting for Lefty that led to a run — to tie the score and take Grove off the hook. The Indians won in extra frames.

In his next start — again on two days rest — Wes was hammered, allowing thirteen hits and eight earned runs in less than four innings of a 14–5 loss. Roy Weatherly made his major league debut in the contest and had two triples and a single. The May 1954 issue of *Baseball Digest* included a story called "The Day Ferrell Met Weatherly" that was about this game. As always, Wes was uncomfortable facing hitters he didn't know. Seeing Weatherly, he asked, "Who's that guy?" Rookie hurler Jim Henry had faced Weatherly in the Southern Association and offered some advice. "He's a left-handed batter who pulls the ball. I used to get him out by keeping the pitches outside the plate." In his first trip up, Wes tossed him a slow out-side curve and the Cleveland batter poked it down the left-field line for a triple. Ferrell shot a glare at Henry, who quickly looked the other way.

New York pounded Grove for eight hits and five runs before knock-ing him out in the fifth inning at Yankee Stadium on June 30. New York also took the nightcap 6–3 and two of the three Boston errors in the twin bill were committed by Cronin.

Wes was the loser the following afternoon, dropping his game 5–0 to Red Ruffing. "The score does not do justice to Ferrell's performance," reported the *Globe*. "Wes yielded eight hits to the seven collected by the Sox off Ruffing, but two of the hits and three of the runs came after field-ing lapses by Jimmie Foxx, that would have retired the side scoreless." New York scored in the first inning when Joe DiMaggio hit a liner to Foxx. "With a double play in sight, Foxx dropped the ball and came up with only a force play at second." With runners on first and second and one down in the eighth, Jake Powell hit a grounder right at Foxx. "With another dou-ble play in prospect, the $150,000 beauty let the ball roll right between his legs and on into right field for two bases." This was the second time Wes faced the Yankees' new phenom, and "the feature of Ferrell's pitching was his rendering the sensational DiMaggio hitless and keeping Joe from hit-ting the ball out of the infield."[28]

Grove stopped Boston's seven-game skid with a 1–0 shutout of Philadelphia at Fenway on the Fourth of July. Singles by McNair, Kroner and Rick Ferrell in the fifth inning loaded the bases and Lefty pushed across the contest's only run by hitting into a double play. Wes won next afternoon with a 16–2 thrashing of Mack's boys; never challenged after his mates scored 11 times in the second. He allowed seven hits and one earned run. Cronin, Foxx and Rick Ferrell all made errors. Rick had four of the Red Sox's 19 hits.

At the All-Star break, the Red Sox sat percentage points behind Detroit, in third place with a record of 42–34. Grove's pitching mark was 11–3 and Ferrell's 11–8. The rest of the staff was a combined 20–23. The All-Star game was played at Boston's Braves Field and Rick Ferrell, who had been named to his fourth consecutive squad, went to the plate twice, fanning against Dizzy Dean and Carl Hubbell. "The Red Sox," observed the *Globe*, "all sat together in the stands, behind the American League

bench. Notable absentees were Wes Ferrell and Moe Berg. Wes allowed as how if he wasn't good enough to play in the game, he didn't want to see it, while the professor was deep in the Modern Language Library in Ogunquit, Me."[29]

* * *

The North Carolina pitcher opened the second half of the season with a 7–2 victory against the visiting White Sox on July 9. Wes

Wes (top, at left; right, at right) and Lefty Grove. The best pitchers in the American League were the best of friends (Gwenlo Ferrell Gore).

was on the ropes early, allowing eight hits and four walks in the first four innings. Cronin had a great day in the field, making a couple of nice plays to extract Wes from additional damage. When Wes glanced out to the bullpen in the fourth inning and saw Ostermueller warming up, he made a "motion indicating his willingness for Manager Cronin to take him out right there if he wanted to. Joe, however, ran to the box and with a few encouraging words quieted his problem child."[30] Wes got out of the inning and then allowed just two base hits over the last five frames. Bill Werber was Boston's big stick with four RBI, and the Ferrells smacked consecutive singles in both the sixth and eighth innings.

Cleveland arrived on July 12 and proceeded to sweep three games that dropped the Red Sox from third to fifth place. Grove lost the first game 5–2 as Boston's impotent offense managed but four hits off Johnny Allen. Two days later, when Wes dropped a 5–1 contest, all three of the Red Sox safeties came from Ferrell bats; a double by Wes and two singles by Rick.

The Red Sox managed to take four of five games for the cellar-dwelling St. Louis squad who came into town next; their only defeat being a 6–3 game that Grove dropped in a doubleheader opener on July 16. Five of the runs Grove allowed were earned; the other came via a Cronin error. "Grove can blame himself for the Sox losing what might have been an important run in the opener," noted the *Globe*. "With one out in the sixth, the Sox trailing only 4–3 and with Rick Ferrell on second, Mose neglected to run out his grounder that Carey kicked all around. As a result, Melillo's fly was the final out instead of the second, which would have scored Rick."[31]

The pitching Ferrell allowed eight hits the next afternoon in besting Ivy Andrews 2–1. Trailing 1–0 with one out in the bottom of the ninth, Wes doubled off the left-field wall with his third hit of the game. Three batters later Jimmy Foxx singled in two runs to win the contest. "Wes won his game. They didn't have to bolt down the clubhouse furniture after all," reported the *Globe*. "In the turmoil of the clubhouse it was obvious that here was a ball game of satisfaction in winning. Foxx was pummeled. Ferrell, the temperamental scuffer who would have been the victim of rank injustice had he lost, had a grin. Cronin beamed. The gang whooped it up. They don't give a hoot, huh?"

Lost in the celebration was the fans' inappropriate booing of Wes. Back in the fifth inning, with the pitcher on second and Werber on first, Foxx smashed a hit into center that looked sure to tie the game, but Werber — before Wes could cross the plate — was nailed at third for the final out of the inning. The fans blamed it on the pitcher. "From where I sat," wrote Jerry Nason in the *Globe*. "Ferrell was going full blast all the way home, and in their eagerness to cast verbal grapefruit at Wesley's sprint form they completely overlooked the fact that Sammy West pulled off one of the prettiest plays seen at the park this season. His fielding the ball and his throw to Clift were both beautifully executed."[32]

After the game Cronin boarded a plane for San Francisco where his mother had fallen ill with pneumonia. She rallied upon his arrival but passed away the next day.

After Lefty and Wes were both hammered in Cleveland on July 21 and 22 — Grove allowing eight hits and five earned runs in two innings, and Wes six hits and four earned runs, also in two innings — Hy Hurwitz of the *Globe* opined that pitching was killing the Red Sox. "From the very beginning of the season," he wrote on July 24, "the Sox have had only Lefty Grove to rely on. Outside of Mose there isn't a pitcher on the staff whom you can count on to consistently stop any enemy.... Mose worked his arm off trying to keep the Sox in the pennant race. He was never supported with a flock of runs, but he went right along winning his games." It is hard to follow Hurwitz's line of reasoning since Grove, after his incredible start, had gone just 2–5 with an ERA of 6.22 over his last eight starts. Ferrell, over the same period, had been 5–5 with a 4.64 ERA in ten starts and three of his assignments had come on two days rest. If anyone was literally working his arm off for the team, it was he, not Grove.

Detroit was the next stop, and the Red Sox swept a three-game series there to move past the Tigers into third place. Boston won the first game 7–4 when Rick Ferrell broke a tenth inning tie with a bases-loaded single. The next afternoon, July 25, the Red Sox pounded out 20 hits in an 18–3 victory. A 12-run outburst in the fifth iced the contest for Grove who won his twelfth game, his first in almost three weeks.

The Sox kept hitting the next day in a 10–3 victory, Ferrell's fourteenth. Wes allowed a run in the third inning and two more in the ninth when he had a 10–1 lead, but when the contest was close he was an entirely different pitcher. "For seven innings Ferrell was engaged in a tense twirling hookup," wrote the *Globe*. "With nine runs to work on, Ferrell eased up in the ninth. He permitted three safe cracks in succession for the final pair of Tiger tallies. When the home fans began clamoring for Ferrell's scalp, Wes put on the pressure to retire the next pair of Detroit batters on easy infield chances."[33]

Joe Cronin met the team in St. Louis after a ten day absence and flip-flopped Wes and Lefty in the rotation — a rotation such as it was — and started Ferrell against the Browns on July 30.

Tony Lupien, former Harvard University baseball captain and baseball coach at Dartmouth College, played first base for Boston in 1942 and 1943. "I don't believe he understood the rotation of pitchers," said Lupien of Cronin's managerial style. "When he began his managing career with Washington, he had some older heads like Clyde Milan to help him run the club while he played shortstop; then with Boston he had veteran pitchers like Grove and Walberg who pitched when they wanted to and how they wanted to.... He either didn't understand or just didn't use the method of choosing a rotation and staying with it no matter who we played.

"Cronin had good ideas offensively and was an excellent man to play for. He'd let you do a lot of things on your own. The handling of pitchers was the one flaw in his managerial makeup."[34]

Wes allowed seven hits and four walks; but three of the passes, all coming in the same inning, cost him a 4–3 defeat. St. Louis, trailing 3–2 in the eighth, filled the bases on walks and had two down when the next hitter, according to the *Globe*, "slapped a bouncer along the right field foul line. Jimmy Foxx stuck out his mitt, the ball hit the center of the glove and bounced out into short right field as Harlond Clift walked home with the tying run and Beau Bell just beat Foxx's throw home to score the winning run. It was scored as a hit...."[35] Cronin made the only Boston error of the game and Rick Ferrell took a foul tip off the thumb of his throwing hand and split a nail, putting him on the sidelines for several days.

Grove — working on five days rest — started in Chicago July 31, winning 7–3 before Ferrell — on two days rest — began the second game of a doubleheader the next day. Wes was given an 11–3 lead after six innings but couldn't hold it. The White Sox, who swept both games, took the contest 12–11 in extra frames and the press immediately pointed the finger at Wes, who was not involved in the decision, for being unable to hold the lead. It was the fifth time in 1936 that Cronin had started him on two days rest.

The Yankees took two games in Boston on August 4 and 5. Grove dropped the opener 4–2, allowing seven hits and six walks in eight innings. Wes' start was rained out the next day. He then dropped a 3–2 contest in ten innings to Earl Whitehill in Washington on August 7. The *Globe* reported that Wes "pitched a masterly game" and that the "Senators were as helpless as babies against the pitching of Ferrell."

"Of the six hits made against Ferrell two of them were negotiated in the first inning and were for extra bases, which in conjunction with a fly to the outfield were good for two runs; two were made in the sixth inning which were negative as to results, so far as runs were concerned, and two in the 10th, through the agency of which the winning run was developed.

"So the Senators got big returns on their meager hitting while the Red Sox' harvest in their fine stick work was very poor indeed because their hits were not made when they would do the most good."[36]

Wes beat the Athletics 6–4 at Fenway Park on August 12. The game was a Ferrell classic, for he had three of his club's seven hits, powdered two balls over the left-field wall, and drove home all six Boston runs. "Ferrell was the whole works," noted the *Globe*. "In the second he presented the visitors with a two-run lead by some chuckleheaded fielding, but in the third he squared accounts by hitting a homer over the left field fence with his brother Rick aboard.

"In the fourth, Wes faced [Hod] Lisenbee with the bases full as a result of Cooke's single, a base on balls to Rick Ferrell, and [Skeeter] Newsome's boot of Melillo's grounder. Wes immediately lined the ball over the amplifiers for another homer and four more Sox runs. In each case the count was one and one on Wes."[37]

Grove shut out Washington at Fenway Park on August 14. The final score was 9–0 and, "for once," said the *Globe*, "the Sox gave their doddering old ace some hitting support." The game was Grove's twenty-fourth start and it was the thirteenth time that the Red Sox had scored at least five runs for him. Ferrell had made 28 starts and been presented with five or more runs on sixteen occasions; thirteen if his own RBI were removed.

Ferrell began the first game of a doubleheader on August 16 by throwing nine straight balls. The Fenway crowd broke out with a cheer after his first strike and Wes responded by doffing his cap. The contest was knotted at three when Washington's Buddy Lewis reached on an infield safety to start the eighth. He was erased on a fielder's choice, but a Texas Leaguer and a walk loaded the bases. Cecil Travis then hit a bounder past both Wes and Eric McNair into center field. "Up to that point," noted the *Globe*, "Ferrell had been involved in a tight pitcher's contest, but the instant Travis pulled up at second in the eighth inning after rolling a grounder through the box that just escaped shortstop Booby McNair and went for a double when center fielder Doc Cramer was playing deep, Wes left the box and started for the dugout.

"He had given no previous hint to anybody that he felt like quitting and consequently left the Sox without a relief pitcher sufficiently warmed up."[38]

The Boston *Post* reported a similar story. "Peeved when the Senators were lucky enough to acquire two unlooked for hits in this round, and unable to conceal his disgust at what he may have regarded as tough breaks, Ferrell left the pitching box, walked to the dugout without giving any warning...."

Washington went on to win the game 7–6 and Wes pinch-hit in the nightcap. There were no follow-up stories— no comments for Cronin, Wes or any other player — regarding Wes leaving the box on his own volition.

WES STEALS SHOW AS SOX SPLIT

August 13, 1936 — Wes was a one-man show (reprinted courtesy of *The Boston Globe*).

The day after Grove beat the Athletics 6–2 in Philadelphia on August 18 for his fifteenth victory — a game which Rick Ferrell drove home two runs with a double, a triple and a home run — Boston dropped a double-header that saw them fall to .500 and into sixth place.

Ferrell opened for Cronin at Yankee Stadium on August 21 and the game was a tight one. The New York *Times* reported that Wes "had done some brilliant hurling," puzzling "the Yankees with slow curves." The *Post* also said the Wes had pitched a "fairly brilliant game of ball." Monte Pearson held Boston hitless until Rick Ferrell homered in the fifth to give his brother a 1–0 lead. New York tied it up in the bottom of the inning via a Tony Lazzeri double. Wes walked Gehrig with one gone in the sixth. Bill Dickey punched a single to right and Gehrig raced to third. George Selkirk lifted a foul pop for the second out and that brought up Jake Powell. "I turned to McNair and told him to play deep," said Wes. "Then I threw my best 'sailor ball' and Powell hit it right where I thought he would. McNair was not there. He came over, failed to scoop up the ball, tripped and almost fell."[39] Ferrell passed Lazzeri on four pitches and Pearson drove a grounder back through the box that eluded Wes. The ball rolled into center field and New York had a 4–1 lead.

"Wes exploded," wrote the *Globe*. "He fired his cap and glove into the air and marched off the field. He didn't even allow relief pitcher Jack Russell a chance to warm up. According to a majority of the players, Wes did the same thing in Boston last Sunday in a game against the Senators. Ferrell made straight for the clubhouse, took a shower and didn't wait for the game to finish before starting for the hotel. When manager Cronin came in after the game and saw that Ferrell had departed, he decided that Ferrell had been allowed enough and announced the fine and suspension."

Cronin said to all within earshot that he was fining Wes and suspending him for ten days. "I'm all through with him," declared Cronin, "he's going to be fined $1,000, suspended and sent home. I don't care if he goes to Boston, to his North Carolina home or to the Fiji Islands. I'm washed up with that guy."[40]

Wes was back at the hotel when a writer notified him of Cronin's decision. "What the hell does he mean fining me for my actions on the field?" he roared. "I didn't walk out of that game myself today. Yeah and I didn't walk out of the game in Boston last Sunday." Asked if he were going to Boston that night, Wes declared, "I want to see Cronin first and get an explanation. They can suspend me or trade me, but they're not going to get any dough from me."[41]

"I was upset," Wes tried explaining to the *Times* writer the next day. "I walked Lazzeri on four pitches and the bases were full. Then Pearson singled and three runs had scored. I looked over to the bench and Cronin was making signs with his hands.

"They were horizontal. There was a hush over the field like there is when a pitcher is being taken out.

"I thought I was out of the ball game and walked straight to the Yankee dugout, which is on the way to the clubhouse, and never looked around. If Joe came after me, I never saw it.

"I made my mistake in not looking around. All I keep saying to myself now is that if I'd only looked around, all of this trouble would have been averted. That's where I made my mistake.

"The first news I got of my fine and suspension was when a newspaper man called me up at my hotel room. I was never so stunned in my life. I was so mad I'd have hit anyone then. Yes, I may have said some things about Joe then.

"I don't know what I said, but that was all forgotten when I talked with Joe and Tom Yawkey later. We parted friends."[42]

Wes told the *Post*'s reporter, "I left the game because I looked around after Pearson hit and I saw Melillo beckoning to the bull pen and I figured I was done. I looked over to Cronin and he yelled, 'Come on Wes,' or something like that and I left the game." Melillo denied that he had any role in the incident, responding with "Ferrell is putting me on the spot when he says that, and I absolutely will not stand for it."

The *Post* reported that the incident surprised no one. Most of the players—all familiar with Wes' competitive makeup—anticipated that he would lose his mind the moment Pearson's ball rolled into the outfield. Rick Ferrell made no statements for or against his brother. Neither he nor Cronin had made any attempt to go to the mound to settle Wes down.

Cronin and Ferrell met the night of the incident with Yawkey, who did his best to smooth things over. He stated that he stood behind his manager and downplayed the incident, declaring that it would soon be forgotten. "The Ferrell case is one that has a lot of you folks aroused," said the Boston owner. "I think it is the best thing that could have happened for Wes. I think it will go a long way toward making Ferrell the pitcher he is capable of being. I gave him a good going over last night and I believe Wes will be a changed person."[43]

"It was just another one of those mistakes that have been holding us back all year," Wes said. "I don't think the manager should be exempt either. Something was bound to happen, and I guess they picked on me for the goat because I could take it." He then added that, "a lot of mistakes that haven't been corrected," were to blame for the collapse of the team, and "everybody has made mistakes on the team."

Cronin denied that Wes had walked out of the August 16 game with Washington. "It is not true that Ferrell walked out on me before. There's also nothing to this story about Ferrell thinking I waved him off the mound. He knows I don't wave my pitchers off. If that were true, there wouldn't be anything to it and the case would be closed. I'll see him in Boston on Monday."[44]

Wes went back to Boston to await the return of the team and Cronin took a couple of days off, leaving Coach Al Schacht—who confounded all subsequent queries by spinning Moe Berg yarns—in command. Grove dropped a 3–2 heartbreaker to the Yankees the next afternoon in 13 innings.

Back in Boston, Yawkey and Eddie Collins waffled on both the fine and the suspension. They decided to see how the rest of the season turned out. "We don't want to take that $1,000 from Ferrell," said Collins. "But the fine sticks until the end of the season, at least. At that time it will be up to Cronin to say whether his conduct warrants the return of the money. Ferrell is a fine pitcher, but no player is bigger than a ball club and I think Wesley has been brought face to face with that realization."[45]

On August 26, just five days after the blow-up in New York, Wes fired a five-hit shutout against the Tigers in Fenway Park. The 7–0 final was tight until Boston scored four times in the sixth inning. "Compared to his walk-out performance at Yankee Stadium last Friday, Wes was Little Lord Fauntleroy," opined the *Globe*. "He raised no outward fuss when Heinie Manush lost a fly in the sun that went for a single. He was emotionless when Eric McNair, the goat of the Yankee Stadium episode, made a wild throw on a fielded grounder.

"Not only was his deportment noteworthy, but his pitching brilliant. He was touched for five singles, one of them a very scratch hit, and didn't allow an enemy to advance farther than second base. At times a trifle off on control, Wes walked four Tigers, but in the clutch he had the stuff to get the opposition out."[46]

The only squawk Wes made came in the top of the sixth inning when, leading 1–0, he thought he had slipped an inning-ending third strike past Marv Owen. The umpire called it a ball and the pitcher started to say something before checking himself. Owen fanned on the subsequent pitch.

"Ferrell was given a heart-warming reception as he walked out to pitch," wrote the *Globe*. "It was obvious from the greeting the fans on hand at the game had forgiven Wes for his two walkouts of the last week. Each time Wes came to bat he was also applauded and there was no doubt Ferrell is one of the real favorites of the fans."

Boston and St. Louis split a doubleheader on August 29. St. Louis took the opener and the nightcap was deadlocked at 1–1 when Wes drove home the game winner as a pinch-hitter in the bottom of the ninth. "Cronin singled with one down," reported the *Globe*. "McNair had one ball and one strike on him when he decided to shift bats. The exchange was just what the doctor ordered for Eric lashed a double off the left field fence that put Cronin on third. Rick Ferrell was walked on purpose and Brother Wes came through with his high poke to Solters that scored Cronin after the catch."

Wes ran his record to 17–14 with a 3–2 victory over the Indians at Fenway on August 30; allowing a first-inning run on a double and a single, and then an unearned run in the third. "After that third-inning score, Ferrell was very effective," wrote the *Globe*. "He allowed only two hits over the last six innings and seemed to have more stuff and speed then he has shown in some time." Wes lashed out at Umpire Lou Kolls in the fifth inning, claiming that Cleveland catcher Billy Sullivan tipped his bat while he was hitting. Cronin was out of the dugout in a flash to support his pitcher-batter and he and Ferrell piled it on the arbiter.

Grove allowed just an unearned run in pushing his record to 16–10 with a 4–1 victory over the Tribe on September 1. The Red Sox did all their scoring in the fourth with a double by Foxx and singles by Cronin and Rick Ferrell being the crucial blows. Afterwards, the team, with a 65–65 record, was just five games out of second place.

Ferrell lost a 3–2 game to the White Sox under threatening skies on September 3; a 30-minute rain delay occurring after the eighth inning. Chicago scored twice in the first on three hits and a walk and again in the sixth on a walk, a double and an infield out. "The loss was Wes' first since being reinstated by the Sox," observed the *Globe*. "Incidentally Wes did quite a bit of kicking up yesterday but it was mostly at himself. He raised a cloud of dust around the mound with his toe after Zeke Bonura had belted his third straight hit in the eighth. He heaved his glove from the mound almost into the dugout after getting the Chisox out on a double play which he started in the same inning."[47] Wes halted Luke Appling's hitting streak at 27 games. Rick Ferrell opened the last of the ninth with a single and his brother sacrificed him to second but Manush and Werber flied out to end the game.

Thirty-one thousand Fenway fans watched Wes and Lefty beat the Yankees, 14–5 and 4–2, in a doubleheader on September 6. Ferrell was starting on two days rest and Grove on four. "Ferrell, who pitched the first game, also did some hitting, turning in two singles and a home run which were prime factors in his 18th victory of the season.

"Grove dazzled the Yankee sluggers with his speed and caused them to wrench their backs trying to connect with his slow ones as he gained his 17th victory."[48]

"Ferrell's pitching was a rare piece of audacity," noted the New York *Times*. "At times he merely lobbed the ball to the plate. Yet though the Yanks cuffed him for fourteen hits, they had a most exasperating time of it." In the eighth, the Yanks "fell victim to a most astonishing cycle of hits. Cronin singled, Eric McNair doubled, Rick Ferrell tripled and Brother Wes jogged jauntily around the bases after belting a homer over the left-field barrier."[49]

Boston's record after those Ferrell-Grove victories was 69–67, and despite being in sixth place they were just three games behind the second-place Tigers. The team, though, appeared to be in open revolt against its manager and finished the season going 5–13.

Boston recalled Babe Dahlgren from Syracuse on September 8, and Cronin installed him at the first base and moved Foxx to left field. Grove dropped a 3–2 decision in relief to the White Sox the next day. Jackie Hayes hit Grove's second pitch into center field to tie the game in the ninth and Mike Kreevich began the thirteenth with a double. Grove fielded the ensuing sacrifice but threw wildly to first base where Dahlgren, in stretching for the ball, collided with the runner. Both players had to be carried off the field and the winning run scored on the play. Bill Werber had started the game at second base but left in the third inning due to what was initially reported as a hand injury. The next day, however, the *Globe* said that Werber had walked off the field after Cronin questioned his hustle in running out a grounder. With John Kroner absent from the team and McNair nursing a sore leg, Cronin had to adjust his infield mid-game, moving himself from third to short and Foxx from left to the hot corner. Tom Yawkey was at his South Carolina plantation, reportedly disgusted with the whole team.

Wes won his nineteenth game, 6–2 in St. Louis on September 11, having a perfect day as a batter with two hits and three walks in five trips to the dish. "Ferrell was rather loose on control as he walked five of the Brownies," opined the *Globe*, "but he was so effective with men on the paths that not a free ticket developed into a run. Other than the fifth, when the Grand and Dodier boys bunched three of their six hits for their runs, the Browns never got a man past second base."[50]

The Red Sox took a 7–4 decision two days later in Detroit. Billy Rogell tried scoring in the second inning on a double but the relay throw to Rick Ferrell had him at the plate by a good ten feet. "Rogell continued on in and jumped into Rick as the latter made the put out.

"Ferrell turned and threw the ball at Rogell and the two players went into a clinch. However, the players of both clubs broke them up and umpire Moriarty chased both boys out of the game."[51] Both were suspended for three games.

Wes and Lefty made their last pitching appearances of the year on September 19 and 20 in Philadelphia. Grove dropped his game 5–4 to finish the season at 17–12 while Wes won his game 5–1 to end at 20–15. Only three of the runs Grove allowed were earned and he had taken a 4–1 lead into the sixth before errors from Cronin and Foxx on successive plays contributed to his downfall.

"With Wes Ferrell taking due care to keep the hits scattered," noted the Boston *Post*, "there was never much doubt as to who was going to cop the marbles.

"The closest the Athletics came to getting in the running was in the fifth, when following a bonafide single to left by Frankie Hayes, Ross, Moses and Dean were all safe on dinky infield singles. Dean's scoring the Mackmen with the lone Mack run of the day.

"With the bases filled, one out and the husky hitters on deck, Ferrell proceeded to end the gesture by retiring Cherokee Bob Johnson on a puny foul behind the plate and Pinky Higgins on a long fly that Rog Cramer gathered in.

"Then in the next stanza, following Babe Dahlgren's sandwiching of a single between two outs, Wes took personal charge of recovering the run. He did so by plowing a triple over Lou Finney's head in deep centre."[52]

Rick Ferrell did not appear in any of Boston's last four games, his last appearance coming on September 22 in Washington. On September 29 it was reported that Cronin would not be rescinding Wes' fine. "What definitely convinced Cronin not to return the fine to Ferrell was Wes' departure from the Red Sox hotel in Washington last week without notifying the Boston manager," reported the Globe, "Cronin wished to pitch Wes in one of the last two games in Washington but had to scratch Ferrell when he learned that Wes had left without a word of warning."[53] The Sporting News contradicted this report. "No statement has of yet been given out by the Red Sox administration as to that $1,000 fine having been lopped from the pitcher's pay, but it is generally believed that the cut was restored to him.... Ferrell swung into line, mended his ways, and was allowed to go home a week before the schedule closed. It is only reasonable to assume," wrote Boston correspondent and one-time BBWAA President Paul Shannon, "that he patched up his differences with the front office and left the club eminently satisfied."[54]

* * *

An incident against Washington on September 25 summed up the Red Sox's season nicely. Jim Henry was Cronin's choice as starting pitcher and he dropped a 9–3 decision. On an attempted double steal in the third inning, Henry — standing on the mound with both the ball and the resin bag in his hand — threw the ball to the ground and the resin bag in the general direction of two of his infielders.

* * *

Johnny Vander Meer had retired 26 batters without allowing a hit as he looked in at his manager-catcher Johnny Gooch — a veteran of 11 big league seasons—for the sign. He had punched out thirteen batters in the game to run his total for the season to 272. It was September 1, the tail end of a year in which Vander Meer would be named The Sporting News Minor League Player of the Year. Vander Meer's club, the Durham Bulls, had a 7–0 lead so the outcome was not in question. The lefty already had notched single-game strikeout totals of 18, 19 and 20 that season, and he had overpowered the visiting Richmond Colts all afternoon with his fastball. With one batter to go, Vander Meer pumped a fastball to the plate. George Ferrell swung, made contact, and sent a rocket back up the middle that hit

Vander Meer on the foot and bounded into left field. "The Dutch Master" would have to wait a little longer for his no-hit fame.

1936 was another typical season for George Ferrell in the Piedmont League. He started the season as Richmond's manager but resigned in May after the team had gotten off to a slow start. "Ferrell is too fine a boy and too valuable as a hitter to be saddled with the manifold worries of the job," wrote the Richmond-Times *Dispatch*. "It's something else simply playing the outfield and then having to play and manage, too. Ty Cobb and Tris Speaker found this out." Ferrell put up his standard numbers, 21 home runs, 114 RBI and a .335 batting average and was named the left fielder on the league's All-Star team.

* * *

Bev Ferrell had a bang-up season in the Georgia-Florida League, leading the circuit with a .338 mark, and was drafted by the Washington Senators at the end of the season for $2,500.

The annual draft took place in New York City on September 29 and Washington owner Clark Griffith snatched Ferrell right from under the nose of the St. Louis Cardinals.

"Griff and Bucky Harris went into the meeting practically empty-minded.

"Midway in the meeting which was supervised by Kenesaw Mountain Landis, Griff got up from his seat and went over to where sat Branch Rickey, guiding genius of the Cardinals' vast chain system.

"'Hello, Branch, old pal,' said Griff, who hates Mr. Rickey to pieces.

"'Hello, Griff.'

"'Who do you like, Rick,' Griff asked negligently.

"'Rickey couldn't hold his information. 'We're set to claim that young Beverly Ferrell. We've looked him over pretty well and he's going to be one sweet ballplayer, if you ask me.'

"'Ferrell? Hmmm. Never heard of him.' Griff said, and went back to his seat.

"The old gentleman who runs the Washington club hadn't been in his chair a minute before Judge Landis called for him to stand and choose one of the unclaimed minor leaguers.

"'I claim Beverly Ferrell,' said Griff.

"Rickey leaped up with a protest, but Landis, after listening to both sides, upheld Griffith."[55]

◆ 12 ◆

1937 — On to Washington

The infield was again Joe Cronin's biggest on-field worry in the Red Sox's spring camp in Sarasota. Mike Higgins had been acquired from Philadelphia to play third base, so Cronin planned to start himself at second and Eric McNair at shortstop, but after teenager Bobby Doerr impressed everyone with his play, Jimmy Foxx opined that there was no room in the infield for Cronin. "I'm sure everybody is going to like him," said Eddie Collins of Doerr. "He's an excellent fielder, fast and sure of himself. He hasn't been breaking any batting records in the exhibition games but he's hitting as well as anybody on the club. The boy has spirit and seems destined to become a fixture for years."

It was the off-field misfortunes, however, that set the early tone of the season and all eyes were on Booby McNair, the man Connie Mack once called the greatest player, "pound for pound," he ever managed. McNair's wife had died in January, just a week after giving birth to a baby son. "McNair's case is a sad one," said Collins on April 5. "Time is the only healer. He's in good physical shape but he is still broken up. There isn't a thing you can do about it but we're all hoping it wears off soon." With McNair hurting and Doerr excelling, Cronin moved back to shortstop. "When Joe saw how depressed Booby McNair was over the loss of his wife," said Collins, "he decided to return to shortstop himself and he sure has played as well as he ever did in Washington. He lends a lot of encouragement to everybody with his presence on the diamond and the club seems to have more life with him in action. There isn't anything wrong with Joe's wrist and his mental condition is vastly better than last Spring when he thought the club was going to win the pennant and then collapsed."[1]

Two days later, on April 7, Mildred Cronin delivered twins in Sarasota and, tragically, both babies died. It was touch and go before Mrs. Cronin was declared out of danger. The manager, after seeing to his wife, tried addressing the team but was unable to do so, breaking down in the

1937 — Wes (left) and Rick begin their fourth season with the Red Sox (Gwenlo Ferrell Grove).

process. He placed the club under the direction of Herb Pennock. Incredibly, on April 8, Oscar Melillo received word from Chicago that his wife, who had delivered a baby a week earlier, had taken a turn for the worse. He headed home, leaving the club short of infielders, for McNair had been given permission to visit his infant son in Mississippi, promising to catch up with the club in time to play in an exhibition game that Grove was scheduled to start in Atlanta on April 11.

Atlanta's Dutch Leonard beat Grove 8–3 and Lefty's pride took a huge wallop when he gave up four first-inning runs on four hits, a walk and an error by Higgins. "Mr. Grove staged one of his typical temperamental outbursts that are fast ceasing to be even slightly funny," commented the *Globe*. "He divided his time between tossing up his sandlot-ish balloon ball and his medium fast ball through the slot for the Crackers to take batting practice. Even the numerous local rooters, who love their heroes to win, didn't appreciate Mr. Grove's humor and sat in stunned silence throughout the Grove-ian burlesque."[2]

Herb Pennock was incensed, allowing Grove to walk to the plate in the sixth inning before calling him back for a pinch-hitter. Words were exchanged and Grove grabbed his gear and stalked back to the hotel. "While little has been said about the matter," continued the *Globe*, "it was such ructions by Mr. Grove on occasions last year that helped considerably to undermine the morale of the Yawkey forces. And the same club has been hampered enough by events beyond its control already this season not to care for any handicaps manufactured under their own steam."

Wes beat the Cincinnati Reds in Winston-Salem the next afternoon. After the game he hustled Lefty off to the Ferrell farm — 21 miles away — to get some distance between his pal and Pennock.

Two days later Mel Almada was badly beaned and hospitalized. Foxx also went into a hospital when the Red Sox arrived in Philadelphia to open the season. Pneumonia was the official reason, although Cronin "believes the night dampness of the local track caused Jimmie Foxx' relapse, about which the Boy Manager is more than a little disturbed."[3] Grove was lost in a deep and dark morass, going on the sick list with a stiff back and a bad cold being the bandied-about diagnoses. McNair was suffering from a sore throwing elbow which prevented him from playing.

Wes opened the season with an 11–5 win against the Athletics on April 20. "Of course, I'm taking it, but I was lousy," he said after the game. "I couldn't put the ball where I wanted it for a thousand bucks. It takes me four or five games before I get warmed up." Rick Ferrell drove in the first run of the game and Boston had a 10–1 lead after five innings. Wes drove

Opposite, top: The 1937 Red Sox catching corps in Sarasota, Florida. From left are Moe Berg, Johnny Peacock, Rick Ferrell and Gene Desautels. *Bottom:* The 1937 Red Sox pitching corps in Sarasota, Florida. From left are Fritz Ostermueller, Rube Walberg, Wes Ferrell and Lefty Grove (both courtesy of Gwenlo Ferrell Gore).

home a fifth-inning run with a double and said after the game that he was prouder of his hitting than his pitching.

Cold and wet weather cancelled the scheduled home opener with the Yankees on April 23, and Cronin announced that if it were too cold for Grove to start the next day he would instead select between Marcum, Walberg or Ferrell. Lefty did amble to the mound, allowing eleven baserunners before retiring after six innings with the game tied at three. Grove did not pitch again for two weeks, and by the time he made his third start of the season, Ferrell had already made six. While bad weather played havoc with the early schedule — and Cronin never used Wes on short rest — the distribution of the starting assignments doled out by Cronin during the first month of the season seems odd. Ferrell started seven games, Marcum six, Walberg and Grove three apiece and Jack Wilson one.

Wes started the third game of the season on April 25. Thirty-five thousand patrons filled Fenway Park and in the middle of the first inning 1,000 wandering bleacher fans, unable to find seats, opened a gate and spilled out onto the field. It took 15 minutes to restore order and Wes was forced to try and keep loose by slow-tossing with his brother. The final was a 6–3 New York win. Ferrell allowed ten hits and half a dozen walks before leaving in the middle of the seventh inning. The crowd — thinking the pitcher was taking another powder — booed him as he walked from the hill. Cronin defended his pitcher after the game, explaining to the press that he had informed Wes ahead of time that he would be relieved after pitching to just one more batter.

Rick Ferrell had two hits in the game and three more the next day in a 12–5 win over Washington. "There's no doubt now that Dandy Rick Ferrell is in the midst of one of his inimitable Spring batting streaks," noted the *Globe*. "His average at the instant is a cool .600, with nine blows in 15 trips. His surge last Spring was stopped only when Richard twisted his ankle in pulling up at second base on a double. Let us hope no such odd accidents overtake the captain of the House of Ferrell right now."

Wes started the fifth game of the season with Philadelphia on April 30, a 15–5 Boston victory. Jimmy Foxx made his first appearance of the year and both he and Wes clouted home runs. The pitching Ferrell — allowing nine hits and three walks — had a 6–0 lead before Philadelphia scored its first run, a 12–1 edge when the Mackmen scored two in the fifth inning, and a 15–3 lead before giving up the final two tallies in the ninth. Each of the Ferrells had two hits and scored two runs.

Wes, following a 22-hour train ride from Boston, and with Grove still complaining of a sore back, started the eighth game of the season in St. Louis on May 4. The Red Sox were 11–6 victors but he wasn't around at the end of the game. "Wes Ferrell," wrote the *Globe*, "who beat the Browns five times last season, didn't even have his 'nothing' ball this afternoon, and the Hornsby clan rapped him all over the lot before he was removed in the fourth. Before retiring, Wes made a couple of hits, drove in two runs and scored one himself."

Though Rick had three hits in the game, Cronin overlooked his catcher and pointed to the work of four batters— Higgins, Doerr, Cramer and himself— when asked to comment on the team's fast offensive start. When the inquiring writer reminded Joe that the catching Ferrell was the club's leading hitter, he replied, "Well, Rick is only hitting the way he did for us last spring and if the rest of us had been bashing it last spring on the same level with Ferrell, then we would have been a different club. Rick is always a great spring hitter and I've become accustomed to counting on him and he hasn't disappointed me."[4]

Rick blasted a home run into the left-field pavilion at Comiskey Park on May 8 when Wes started for the fifth time in the just the team's eleventh game. The pitching Ferrell singled in the third inning and rode home on Mel Almada's home run, so the catching Ferrell's clout made the score 3–0. "The temperamental Boston twirler," wrote the *Globe*, "had Kibitzed along with customary success for four innings. It looked like he was all set to carry on as he had retired two men and there was only one on in the fifth." Quickly things fell apart. Hank Steinbacher hit a two-run homer. An infield hit and a clean single came in front of a slow outside curve that Zeke Bonura shoved 400 feet into the right-field stands. All of a sudden Boston was behind 5–3 and the Chisox chased Wes from the game with three seventh-inning singles, two of them flares. The final score was 6–5 with Ferrell taking the loss.

The tall Carolinian also dropped his next start — his sixth in Boston's fifteenth game — in Detroit on May 13 by a 4–0 score. "Despite his best pitching performance of the year," wrote the *Globe*, "Wes Ferrell lost his third straight. He gave up but five hits and the only untainted Tiger run was produced by Charley Gehringer who lofted a lazy Ferrell delivery into the upper deck of the right-field bleachers in the eighth inning."[5] Wes, the batter, went hitless for the first time that year. "If only I could pitch the way I've been hitting, I'll win a lot of ball games," he exclaimed. "Every time I've been pitched I've knocked old Harry out of the ball, but I haven't pitched a plugged nickel's worth."

Boston's record fell to .500 (9–9) when Wes dropped a 4–3 decision at Griffith Stadium on May 17. He had taken a 3–2 lead into the bottom of the eighth inning. "Aided by five double plays, one shy of the big league record, Ferrell had gone along in fine style," reported the *Globe*, "and seemed on his way to breaking his three-game losing streak...."

"Jesse Hill opened the ill-fated eighth with a slow roller down the third-base line. Pinky Higgins came in fast and tried to catch Hill with a lightning peg, but the ball shot by Jimmy Foxx as Hill went down to second. Buddy Lewis laid down a bunt toward third, which he beat out and Hill reached third.

"The Sox infield came in and Joe Kuhel rapped a high bounder through the box that sent Hill home with the tying run and moved Lewis to third. The Kuhel rap would have been an easy one to handle if the infielders hadn't been forced to play short. Johnny Stone then sent a harsh grounder to Eric McNair. Eric feinted Lewis back to third, but the moment he let the ball go to first Buddy sprinted home and slid under Jimmy Foxx' perfect throw for the winning run."[6] Rick Ferrell left the game with a fractured finger on his throwing hand. It was his last appearance in a Boston uniform.

Trade rumors that previous winter which had Wes headed to Detroit now heated up again. Mickey Cochrane had seen enough of Wes over the years to know what he still had left. "They will recall such cases of that of Wes Ferrell who pitched so effectively for the Red Sox after he was, to all intents and purposes, washed up," wrote the Detroit manager in his book, *Baseball, The Fan's Game.* "From a press-box seat Ferrell had a 'nothing ball.' And at the plate hitting it, it was just about that. What he had was superb control, an endless file cabinet in his mind of the likes and dislikes of every batter who faced him, and not to be underestimated, confidence that he could still win."[7]

"Cochrane," noted the *Globe* on May 21, "is the only other American League manager who has come right out and said he is willing to take a chance on Wes Ferrell and his highly publicized temperament." It all became a moot point a few days later when Cochrane was beaned and fighting for his life after undergoing emergency surgery. He might have changed his mind anyway, after watching his club pound Wes for 11 hits in four innings on May 22. Hank Greenberg hit a home run that cleared the wall above the bleacher seats in left-center field.

Though the winning pitcher, Wes allowed the Browns twelve hits and eight earned runs on May 26. Presented with an 8–1 lead, he gave up four

Opposite: The 1937 (or possibly 1936) Red Sox at spring training in Sarasota. Moe Berg and Jimmy Foxx are in the top row, second and third from left. Wes Ferrell is in the second row from the top, first player at left. Rick Ferrell is in the third row from the top, third from right. Lefty Grove is in the second row from bottom, fourth from left, sitting next to Tom Yawkey (light suit). Joe Cronin and Herb Pennock are two and three seats to the right of Yawkey. The front row is made up of the Boston media (Wes Ferrell, Jr.).

runs in the fifth, one in the sixth and finally two in the seventh before Cronin yanked him. As a hitter he had two hits and two RBI. "The boys down stairs later told us that Wes Ferrell really had a lot of good stuff, but simply put it over the middle of the pan. Our vote is 100 percent for the charitable angle on that," commented the *Globe*.

There was plenty of discussion regarding what was wrong with Ferrell. "It's his control," offered Cronin. "Wes has had his curve ball breaking and has had more speed than in the past two years. But he hasn't been able to put the ball where he wants to. Control was once Wes' chief stock in trade, and he hasn't had much control this season."

The *Globe* also offered an opinion. "Even Ferrell cannot deny that he isn't as fast as he was when he first came up with Cleveland. The opposition apparently has caught on to all of Wesley's tricks. If you watch the batters when Ferrell is pitching, you will notice them stepping in on Ferrell's delivery. They no longer try to take toe-holds on his slow ball but are punching at it for short hits.

"The batters aren't biting for outside curve balls but make Wes come in there with a pitch over the plate. They have been working Ferrell down to a 3 and 2 count on innumerable occasions and when he tries to pour the big one through they just powder it out of the park. Beau Bell did it twice yesterday and so did Harlond Clift."[8]

Reports on June 1 had the Ferrells heading for Washington in a trade. The front-office relationship between Washington and Boston was a complex one. Cronin, who was Clark Griffith's adoptive son-in-law, had essentially swapped managerial jobs with Bucky Harris after the 1934 season, and Harris still harbored resentment toward Eddie Collins over that move. Harris was well-liked, and a group of Boston players— headed by Grove and the Ferrells— approached Yawkey late in 1934 when they heard he might be replaced. When it was rumored in 1938 that Collins and Cronin were having problems, and Cronin would be returning to Washington to run the team, Yawkey quickly denied any discord between his lieutenants.

"Wesley Ferrell started like a champion, bowling out Jimmie Dykes' crew for the first two frames," wrote the *Globe* of Wes' June 3 game. "But in the fourth the Carolinian lost all his cunning. He was hit for a homer, a single and double before finally taking to the showers with the score tied 4–4."

The next stop was St. Louis. Rick Ferrell, who had been at home in North Carolina while his hand was mending, phoned Eddie Collins to say he would be rejoining the team. Speculation was growing that a Wes Ferrell to Washington for Bobo Newsom trade was imminent. In his final Red Sox mound work, Wes tossed a complete game against the Browns on

Manager Bucky Harris (center) welcomes Rick (left) and Wes to the Washington Senators in June 1937 (Gwenlo Ferrell Gore).

June 7, allowing 17 base runners and nine earned runs. The score was 9–6. As a hitter, Wes had a walk and two of the six Boston hits; his bat involved in three of the team's four run-producing innings. The next afternoon against Cleveland, the Red Sox scored eight runs in the last inning in a 10–8 win. Wes drove in the last run as a pinch-hitter.

The trade that sent the Ferrells and Mel Almada to Washington for Bobo Newsom and Ben Chapman was announced late on June 9. "I think Rick Ferrell is just what we need to make Washington a steady winner," said Clark Griffith. "He is a great catcher and a fine fellow. We haven't had a good catcher in a long time and were sorely in need of one. When Wesley Ferrell is in shape there are few better pitchers. He has had tough going this year but we expect him to come through for us."

Cronin had little to say in the way of parting words, nothing, in fact, about Wes. "Funny the difference between those two brothers," said the Boston skipper. "I sure hated to lose Rick — good ball player, hard worker, easy to get along with."

Rick was the key player in the trade. "There has never been any doubt of his catching skill nor his hitting talents," wrote Shirley Povich in the Washington *Post* the day after the trade. "The Nats are gambling that his broken hand will heal." Whether it was his hand or his finger, the injury had not mended properly and a persistent pain affected Rick's batting grip for the remainder of the season. A foul tip that split open his right thumb on July 30 cost him two more weeks.

Harris felt that Wes was trying too hard to work his fastball back into his repertoire. "That is an item Harris has promised to take up with Ferrell," continued Povich. "The Nats' manager has said he will ask the temperamental right-hander to revert to his slow curves over which he used to have superb control.

"We'll let 'em hit Ferrell's slow stuff,' he said. 'In that big Washington park, they can't knock it anywhere, anyway. A fellow with his control can get away with slow-ball pitching."[9]

Harris was happy to have Wes back. When the pitcher and Cronin were at odds the previous season, the Washington manager was quick to defend him, simply stating "I always got along with Wesley." *The Sporting News* reported at the time that "Harris would like to have the veteran right-hander under his command again and would eagerly join negotiations with the Boston owners."[10]

Wes obviously listened to Harris, for he tossed a four-hitter in Chicago on June 12, winning 6–2. "Out of the skilled fingers of Wesley Ferrell spun a magnificent assortment of slow-winding curves," wrote Povich. "Wes served up those deceitful slow balls that literally slithered off the Chicago bats, popping harmlessly into the air or resulting in anemic grounders into the infield." Chicago made two hits in the third inning, one in the sixth and one in the seventh. When Washington broke the game open with four tallies in the eighth, Wes drove in the third run with a single to right. He had doubled earlier in the game. "And Brother Rick behind the bat, was no drawback to the Nats either, for because it was in the seventh inning, with the score tied tightly at 2–2, and the Chicagos having a runner on base with none out, that Rick erased the tension for the Washingtons by making a suburb throw to second base to catch the fleet Tony Piet stealing."[11]

Washington dropped a 9–8 decision in 15 innings to the Tigers on June 15, but not before overcoming an 8–1 deficit with seven runs in the ninth inning. Rick drove home two of those runs with a single. Wes followed as a pinch-hitter and "rocketed a line drive two-bagger to right" that cut the Tigers' lead to 8–6.

The next afternoon Rick went three for five and drove in the winning run in the twelfth inning as Wes beat the Tigers 2–1. "For Ferrell," wrote Povich of the pitching brother, "it was a magnificent triumph, added proof of salubrious effects of the recent trade."

Wes gave up three quick runs in his 5–3 win over the Browns on June 20. "He stuck in there, undaunted, through three harrowing innings, during which the Nats threatened to boot the ball game away, and then given a lead in the third he made it stand up nicely," wrote Povich. "He gave up only two hits to the Browns in those last six innings— one of 'em an infield affair — and the St. Louis run that Cecil Travis kicked over the plate in the second inning was the last run the Browns were able to score."[12]

Ferrell lost 7–6 to the White Sox on June 25. He allowed 11 hits and two passes. He did not record a strikeout. "The Nats," noted the *Post*, "scored in all of the first four innings, but they never could catch up with the White Sox, who were wrestling some cheap runs out of Ferrell, which caused the big right-hander to pitch his glove in disgust at the end of the fourth inning...."

"It was a cruel defeat for Wes Ferrell....

"A pair of grievous errors cost Ferrell three runs, including the runs in the eighth that gave the Sox their winning margin." Rick Ferrell had three hits in the game, but poor baserunning cost Washington a chance to tie the contest in the ninth. Buddy Myer led off with a single and Rick moved him up with a sacrifice. Wes walked. Mel Almada followed with a base hit up the middle but Myer, misinterpreting the coach's instructions, stopped at third base. "Harris was waving for Wes Ferrell to stop at second base," said Myer after the game. "I thought he was motioning to me to stop at third. We got mixed up, that's all. I'll take the rap."

The Red Sox were due in town next and Clark Griffith, anticipating a big gate, wired ahead to Cronin to suggest a pairing of Ferrell and Newsom. Cronin agreed and the press played it up big.

Babbling Buck Newsom was a natural when it came to the media, in the same mold as Dizzy Dean or Lefty Gomez. Wes, though prodded, had little to say. Rick quickly spoke his mind. "We're ready for him," declared the catcher. "He's got six left-handed batters to face and three pretty good right-handers."

The series opened with intense bench jockeying emitting from both dugouts. The Boston players poured it on Wes.

"Have you been breaking up any lockers lately, Wes?"

"How are the stars for tomorrow, Wes?"

Washington gave it right back to Newsom, Chapman and Cronin. Wes finally gave in to the barrage of questions from the writers. "I don't have to build up my courage in the newspapers," he said. "I know what I've got. I beat him the only time we met last year, but I didn't think beating him was even worth talking about." When it was brought to his attention that he had beaten Newsom in 1935 with his own two home runs, he replied: "That's right, too, but I don't go around bragging about hitting homers off a guy who can't win 12 games in a season." Comments then shifted to a congratulatory mode regarding the Ferrells being named to the All-Star team by Joe McCarthy. "I'll admit it did come somewhat as a surprise," said Wes, "but that isn't saying I'm not good enough to be on the team. And I'll show Newsom tomorrow if he wants to say anything about it."

Twelve thousand cash customers and 8,000 Boy Scouts watched throughout a constant drizzle as Wes took the game by a 6–4 score, driving across the deciding runs himself in the eighth inning. Washington scored twice in the second but the Red Sox got those back when Jimmy Foxx crushed a three-run, 450-foot homer to center field in the fourth. A double by Newsom in the fifth led to another run, and the Boston pitcher — who banged the ball off the left-field fence — waited calmly on second while Wes walked out to shake his hand. Before the game Bobo convinced Wes to make a wager whereas the pitcher who allowed the first hit to the other would halt the game in order to congratulate him.

"The fans are all yelling and cheering, and I'm standing out on the mound, knowing what I've got to do," Wes told Donald Honig years later. "I didn't know whether to cuss or laugh. Finally I turn around and here I go, walking toward second base. The umpires thought I was going to fight, and they start coming over. I walked up to Bobo, and he's grinning a mile across his face, and I start laughing too, couldn't help myself."[13]

Wes scored a run in the seventh inning to make the score 4–3. Then Cecil Travis tripled with one down in the Washington eighth. Newsom walked Buddy Myer and hit Rick Ferrell with a pitch. Bobo, with the count one and one, tried jamming Wes with an inside fast ball. Ferrell fisted it into right center and two runs scored to put Washington up 5–4. Boston made one last run in the ninth when Chapman and Cronin singled with two down. A double steal followed which essentially took the bat out of Foxx's hand — Wes passed him intentionally — and the game ended on a ground out. The Boy Scouts swarmed onto the field and mobbed Wes as he walked from the hill.

Wes got trounced by the Yankees on the Fourth of July. Joe DiMaggio boomed a first-inning home run to left and Lou Gehrig followed by plastering the ball off the right-field fence. The final straw was a hit by Lefty

Gomez in the third. "Ferrell," noted the *Post*, "figured correctly that if Gomez could make a hit off him he had very little on the ball, indeed, and walked out of the box even before Manager Bucky Harris could wave him out." Wes was also hammered in his next two starts, again by the Yankees on July 10 and then the Indians on July 16. He allowed 18 earned runs in just seven innings over those three games, the only starts he did not complete for Washington in 1937.

Thornton Lee beat Wes 4–2 on July 20. The loss was the tenth straight for the Nats and only two of the four runs Wes allowed were earned. "For Wesley Cheek Ferrell," wrote Povich, "it was a galling experience. The handsome hurler was deprived of a richly deserved victory in regulation innings because of an ugly error by outfielder Johnny Stone that directly produced two vital Chicago runs."[14]

Washington took a doubleheader in St. Louis on July 24 and pinch-hitter Wes Ferrell drove home the winning runs in both contests. "When the Nats needed a run in that first game with the score tied at 5–5, Bucky Harris sent Wes Ferrell to the plate as a pinch hitter in the eighth inning and Ferrell produced that run with a full-brassie fly to left field that scored Myer from third," wrote the *Post*. "And when the Nats needed a run in that second game with the score tied, again at 5–5 in the seventh inning, Bucky Harris again sent Wes Ferrell to the plate as a pinch-hitter and Ferrell produced that run, too, with a hot single into centerfield."[15]

Wes pitched the next afternoon, winning 16–10. He allowed the Browns 14 hits and nine earned runs, and had a 16–6 lead before allowing two runs in the seventh and ninth innings. He had two hits himself.

Thornton Lee beat Wes again on July 29, this time 2–0. "Down to defeat with them, the puerile Nats dragged Wesley Cheek Ferrell who was giving young Lee a valiant battle out there on the pitching mound," wrote Povich. "Ferrell held the Sox to eight hits and shut 'em out for eight of the nine innings, but the two runs they scored in the fifth were two more runs than the Nats could get for Ferrell."[16]

Wes' next contest was a 3–2 victory in 12 innings over the Browns and Elon "Chief" Hogsett on August 3. "It was a cock-eyed sort of a pitching duel, the affair in which Ferrell and Hogsett found themselves engaged," wrote Povich. "The Nats made 17 hits off of the old left-hander, while Ferrell was giving up but seven to the Browns, yet the Nats could wangle only a single run out of Hogsett until the twelfth."[17] Wes scored the only Washington run made in regulation following his fifth-inning double. He was in trouble only in the eighth and twelfth innings; the Browns scoring one in the last frame and the Nats twice.

Next up for Ferrell were the Tigers who beat him 3–2 in the first game of a twin-bill on August 7. "Ferrell, mixing some new-found speed with his usual assortment of mush balls, was doing nicely in the first game. He didn't give the Tigers the faintest semblance of a hit until the fourth, when Hank Greenberg banged a futile single to left with one out, and in the fifth, when they threatened to do something about it — Rogell and Lawson rapped consecutive hits— our boy Wesley upped and struck out Gerald Walker."[18] Wes had driven in a run in the second inning and was protecting a 2–0 lead late when Rudy York hit a three-run homer in the seventh to snatch the game away.

Ferrell beat Philadelphia 5–4 on August 11. His mates scored four times in the first inning and Wes was working with a 5–1 lead when the Athletics scored three times in the seventh. "The A's first run was almost a gratuitous affair, eventuating from a ludicrous double by pitcher Thomas after Peters had drawn a walk. Al Simmons was poised for the catch of Thomas' ball when his feet flew out from under him in the wet grass....

"Those three runs that narrowed the Nats' lead to 5–4 were not exactly honest affairs. Brucker drew a walk and was safe at third only because Buddy Lewis dropped Almada's perfect throw. Peters dashed to second on the play and thus both runners were in a position to score on Newsome's drooping double that dropped at Simmons' feet in short left. Wally Moses prolonged the rally with a single to center that scored Newsome but at that point Ferrell called a dead halt, retiring Finney on a short fly. Brother Rick helped him over the hump when he threw Moses out on an attempt to steal. After that, Ferrell didn't take any chances. In fact, the A's never saw first base in those last two innings."[19]

Next up were the Red Sox and Lefty Grove on August 15.

Many years after his retirement, Wes spoke about his relationship with Grove to historian Donald Honig. "He was my idol," said Ferrell. "Fastest pitcher I ever saw. The greatest. Why, I wasn't good enough to carry his glove across the field. Dizzy Dean was great, and so was Koufax. And Bob Feller was fast, of course.... But Grove was faster.... He was just about the finest friend I ever had."[20] So, for Wes, besting Grove in this contest was significant.

Twenty-two thousand thousand fans watched the Nats sweep a pair that left the Red Sox with a 58–45 record, 12 games behind the first-place Yankees. Hy Hurwitz of the Boston *Globe* described the losses as extracting the last spark out of Boston's pennant chances. "Wes Ferrell was in the pulpit as the exercises opened at 1:30. No more appropriate gent could have been selected to officiate. He made it doubly effective as he beat Lefty Grove for the first time in his nine-year American League career."

Washington scored once in the second and twice in the third; Wes singling and riding home on Mel Almada's home run. Ferrell allowed just one hit in the first three frames, but four hits— singles by Cronin and Foxx, a double by Higgins, and a flare-single by Eric McNair— produced three runs and a tie game. "It was a shaky session for Ferrell and there were anxious looks toward the bull pen where a couple of pitchers were warming up, but Ferrell reformed suddenly. He gave the Red Sox only four hits during the last five innings and only one runner advanced as far as third." Grove retired after seven innings, allowing seven runs on nine hits and three walks. The score was 8–3.

Four days later Wes dropped a heartbreaker to Red Ruffing and the Yankees. The Nats had given Ferrell a slim 2–0 cushion but New York scored three times in the third. "The Yanks scored those three runs," noted the *Post*, "on one legitimate hit, one cheap hit and one damaging error by Joe Kuhel." Rick Ferrell scored the tying run in the fifth inning on a single by his brother. The Yanks had a chance to win in regulation when they placed a runner on third base with no outs in the eighth but Wes stopped them. Again in the eleventh a New York runner managed third but Ferrell held them then, too.

The Bombers were limited to four hits over the first nine innings and just six through eleven. Red Rolfe led off the twelfth with a single to right. DiMaggio followed with a double to left. Wes walked Gehrig on purpose. Bill Dickey laced a liner toward left that looked like a winning hit, but shortstop Cecil Travis leaped high in the air, speared the ball and converted it into a double play with a long throw to first.

Tommy Henrich received Ferrell's second intentional pass of the inning. Tony Lazzeri was next. The count went to three and one before Wes sent a second strike across the plate. Lazzeri then hit a grounder to short and Travis, who moments earlier saved Wes, erred with a wide throw to first. "Big Wes Ferrell," wrote Povich, "pitched a winning ball game today and lost — beaten by a brutal break in luck which endowed the Yankees with a 4–3 victory at the end of the 12 most tense innings in which the Nats have figured this season."

It would not be unexpected that Wes, after losing a close game in such a manner, would be in a foul mood. The aftermath of this game, however, had a different twist. On his way to the dressing room, Wes happened across a crowd circling two players who were having a fistfight. Wes broke through the ring of spectators only to find his brother and Tony Lazzeri going at it. The Yankees' second baseman had accused Rick of tipping his bat in the last inning, and the Washington backstop took umbrage with the charge. Wes waded in and broke up the fight, which "impartial observers voted a draw."

Ferrell's next start was a 9–6 win in St. Louis on August 24. It wasn't an easy one as the Browns scored four early runs. "The knock-kneed right-hander, who appeared in for an awful drubbing in those first two innings when the Browns belted him for seven hits, deflated the St. Louis boys with some near-perfect pitches for the next five frames during which he have up only one hit." Wes gave up two final runs in the eighth inning after the score was 9–4. "Ferrell, himself, was no drawback to the Nats up there at the plate," noted the *Post*. "He bashed out three hits that figured in five runs and pitched three-hit ball for the last seven innings."[21]

Ted Lyons took a 3–2 decision from Wes on August 28. "Wesley Cheek Ferrell cast his sinister spell over his Washington teammates today and under the influence of the old Ferrell hex, the Nats went into a batting trance," observed Povich. The game was knotted at 1–1 when Luke Appling and Jimmy Dykes hit home runs into the left-field seats. "After that blow-off in the fourth Ferrell was some shucks out there on the mound, holding the Sox to a lone hit for the rest of the afternoon, but securely in the grips of Lyons, the Nats were a beaten bunch."[22] Washington trailed by a run in the eighth when Wes hammered a two-out double off the left-field wall and scored on an ensuing base hit.

Four days later Wes confounded the Tigers in Detroit by an 8–2 score. "Wesley Cheek Ferrell, smart guy that he is," wrote Povich, "was wary of the slugging Detroit Tigers and pitched accordingly as he took the mound. With each passing inning, the wariness plus a high degree of disgust were transferred to the Tigers, who were thoroughly bamboozled by the old fellow's pitching.

"For seven innings the Tigers accomplished a great deal of nothing against the tantalizing slow balls of Ferrell, and one lone hit — Charley Gehringer's double in the first — was their share of the proceeding. During those seven innings Ferrell was something to watch. With Brother Rick handling his pitches, Wes gave the Tigers a mixture of slow curves and slower curves that the Detroiters could only beat into the dirt or lift harmlessly overhead."[23]

The next stop was Boston. where Lefty and Wes were each looking for their fourteenth victory in the first game of a doubleheader on September 6. The adrenaline was flowing as Grove fanned nine and Ferrell seven. Joe Cronin went down on strikes three times. Each hurler passed five batters. Wes was working with a 2–0 lead when the Red Sox tied things up in the sixth inning on a walk, an infield hit, a double and a Washington error on a relay throw. Boston scored four more times in the eighth to give Lefty the 6–2 win. Two doubles, a single, two walks — one intentional to Foxx — and some daring base-running by Ben Chapman produced the runs.

Wes dropped a 5–3 decision in Philadelphia on September 10. Five days later he took a 3–1 lead into the top of the ninth against the Tigers in Washington, having allowed just seven hits and one unearned run that had come back in the first inning. Five Detroit singles in the ninth gave Detroit a 4–3 lead. "When Goslin finally ended the inning with a fly," observed Povich, "Ferrell was seen to tear up his glove on the dugout steps. He probably would have eaten it had it not been a half hour before sundown."[24]

Wes' next start was almost as bad. It was a 6–3 loss to the visiting Indians on September 21, and Johnny Allen's thirteenth consecutive victory. "Strictly on the merits of pitching," wrote Povich, "Ferrell should have been returned a 3–2 winner. Because the four runs the Indians came up with in the fifth to take the lead were as unearned as a foundling's fate. Ferrell apparently was out of that inning without damage. He had two Indians on base, but he also had two out when Averill smashed a hard grounder at Myer. The ball tore its way through Myer's glove and the error filled the bases. Hal Trosky looped a modest fly ball to center field. Mel Almada dashed in for a shoestring catch, missed the ball, and it rolled to the center field fence, evolving as cheap a home run that scored four tallies."[25]

Wes' last start was a 4–3 victory against his former team on September 30. "The Red Sox hopes of finishing in the first division," wrote the Boston *Globe*, "received a staggering blow here today and the thrower of that wallop was none other than Wesley Cheek Ferrell." The Red Sox looked pitiful against Wes for eight of the nine innings, scoring all of their runs in the seventh inning on two singles and a home run by Fabian Gaffke. The Boston batters went down in order over the last two innings.

* * *

The Piedmont League in 1937 was full of future major league stars. The Red Sox, Tigers, Yankees, Cubs, Reds, and Cardinals all supported farm teams in the circuit, and Clark Griffith had just put a team in Charlotte, North Carolina. The Richmond Colts, while still independently owned by Eddie Mooers, had a close working relationship with the New York Giants.

George Ferrell, the Colts' perennial cleanup hitter, had a big night on June 25 with four hits. Richmond came up a little short in the run department, though, dropping an 8–6 contest to the Charlotte Hornets. George's two-run homer in the eighth pulled his club to a one-run deficit, but the

Cousin Bev Ferrell in Washington's 1937 spring training camp (Deta Ferrell).

difference in the final score was a home run hit by Cousin Bev Ferrell, the Charlotte center fielder, in the top of the inning.

Harry Brecheen — the pitching star of the 1946 World Series — won 21 games for the Portsmouth Cubs in 1937. On May 27, Bev Ferrell belted a ninth-inning home run off Brecheen to send the game into extra innings only to see Bill Nicholson — the National League's home run and RBI leader

TRUE TO THE FERRELL TRADITION

Rated as one of the best looking prospects below the majors today is Durham's own Beverly Ferrell. Diamond experts maintain young Ferrell is destined to take his place in the Big Show along with his famous cousins, Wes and Rick, the Red Sox plutocrats. According to latest reports from the Hornet front office, Ferrell will tarry long enough to brush up on a few rough spots, gain a little more "upper minor" experience, and then will be given every opportunity to make the Senators either this fall or next spring. And the way he has been massaging the apple thus far, it wouldn't be at all surprising if foxy old Clark Griffith recalls Beverly before the current season is completed. Latest figures show his bat mark to be .353.

Bev Ferrell in action — a Piedmont League favorite (Deta Ferrell).

in 1943 and 1944 — win the contest for Portsmouth with a tenth inning round-tripper.

Colts lefty Clem Dreisewerd, who fanned a Piedmont League high 195 batters in 1937 — and whose wife Edna would later pen a forgotten classic baseball book called *The Catcher Was a Lady* — tossed a three-hitter in Charlotte on July 22, winning 3–2 in ten innings. All three Charlotte hits came in the ninth inning. George Ferrell belted a long homer in the sixth inning to give Dreisewerd a 2–0 lead. "While Dreisewerd was not hit safely until the hectic ninth, Bev Ferrell cracked a long ball out of the park in the seventh with Bobby Estalella on base which spectators proclaimed was fair. Umpire Vaught, who ruled the ball foul, was razzed unmercifully the rest of the game. It was rapped down the left field line and would have tied the score in the seventh."[26]

Bev hit .275 with 15 homers and 94 RBI in 1937. George finished the season with a .321 batting average, good enough for seventh in the Piedmont batting race. He hit 18 home runs and drove home 110 runs. Tom Ferrick, who won 20 games for Richmond in 1937 before going on to pitch nine seasons in the majors, told the Richmond *Times-Dispatch* in 1982 that George Ferrell was the best minor league hitter he ever saw.

◆ 13 ◆

1938 — On a Wing
and a Prayer

President Roosevelt "heaved a crisp, low fast ball toward the diamond" to open the season on a drizzly April 18 in Washington. "That," lamented the Washington *Post*, "completed the good pitching for the day." For Wes Ferrell it was the sixth opening day assignment of his career, and the 12–8 victory pushed his mark in those contests to a perfect 6–0. He surrendered 16 hits, allowing four runs in the third inning and another in the sixth before collapsing at the finish. It would be a long season.

"Ferrell, pitching with a sore shoulder that had received treatment until game time, lasted the nine-inning route because the Nats gave him a large and comfortable lead," wrote Shirley Povich. "But he was wavering in the ninth, when the A's, in a last-ditch uprising, pushed across three runs."

His second start, a 7–4 victory over Lefty Gomez, came five days later at Yankee Stadium. "Bases on balls plagued Ferrell from the start," reported the *Post*. "He issued eight. But when he wasn't passing the Yankees he was effective, for the New Yorkers were able to reach him for only seven hits."[1] He again suffered a ninth-inning meltdown, walking three before Al Simmons and John Stone saved him with superb catches. Wes sprinted out to hug Stone after he corralled Bill Dickey's liner at the base of the right-field wall to end the game.

Buddy Lewis drove in six runs in Wes' 7–2 victory in Philadelphia on April 28. "It seems that the Ferrell Brothers, one or both of 'em," wrote Povich, "were always getting on base because when Lewis arrived at the plate in the fifth inning there they were on second and third — the pair of 'em. There was nothing cheap about Rick Ferrell's smashing single to left that opened the fifth inning. And Brother Wes tossed in a two-bagger that moved Rick to third." The pitching Ferrell also managed to keep the

Wes (left) and Rick go over the signs in Washington's 1938 spring training camp (Gwenlo Ferrell Gore).

Philadelphia batters off stride. "Ferrell served a heady game in holding the A's to a run in the first inning and another in the sixth. His own wild throw was responsible for the first run, and after Lewis' homer put him in a commanding lead, the temperamental right-hander was the personification of care and caution."[2]

Wes' first loss of the season came against Cleveland on May 3. He began the fifth with the score tied at 3–3 but five straight hits knocked him from the box.

* * *

The next afternoon Emil "Dutch" Leonard outdueled Bob Feller 1–0 in thirteen innings. Leonard had resurrected his career by perfecting his knuckleball while with Atlanta in the Southern Association, and now he was about to change baseball. Other pitchers had used the knuckler before him but none had relied on it exclusively. Leonard's success would be tentacled, for even history's most famous knuckleballer, Hall of Famer Hoyt Wilhelm, began fooling with the pitch while still in high school after reading about Leonard's success. Leonard's catcher at Atlanta, Paul Richards, later introduced a new catcher's mitt specifically designed to handle the pitch. While Wilhelm's manager at Baltimore, Richards converted him to a starting pitcher.

Clark Griffith, Bucky Harris and Rick Ferrell conferred often that spring to discuss the pitch. Could Leonard win with it, they wondered? Yes, they decided, he could and all three quickly grasped the possibilities. "All he needed right along," Griffith told Denman Thompson of the Washington *Star*, "was a catcher who wasn't afraid to call for his knuckle ball. It so happens that Washington has that kind of catcher in Rick Ferrell."

Leonard's floater was the whole story in his victory over Feller. "Showing the Indians a knuckle ball that fluttered and wobbled as it neared the plate and forced Catcher Rick Ferrell to be on the alert," wrote the *Post*, "Leonard was in command from the start." The pro behind the plate was master of the situation. "Don't know how Ferrell escapes the passed balls," said Leonard, "When I, myself, do not know always just where my knuckler is going."

* * *

Wes ran his record to 4–1 with a 9–7 victory over the Browns on May 8. He took an 8–2 lead into the eighth before St. Louis blasted him from the hill. "In the eighth," wrote Povich, "pinch hitter Mazzera singled to right and so did Mills and Sullivan. With one out, Bell singled to center and there were two runs across. Then Sammy West blasted a tremendous fly high over the right-field wall and the Browns had five runs for the inning and Washington had a new pitcher."

A pattern was emerging for Wes, who could still pitch well enough for six or seven innings but was increasingly vulnerable late in games. That might have been sufficient had it been 2003, but pitchers in 1938, especially those of Wes' reputation, were expected to finish what they started. Ferrell had worked harder than any other hurler from 1935 to 1937, topping the majors with 111 starts, 85 complete games and 904.1 innings. Dizzy Dean turned in 74 complete games over the same period. He was followed by Carl Hubbell and Tommy Bridges with 67 and then Grove and Red Ruffing with 66.

Leonard's floater was masterful the next day as he beat St. Louis 7–1 to move Washington a half game in front of New York for the top spot in the standings. Rick Ferrell's second-inning triple put the Nats up 3–1, and they broke it open in the eighth, which began with a Cecil Travis double and an intentional pass to Buddy Myer. "This obvious insult to Ferrell's batting was met with a sharp single off the bat of the Washington catcher and Travis scored." Leonard followed with a triple to plate Myer and Ferrell.

Washington remained in first place despite Wes' 10–0 loss to the Red Sox on May 13. Ferrell went the distance, looking good before a Jimmy Foxx double began the Boston fourth. Successive singles by Cronin, Higgins, Doerr and Desautels made the score 4–0. The Red Sox scored four unearned runs in the sixth on three hits and two Washington errors, and two final runs in the eighth on three straight singles. All told Wes was battered for 13 hits.

Wes beat the Tigers 5–1 in Detroit on May 18. "Out of their slump emerged the Nats today," penned Povich, "riding to triumph on a superlative performance by Wesley Cheek Ferrell ... the tall right-hander was in complete command from the opening inning and it was with near ridiculous ease that he subjugated the Tigers." He allowed six hits, three of which were described as "cheap, luck-anointed blows." Before Chet Laabs homered to begin the seventh, Ferrell had limited the Tigers to just two singles. "He was something to watch today, Ferrell was. Bereft of the fast balls he used to own before his arm collapsed a half-dozen years ago, the wily Ferrell served up his slow stuff with consistent success. Gehringer, Greenberg and York, the big three of the Tiger batting order failed to collect a hit." Povich described York, who went down on strikes four times, as looking both pitiful and pathetic against Ferrell. The Nats were up 2–0 when Wes came to bat in the fifth. "Ferrell, who used to be one of the better hitting pitchers in the league, also reclaimed a bit of his slugging glory. Far, far into the left centerfield bleachers he swatted a home run."[3]

Ted Lyons won his 200th game with a 9–2 victory over Washington in Chicago on May 22. Ferrell was the losing pitcher, though for five innings it was a pitching duel that Wes led 1–0 before giving up five runs in the bottom of the sixth.

Washington dropped a 4–3 contest in St. Louis on May 25. Rick Ferrell had three hits in the game and all were doubles. With his club down a run in the second inning, he doubled and scored. In the fourth inning, with a runner on first, "Ferrell pounded out a double against the leftfield wall only inches shy of a home run to make the score 3–3." His third double came with two down in the eighth, but Wes, pinch-hitting for the Washington pitcher, grounded weakly back to the mound to end the threat.

The pitcher upped his record to 7–3 with a 5–3 victory over the Red Sox at Griffith Stadium on May 29. "The Red Sox," noted the *Post*, "nudged him for 10 hits and Ferrell was in continual trouble after the second inning. But mixing his curves with a new found fast ball he left 12 Bostonians stranded on the bases."

Next was a 5–1 six-hitter that he tossed against the White Sox on June 3. Al Simmons hit a two-run homer to give Washington a 3–1 lead in the

Wes as a Washington Senator. His arm was failing but his intensity was not (Gwenlo Ferrell Gore).

third, and "Rick Ferrell caught the spirit of things in the fourth inning and slapped a long two-bagger into left field that was converted into the fourth Washington run." Wes sacrificed his brother along and Ossie Bluege drove him home. "The Ferrell frères knocked [Thornton] Lee loose from the

Nats fifth run two innings later after Brother Rick drew a harmless-looking walk with two out. But a bit later it took on an important aspect because the pitching Ferrell thumped a hefty two-bagger over Leftfielder Gerald Walker's head against the base of the bleacher wall, and Rick scored all the way from first base."[4]

Wes Ferrell's record then stood at 8–3 with a 4.63 ERA. He had completed seven of his ten starts and had beaten every team in the circuit but Cleveland. With the American League's ERA being 4.79 in 1938, Ferrell remained slightly ahead of the curve. He was just 30 years old.

Washington dropped an 11–5 contest to the visiting Browns on June 8. "Ferrell had a harrowing time of it trying to get the Browns out in the second inning. In fact, the third man out in the second inning was Ferrell himself," wrote Povich. "He walked Sammy West with one down and then the next five guys rapped him for hits."

Washington jumped out to an early lead on June 12, scoring seven times in the third inning to give Wes a 7–1 lead over Detroit. The inning had been highlighted by Rick's inside-the-park home run. Then it started to rain. Wes, with the game not yet official, paced nervously up and down the Washington dugout as the grounds crew went to work. That did not go unnoticed, and the Tigers began to pour it on. "We sat around for an hour with the rain coming down and jeered at Ferrell," recalled Hank Greenberg.

"Wes was one of your great competitors," Charlie Gehringer told Donald Honig. "He just hated to lose ... he's was going great guns ... then it started to rain. The skies turned black, and I tell you it just poured. Naturally the game was held up. I was sitting in the dugout, looking across at Wes, and I could almost *see* what he was thinking: God, am I going to lose this easy victory? After about 15 minutes the rain stopped and the sun came out, and even before they could get the canvas off the field, there's Wes out there loosening up. He's determined to get that one more inning in to make it an official game."[5]

The contest resumed and Washington scored four more runs to make it 11–1. Gehringer started off the Detroit sixth with a homer to right. Greenberg walked and Rudy York belted the ball into the left-field seats. Pete Fox doubled. Chet Laabs, Tony Piet and Bill Rogell all followed with singles and Wes was out of the game. The bullpen had no better luck and by the time the inning was over the score was 11–10. Detroit eventually won the game 18–12, and Greenberg recalled seeing Wes sitting at the far end of the Washington dugout, tearing apart his glove with his bare hands while the Detroit bench howled at him. All of Ferrell's teammates had moved to the other end of the dugout. "He should be in the Hall of Fame,"

Wes — always the stylish dresser — watches his Washington teammates (Gwenlo Ferrell Gore).

said Greenberg of Wes in his 1989 autobiography. "Why his name has been overlooked I'll never understand, but his record measures up to anybody's."[6]

Ferrell's next assignment came five days later in Detroit where he took a 10–3 lead into the seventh. Only one of the Tigers' runs was earned and Wes' two hits as a batter had accounted for two of Washington's tallies. He began the ninth with a 12–5 lead but Harris pulled him after the first two batters hit safely. Pete Appleton relieved and gave up a single, a walk and a home run before completing the inning. The final was 12–10.

Harris lifted Wes after six hits and four runs in just two innings in Chicago on June 22. The bullpen surrendered 11 hits and 12 more runs and the result was a 16–3 White Sox victory.

Ferrell's 185th career victory came in a 7–2 contest in St. Louis on June 26, the same day Carl Hubbell won his 200th game. "Big Wesley Ferrell, pitching one of his better ball games after recent disastrous outings, was in complete control," observed Povich in the *Post*. "In the first six innings, he allowed the Brownies only three hits, two of which were infield affairs which skipped just out of the reach of Buddy Myer's full grasp. And he did not pass a soul until he pitched a walk to Kress with two out in the sixth."[7] The victory was Ferrell's tenth, and at the All-Star break he was one of only five American Leagues hurlers that could count as many. The All-Star team was announced on June 27, and Rick Ferrell, who was hitting .324 at the time, got the nod for the sixth consecutive season.

* * *

By the beginning of July, the fans, the writers and even the Washington manager were souring on Wes. "The victim of the Yankees' assault was— you probably guess it — Wesley Cheek Ferrell," wrote Povich after he dropped a 12–2 decision in New York on July 2. "Ferrell pitched five innings and shut the Yankees out — in the second inning. In every other inning he was belabored horribly by the Yanks. By the time Bucky Harris got him out of there, he had pitched ten hits and seven runs to the Bronx bombers, including three home runs."

Ferrell's eleventh win was a 7–4 decision he took from the Athletics on July 9. Wes "pitched masterful ball yielding only two hits," said Povich, before he "encountered evil times in the sixth when the A's came up with three runs. He yielded another in the eighth. When he came back to the mound in the ninth a generous sprinkling of the customers raised a salvo of boos." Once more Ferrell staggered toward the finish. He walked Bob Johnson to start the ninth before retiring the next two batters on fly balls. Then he walked another. When Buddy Lewis erred on a ground ball that should have ended the game, Harris decided that Wes had pushed his luck to the limit, and went to the pen.

Six days later Wes lost 11–3 to the visiting White Sox. He allowed seven hits and six earned runs before the opposing pitcher knocked him out of the game with a home run. "Manager Bucky Harris who had suffered Ferrell's presence until that point with increasing misgivings," noted Povich, "emerged from the dugout as Lee's homer cleared the wall and frantically waved Ferrell out of the box."[8]

Rick Ferrell's tenth inning double plated the winning score in a 4–3 victory over Detroit on July 19, and his brother's Jekyll and Hyde act continued the next day when he beat the Tigers 7–2 at waterlogged Griffith Stadium. It rained much of the day and the game was delayed while the grounds crew worked on the field. "With seeming unconcern of the treacherous footing of the pitchers' mound, where he was ankle deep in goo, Wesley Cheek Ferrell came up with one of his better pitching performances," wrote the *Post*. "He held the Tigers to nine hits and only once during the proceedings—in the sixth inning—did he hear the boos of the 3,000 customers who, at the final, were applauding the unpopular fellow."[9]

His next start ended in a 6–5 Tigers win. Given three leads to work with, Wes couldn't hold any of them. When Harris came to mound to remove him in the sixth, after he had allowed ten hits and five runs, the pitcher fired the ball to the ground in disgust. He left to the jeers of 12,000 Detroit customers.

A 5–3 victory in St. Louis on August 2 boosted Wes' record to 13–7. Harris yanked him with the bases loaded and one down in the last frame. "Until the ninth inning, Ferrell had pitched impressive ball," noted Povich, "yielding only seven hits. Only one of the three Browns' runs was earned, an error by Buddy Myer in the second inning accounting for a pair."

Wes started the first game of a doubleheader on August 7. The Chicago White Sox leadoff batter sent a low liner into center field that went for an inside-the-park homer when an outfielder missed a shoestring catch. A walk, a hit batsman and then four hits drove Ferrell from the game in the second.

The next afternoon the Senators released him. Speculation for the action ranged jokingly from Wes' love for astrology and his poor checker playing to the real reasons, his temperament and high salary, which was $14,000. Povich reported that Wes had recently made a disparaging remark about the Washington owner's frugalness, and flat-out called Griffith cheap. "Ferrell does not figure to help us," said Griff. "I wish him luck, but we are going to rebuild our pitching staff in different lines."

Wes was not happy. "This is a new one — releasing a pitcher who has won more games than anybody else on the club," he said. "But I'm not worried. I'll get a job, not this season perhaps. I think I'll lay off for the rest of the year. But I'll be in the majors next season. You can bet on that." His former teammates wished him luck as he cleaned out his locker. Finally he was left alone with Rick. Long bonded by their ability, they were about to embark on very different paths. Brothers they would always be, but never again would they be teammates in the game that possessed them both. "No stranger individual than Ferrell has ever been part of the modern baseball scene...." Povich wrote trying to explain Wes. "But as a rule, managers have been tolerant of him in deference to his pitching skill and his philosophy of blaming no one but himself for games that he lost, whether by his own pitching or teammates errors."

Two days later, in a move that shocked many, Wes signed with the Yankees. New York had plenty of young arms at Newark in the International League, but Jacob Ruppert promised he would not touch them until the end of the season. When Joe Vance underwent an emergency appendectomy, a spot opened up for Ferrell on the New York staff.

"Bucky Harris will tell you my arm is going dead," Wes told the New York *World-Telegram*, "that it hasn't its old snap, that my fast one doesn't sing and my curve doesn't break any more. And I'll admit my fast one isn't like it was six or seven years ago. You can't pour smoke forever. Mungo, Rowe, Feller — that poor kid never had a chance — and the Deans will tell you that. But my control is good." He then described his "nuthin' pitch" to the press. "All it is is a big change of pace, with plenty of speed in the motion and plenty of 'squash' on the ball. Just kills their timing."

Joe McCarthy was a no-nonsense leader with a reputation for disliking hot-heads, especially Southern ones, and though Wes was hot-headed — when his game was on the line — that was something McCarthy both understood and respected. The New York manager, according to lore, once released Roy Johnson after the outfielder asked after a loss, "Does he expect to win every game?" The answer, as Johnson should have known, was yes.

"The Yankees will have to score 19 runs to win the game Ferrell pitches, because we're going to get 18 runs against him," mocked Griffith on the morning of August 18. Wes, in the only significant game he pitched for the Yankees, beat Washington 5–4 in 11 innings.

* * *

Carl Hubbell was routed over at the Polo Grounds on the same day Wes beat Washington in his Yankees debut. The Giants' ace had been suffering elbow pain for some time, and surgery, performed by Memphis physician J. Spencer Speed, quickly followed.

Dizzy Dean — predicting 30 wins for himself with the Cubs — opened his season with a victory on April 20. Leaving with a big lead after six innings, Dean noted "Charley Grimm is the only manager in baseball who would have taken me out of a game like that to give me a rest." A four-hit shutout followed against the Cardinals on April 24, but never again during the season would Dean begin a game with less than a week's rest between starts. Bursitis shelved him for ten weeks beginning in May, and Grimm, when Diz finally came back — and noting that he had been working with a bum wing for two years anyway — said Dean "will be a better pitcher with a sore arm than half the major league pitchers who have good ones."

Lefty Grove's arm had gone numb in the fifth inning of a game against the Tigers on July 14. He waited a month before trying it again but lasted only two innings on August 11 before calling it quits. "Boys, she's dead as a board," said Grove to surrounding writers as he looked down at his arm.

Two members of the McCarthy-Ferrell mutual admiration society. Joe McCarthy and Wes in 1939 (Gwenlo Ferrell Gore).

Grove, Hubbell, Dean and Ferrell — the greatest pitching thoroughbreds of their generation — were all staggering.

* * *

The Charlotte Hornets, managed by Calvin Griffith, led the Piedmont League race until the last day of the season before losing the flag to the

PIEDMONT LEAGUE BASEBALL
Welcome Home Durham's Own "Bev." Ferrell

DURHAM BULLS VS CHARLOTTE HORNETS
DURHAM ATHLETIC PARK
Friday, Saturday Nites at 8 P. M.
Sunday Afternoon at 3 P. M.

Above: Rick (left) and Wes on opposite teams. Imagine the record Wes would have compiled had he played in New York while his arm was sound (Gwenlo Ferrell Gore). ***Left:*** Bev Ferrell was a crowd favorite (Deta Ferrell).

New York Yankees' Norfolk farm team that boasted the keystone combination of Phil Rizzuto and Gerry Priddy. Bev Ferrell played center field for the Hornets. Joe Haynes, the brother-in-law of both Cal Griffith and Joe Cronin, was the team's pitching ace and Bobby Estalella, who played in nine big league seasons, was the league's top hitter. Jake Early, the Hornets' backstop — and the 1943 American League All-Star catcher — was being groomed to handle the knuckleball.

George Ferrell was still playing left field

for the Richmond Colts. Among his teammates was pitcher John Hubbell, brother of the Giants' ace. George belted a three-run homer in the first inning on May 6 against Charlotte, and Hubbell fanned nine batters in the 9–6 Richmond victory. The next afternoon Bev Ferrell sent two balls out of the park in a 13–5 Hornets win.

Charlotte split a doubleheader in Durham on June 29. A free-for-all broke out in the fifth inning of the first game and when the dust cleared, Cal Griffith was being hauled off to jail for slugging an umpire.

George and Bev finished the season with identical batting marks of .300 and were listed consecutively in the final averages listed in the 1939 *Reach Base Ball Guide*. Bev hit 14 home runs and drove in 92 runs. George hit 18 home runs and had 110 RBI.

* * *

Marvin Ferrell played for Washington's farm club at Trenton in the Eastern League in 1938. The previous season he had recorded a 12–4 pitching mark and hit .316 when playing the outfield for Landis in the Class D North Carolina State League.

As he had done in several other seasons, Marvin got off to a fast start with three wins in May. He fanned nine batters in an 8–2 victory over Williamsport on May 6, holding Bill "Swish" Nicholson hitless in five trips to the plate. Also used in the outfield and as a pinch-hitter when needed, Marvin was optioned to Greenville in the South Atlantic League when his pitching fell off in mid-season.

◆ 14 ◆

The Knuckleball Catcher

The St. Louis pitcher had spun a gem at Sportsman's Park on the night of May 21, 1943, holding Philadelphia hitless until the eighth inning. In the ninth, after tying the game, the Athletics had runners on second and third with one down as the hurler looked in at his catcher for the obligatory but unneeded sign. Johnny Niggeling had bounced around the minors for close to a decade before sticking with the Browns in 1940. A one-trick pitcher, he relied on the knuckleball, a pitch he learned while still in parochial school in Remsen, Iowa. His catcher, as expected, flashed the sign for the floater, and the one Niggeling tossed to the plate was a beauty. The batter swung, missing it by a foot, but the ball got away from Rick Ferrell and rolled to the backstop. The winning run scored and Niggeling, who tossed a two-hitter, was a 2–1 loser.

The pitcher was philosophical about the play, which went as an error, for he understood that his career rode on the whim of the fluttering ball. Every hurler who threw the pitch, he was fond of saying, owed a debt of gratitude to two men — Dutch Leonard and Rick Ferrell. "Leonard showed that a fellow could throw the knuckle ball and win," Niggeling told Shirley Povich in 1944. "He was lucky enough to have a fellow like Ferrell who wasn't afraid to call for it. There were other catchers in the big leagues, supposed to be good catchers, who wouldn't risk their reputations by calling for the knuckler because it was so hard to handle. But when Leonard came up from Atlanta and found out he could pitch to Ferrell and win, the whole league got knuckle-ball conscious."[1]

* * *

Rick Ferrell was slowing up; unable to play through the small nagging injuries like he could in his youth. Midway through the 1939 season, Bucky Harris decided that he was no longer capable of catching every day and began using a two-catcher system. Clark Griffith was looking for a

240

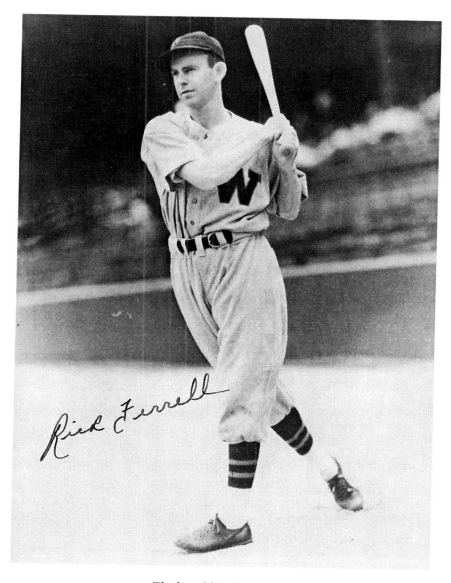

The knuckleball catcher.

younger replacement but finding a backstop of Rick's defensive ability was not a simple task. "Rick Ferrell is still a crack catcher," wrote *The Sporting News* in 1940, "and, when rested, a dangerous hitter."

The St. Louis Browns negotiated hard over the winter of 1940-41 for Rick, wanting him to tutor their young catcher, Bob Swift. "Rick knows all the tricks of the catching trade, and could, in addition helping the pitching staff, teach a few things to Robert," commented *The Sporting News* in January 1941. The list of young catchers that received instruction from Ferrell over the next four decades would be lengthy.

When Rick went down with an injury in May 1941, Jake Early, the catcher the Washington club had been grooming to take Ferrell's place, stepped in and convinced Harris that he was capable of handling Leonard's knuckler. That opened the door for Rick's move back to St. Louis.

* * *

Bob Feller fired a one-hitter against the Browns at Sportsman's Park on September 26, 1941, taking his 25th victory of the season with the 3–2 decision. St. Louis scored both of its runs in the fifth inning on three walks, a fly ball and the lone hit, a bunt single by Rick Ferrell. He was trying to lay down a sacrifice.

* * *

World War II had taken a toll on major league baseball by the start of 1944 and Washington had been hit especially hard, losing their two best offensive players, Cecil Travis and Buddy Lewis, and pitcher Sid Hudson to the armed forces. When Early was inducted following the 1943 season, the team was short an experienced catcher. What the Nats did have — with the acquisitions of Johnny Niggeling and Roger Wolff late in 1943 — was four pitchers who threw the knuckleball.

* * *

Just before Wolff, then with the Athletics, went out and beat the White Sox in August 1943, his catcher, Hal Wagner, turned to umpire Eddie Rommel and said, "I can see I have a great night in front of me." Rommel nodded in agreement, replying, "How about me? I'm behind the plate tonight. Every time I see a knuckleball I wish I had been a bricklayer."[2] That was an odd statement indeed, considering that Rommel had previously been a successful knuckleball practitioner.

Wagner had a tough time in the first inning, just about every pitch squirting out of his glove or hitting him in the chest protector, the mask, arms or bare hand. In the dressing room after the contest, the writers noted that Wagner's right hand was swollen and his shoulders and forearms were bruised. "Frank Bruggy used to catch me," mused Rommel after surveying the scene. "He looked like a feather bed back of the plate. You couldn't miss him. How he fought the knuckleball! When it was my turn to pitch he would ask Connie if he could go fishing that day. His fingers were split and bunged up and he was black and blue from the wrists to the shoulders."

* * *

Washington reacquired Rick Ferrell from St. Louis at the start of spring training in 1944. Over the next two seasons he would catch in 179 games, and a knuckleballer, working as either starter or reliever, appeared in 146 of them. "I know the knuckle ball makes me look bad at times, but what the hell?" said Ferrell. "As long as we get men out and win games, what's the difference? The ones I can't catch, I'll just run down."

Rick's reunion with Dutch Leonard, who had won 77 games for Washington since throwing his first knuckler to Ferrell back in 1938, was immediate inspiration for a Shirley Povich column.

"Leonard may never have made good in the big leagues except for the help he got from Rick, who, unlike the catchers Leonard had in his trial with Brooklyn, kept calling for Leonard to throw his knuckler. Ferrell didn't care about his own catching record. In fact, in the same years when he was acknowledged as one of the great catchers of the league, he was charged with the most passed balls, due chiefly to the butterfly pitch of Leonard....

"It's more than a coincidence too," continued Povich, "that Johnny Niggeling developed as a knuckleballer with the Browns while Ferrell was the Browns' catcher these two seasons. He couldn't win in his previous trials in the majors, but when he found a catcher who could handle his knuckler and wasn't afraid to call for it, Niggeling blossomed as one of the better pitchers in the league."[3]

The Nats were projected by most baseball analysts to finish second behind the Yankees in 1944, and although offense was down throughout the majors as a result of the war, and Washington's hitting was among the worst in baseball, Rick got off to a fast start with the stick, hitting .389, sixth in the league when the stats were reported in *The Sporting News* issue of May 11. The next day a wayward floater from Niggeling split open his right thumb and put the receiver out of service for ten days.

* * *

"Handsome Joe" Fitzgerald had a lifelong affiliation with the Nats, beginning as a batboy in 1912, and then returning as jack-of-all-trades employee after catching for nearly a decade in the low minors. Officially listed as a coach from 1947 to 1956, he had previously been the bullpen catcher. Joe liked to claim he had warmed up all of the great Washington pitchers — Walter Johnson included — and worked with the knuckleballers in 1945. He and Rick were later roommates as Washington coaches.

"Man, those guys could make that ball do crazy things," said Fitzgerald in a 1955 interview. "The fans used to laugh at me when I put on shin guards, chest protector and mask to warm them up. So a couple of times I got brave and warmed them up without all that gear.

"What happened? That Wolff cuts loose one of those butterflies and it smacks me square in the mouth. Knocked out all my lower teeth.

"Leonard broke my finger with a knuckler during another warm-up. I never could figure out how Rick Ferrell did such a good job catching those guys during the game."[4]

* * *

Despite the effort required by his defensive game, Ferrell continued to hit well over the first half of the 1944 season. "Ferrell was expected to hit, because down through the years he has been dangerous with the bat," wrote Povich. He was hitting .353 when *The Sporting News* published averages on June 15, and his .306 mark on July 6 was still eleventh in the batting race.

The league standings on July 18 showed Washington in fourth place with a 41–41 record, just 5½ games behind the front-running Browns. Ossie Bluege, the Washington manager, had been careful to rest Rick, never using him to catch both games of a doubleheader. The Nats had three team members — third baseman Gil Torres, outfielder Roberto Ortiz, and Ferrell's back-up catcher, Mike Guerra — who were Cubans working in the United States as "alien non-residents." When the Selective Service reclassified them as eligible for the draft in mid–July, they left the team, planning to return to Cuba. Clark Griffith was irate and called in his political markers in order to get his players back on the field. He kept the players on the payroll during the several weeks it took to resolve the issue. Things got so desperate that Eddie Boland took a month-long leave of absence from his job with the New York City Department of Sanitation to replace Ortiz in the Nats' outfield. Harlond Clift, who had retired and was working on his cattle ranch in Washington State, came back to play third base.

With Guerra gone, Rick's backup became Al Evans, who having recently been discharged from the service, wasn't in tip-top playing form. The extra work was too much for the 38-year-old backstop and though a modest ten-game hitting streak left his average at .295 on August 5, Ferrell hit just .235 the rest of the way.

"It will be high adventure," Rick had told scribe Frank O'Neill at the start of the season. "Yes, there is an element of danger in catching the knuckleball pitcher, but that's part of the job catching for Washington this season. If we can win the pennant, I'll catch knucklers every day and night, every pitch while my hands last."[5] Washington didn't win the pennant.

They weren't even close, finishing in last place, while Rick's previous team, the St. Louis Browns, copped their only pennant after a tight contest with the Tigers.

* * *

Rick Ferrell was attracting the attention of the media in 1945, something he had spent years avoiding. There were several reasons. Dickey and Cochrane (who was retired as a player) were both away from the game in the military, the baseball public was fascinated with the knuckleball, and the American League record for career games caught was within his reach.

Ed Rumill penned an article in the February 1945 issue of *Baseball Magazine* titled "That Unsung Catching Star, Rick Ferrell." "Rarely is the name of Rick Ferrell included among the all-time greats," he wrote. "And yet, how many catchers can you name who could match his all-around abilities as a receiver and hitter? And, of course, how many were there who could even approach his endurance record?"

Rumill argued that Rick's colorless makeup caused him to be overlooked. "Much as a well-oiled machine, Rick has gone about his chores arousing a minimum of attention from the press box and the stands. Many times during his 15 years he has reached the headlines with timely base hits or slick defensive maneuvers. But most of the time he has been content to remain quietly in the background, hiding in the shadows of nosier and more publicized yet not more efficient individuals."

Rick had been recognized as a stylist behind the bat, argued Rumill, long before his recent fame as handler of the knuckleball. "Men who have played against both, maintain that Ferrell is another Muddy Ruel — in other words, a smoothie back there."

* * *

Washington's baseball fate in 1945 would again float on the hurling of the four knuckleballers, and Ferrell's ability to manage them, for Bluege had placed Rick in charge of the pitching staff. In today's vernacular, the catcher was the pitching coach.

Mickey Haefner was the lone lefty in the group. Wolff threw his knuckler with three fingers, Leonard and Haefner used two and Niggeling pushed the ball with just the middle finger of his throwing hand. "Wolff especially could get the big break with his knuckleball," said Rick. "Leonard and Niggeling had better control, while Haefner used the knuckler as an off pitch."

* * *

Rick's hands—"rather small for a catcher, nothing like the big mitts of Bill Dickey"—were in good shape despite his many years behind the

plate and were not misshapen. His thumbs "have been driven back a little," but that was something Ferrell attributed to his boxing career. Rick
had refined his catching style over the years. He had gone to a one-handed
receiving style — pioneered by Cochrane and Dickey — in 1938. By 1944 he
was using a hinged catcher's mitt; something Dickey had been using for
several years.

"The knuckleball is the number one enemy of catchers," Rick said that
summer. "Going out there day after day to catch knuckleball pitchers is
like going out looking for an accident to befall you. Sooner of later you
find one. Sooner of later you help a knuckleball pitcher to beat himself by
being unable to stop the sort of stuff he throws at you.

"You sign for the knuckler in a pinch because it's the best pitch the
hurler has. You're asking for trouble on the risk of winning or losing on
one ball. So the ball comes. You can see the stitches, and it look easy. But
you can't make a move to meet the pitch. You don't know how it's going
to break. Maybe in, or down, or maybe it will jump up at 45 degrees and
go to the stand.

"Suppose the game is tied, or the home club is one run behind in the
late innings of a game. There's a runner on base like George Case, or that
Cuban boy we had, Jose Zardon. They'll try and pick a knuckleball on
which to run because they have a big edge on the catcher.

"On a fast ball, a receiver can jump up and or out and throw the day-
lights out of the ball. Not on the knuckleball. You have to wait and watch
as it breaks and then you make your peg. Perhaps you'll barely be able to
catch the ball. All those elements favor the runner and reduce your chances
of throwing him out stealing."[6]

* * *

Niggeling took a two-hitter into the top of the ninth against the White
Sox on September 11, leading 1-0. Rick had driven home the game's only
run in the seventh inning. Wally Moses started the Chicago ninth with a
base hit and pinch-runner Bill Mueller, anticipating a knuckler, promptly
stole second base. Johnny Dickshot followed with a single to tie the game.
Ferrell, manager Bluege and shortstop Gil Torres all expected another steal
attempt, and Torres hollered for the second baseman to cover the bag.
Ferrell signaled for a pitchout as Dickshot broke for second. The peg to
second was a strike, but Fred Vaughn was late in covering the bag and the
ball went into center field. The winning run scored on a subsequent
squeeze play. Bluege was furious, and screamed at Vaughn that the play
was so elementary that everyone in the stands knew it was coming.

It was the last year of the war, and the caliber of play in the majors left something to be desired. George Binks was the Nats' top RBI man that year. The year before, he had played at Milwaukee where his manager — Casey Stengel — became so nonplussed with the outfielder that he started referring to him as the "Magnificent Unpredictable Binks." Bluege respected Ferrell's judgment and allowed him to put on his own plays while at bat. Several times that year, with Binks on first base, Rick signaled for the hit-and-run and each time the runner failed to move on cue. When Bluege discussed the plays with Binks—who indicated that he received and understood Rick's signals—the outfielder's reasoning for not running was, "I was afraid he was going to miss it."[7]

* * *

Rick tried going about business as usual, downplaying the attention as he approached the catching record. He joked that his job had been a little hard on his ears. "I guess I've had to listen to more profanity than any other man in baseball. Not that I minded, particularly. When you've got the hitters cussin', your club's in good shape. They don't say anything when they're hitting."[8] Ray Schalk was at Comiskey Park when Rick tied his record on July 5. When Carlton Fisk broke Ferrell's record four decades later, Rick was there to congratulate him.

A thumb injury in April and various other hand injuries hampered Rick throughout the year. An infected leg cost him time in August. The biggest problem for the 39-year-old backstop, however, was the schedule. Conventional wisdom said that the knuckleball was harder to hit under the lights, so Griffith planned as many night games as the league would allow. The team also played 45 doubleheaders; effectively taking Rick out of 44 games, for Bluege felt it too much for Ferrell's legs to play twin bills. Rick caught both ends of a doubleheader only once in 1945, on September 16 — when the pennant was on the line. *The Sporting News* ran an editorial on September 27 called "1945 — The Year of Horrible Scheduling."

Washington was in seventh place on June 5 with a 17–21 record, but by July 17 they were 40–34 and just three games behind the league-leading Tigers. Ferrell's season mirrored the club's. Slow coming out of the gate, he hit .210 (22 for 105) with a .297 on-base percentage from April through June, but .298 (54 for 181) and .404 over the last three months. His only home run came in the ninth inning of a 6–5 win in Philadelphia on August 28, and it was the game-winner. On September 5, Rick's base hit in the eleventh inning gave Haefner a 2–1 victory over the Browns.

Walt Masterson and Bob Feller — both freshly discharged from the U.S. Navy — dueled on September 13, and Masterson's two-hit shutout moved Washington to half a game from first place. Allie Reynolds shut down the Nats for six innings the next afternoon but blew a 5–0 lead as Washington scored six times in the last three innings. Rick had two hits in the game.

Griffith Stadium had been sold out for two weeks when Detroit opened the first of five games in Washington on September 15. The Tigers took the opening doubleheader 7–4 and 7–3. Ferrell had two hits in the first contest and Al Evans caught Haefner in the second. In another twin bill the next afternoon Wolff beat Newhouser 3–2 in the first game. Rick went one for three with a run scored. Detroit almost blew a 5–0 lead in the second contest but held off a late rally to win 5–4. Rick went one for four with a run scored before being lifted for a runner in the ninth. Ferrell had two hits— one a double — scored a run and knocked home a pair when Washington broke a 5–5 tie on September 18 with four runs in the seventh and three more in the eighth to beat Detroit 12–5. The victory left Washington a game and a half behind Detroit.

Rick went 0–1 but drew three passes when Joe Page beat Washington 6–1 at Yankee Stadium on September 20. The next day he went two for four with both a run scored and an RBI during a 5–3 loss to the Yankees.

Washington closed the season in Philadelphia where Rick handled Wolff's twentieth win, a 2–0 shutout on September 22. That left a doubleheader the next afternoon to decide the Nats' fate. The score of both games was 4–3 but Washington — needing as it turned out two wins to force a playoff with Detroit — dropped the first game in 12 innings when the "Magnificent Unpredictable" Binks forgot to put on his sunglasses and lost a routine fly ball in the sun.

That was as close as Rick Ferrell ever got to playing in a World Series.

* * *

Wes Ferrell had surgery following the 1938 season to remove bone chips from his elbow. He made several unsuccessful comeback attempts. In June 1941, the manager of the Leaksville Triplets in the Bi-State League resigned. Several carloads of enterprising local citizens drove to Martinsville, Virginia, seeking out George Ferrell, the manager of the Bi-State's front-running Martinsville's Manufacturers, to ask him if Wes would be willing to take over their club.

George phoned his brother in Guilford, and Wes indicated that he would be open to offers. The caravan continued on to Guilford where they located Wes at the farm. Talks progressed smoothly until Wes asked about salary. The fans went silent, and for the first time Wes realized that they were just fans, not team officials. They piled back in their cars and motored to Leaksville and woke up the team's business manager in the middle of the night.

Leaksville was in last place when Wes took over the team but he quickly turned them around. In the first game they played against each other, Wes picked George off first base. Wes eventually brought Leaksville home in the top spot, two games ahead of George's club. "In the meanwhile," wrote *The Sporting News* on September 18, 1941, "a little personal batting feud had been going on between the two brothers—to see which would have the higher hitting average and make more home runs. In five consecutive games, during the last month of the season, Wes hit five home runs, giving him the round-trip honors over George, 20 to 15. But George proved more consistent with the stick and wound up with an average of .351, third in the league, against .332 for Wes."

Both teams were eliminated in the first round of the playoffs but that didn't stop the siblings from rehashing the season once they reached Guilford. Wes' wife Lois, and George's wife Kate, finally had to seek out their mother-in-law to halt the arguing. Once Mother Ferrell ruled, the boys settled down.

* * *

Sergeant Beverly Ferrell was leading his rifle squad across a field in France in the fall of 1944. It was several months after D-Day, when the former outfielder had come ashore on Omaha Beach with the 29th Infantry Division. They had driven through Normandy into Brittany. "We didn't stop for anything," said Ferrell. "We went right along with the tanks, sometimes walking and sometimes riding in trucks. Whenever we came to any opposition the tanks would move up front and we would go right through. The units back of us cleaned out the pockets we left and units further back mopped up what the second units left."[9] A German artillery barrage suddenly engulfed the squad and when it lifted, the fleetest of the Ferrells would run no more, having to be carried from the field with shrapnel wounds in both legs. Bev's baseball career was over.

* * *

Former major league pitcher, coach and manager Roger Craig was born in Durham, North Carolina, and is familiar with various members of the Ferrell family. "I was in the army with 'Little Rick' and he caught me several games on the post team," wrote Craig. "And I was associated with 'Big Rick' while I was pitching coach for the Detroit Tigers. I knew Charlie Ferrell very well, too. I used to be the batboy for the Durham Bulls," for whom "Charlie and my brother Wilson Craig were very close and both catchers."

Charles Dewitt Ferrell was born in Durham on July 10, 1921. He was

Charlie Ferrell of the Durham Bulls (Eleanor Ferrell Hoover).

the son of Grover Cleveland Ferrell and Bev Ferrell's younger brother. Wes, Rick, George and Marvin were his cousins.

"The Ferrells had tempers and Charlie was no exception," wrote his daughter, Eleanor Ferrell Hoover. "He was in quite a few fights. My mother always said she had a tiger by the tail and loved it! I don't want to make my father out to be a roughneck, but the stories tell me that he came out swinging at the drop of the hat and he dropped the hat."

Like his cousins, Charlie Ferrell was a whiz on the basketball court, starring for the legendary 1939-40 Durham High School team that won both the North Carolina State Championship (for the third of five consecutive years) and the Eastern States (High School) Basketball Championship, to claim — if you will — a national title.

Most of Charlie's teammates continued on to play basketball at Duke University. The team's center, Horace "Bones" McKinney, went to North Carolina State before embarking on a career that climaxed — after playing for the Boston Celtics and coaching at Wake Forest — with induction to the Basketball Hall of Fame.

George Ferrell hit .289 for Winston-Salem in the Carolina League in 1945. Charlie, catching in the same circuit for the Brooklyn Dodgers' farm team at Burlington, hit .347 before being called up to Montreal in the International League.

Charlie was a diabetic, a condition apparently diagnosed at the Dodgers' 1945 spring training camp at Bear Mountain, New York, where he had attracted Branch Rickey's eye with a prodigious home run. Within a week the Brooklyn boss declared Charlie the "best catching prospect I've seen in three years."[10]

Rickey took a parental interest in Charlie's medical problem and set up an appointment at the Joslyn Clinic in Boston. The diabetes was a condition Ferrell never came to grips with, evidenced by this telegram Rickey fired off to Charlie in Durham on October 12, 1945. "Just returned today to Brooklyn to find that you have not been in Boston and that you are not now in Boston and that Doctor Joslyn does not know where you are. How Come? Don't you want to live and don't you want to play ball if you do live? And didn't Dufresne tell you that I wanted Mrs. Ferrell to go with you to Boston and weren't you both supposed to see me here immediately at the close of the Montreal playoffs? How come?"

Branch Rickey, Jr., was a diabetic and that was the likely impetus behind the senior Rickey's empathetic interest in Charlie's condition. "Yes, my father had severe diabetes which began in his twenties and led to his early death in 1961 at the age of 47," emailed Branch Rickey, III — currently the president of the Pacific Coast League — in 2004. "Annually he would

CLASS OF SERVICE		SYMBOLS
This is a full-rate Telegram or Cable-gram unless its deferred character is indicated by a suitable symbol above or preceding the address.		DL = Day Letter NL = Night Letter LC = Deferred Cable NLT = Cable Night Letter Ship Radiogram

WESTERN UNION

1201

(34)..

A. N. WILLIAMS
PRESIDENT

The filing time shown in the ... YA55 ... grams and day letters is STANDARD TIME at point of origin. Time of receipt is STANDARD TIME at point of destination

Y.NC22 LG PD=WUX BROOKLYN NY 12 1111A

CHARLES FERRELL=

2611 CHAPEL HILL RD DURHAM NCAR=   1945 OCT 12 PM 12 2

JUST RETURNED TODAY TO BROOKLYN TO FIND THAT YOU HAVE NOT
BEEN IN BOSTON AND THAT YOU ARE NOT NOW IN BOSTON AND THAT
DOCTOR JOSLYN DOES NOT KNOW WHERE YOU ARE. HOW COME?
DONT YOU WANT TO LIVE AND DONT YOU WANT TO PLAY BALL IF YOU
DO LIVE? AND DIDN'T DUFRESNE TELL YOU THAT I WANTED MRS.
FERRELL TO GO WITH YOU TO BOSTON AND WEREN'T YOU BOTH
SUPPOSED TO SEE ME HERE IMMEDIATELY AT THE CLOSE OF THE
MONTREAL PLAYOFF? HOW COME?=

BRANCH RICKEY.

CLASS OF SERVICE	
This is a full-rate Telegram or Cable-gram unless its deferred character is indicated by a suitable symbol above or preceding the address.	

WESTERN UNION

A. N. WILLIAMS
PRESIDENT

he filing time shown in the date line on telegrams and day letters is STANDARD TIME at point of origin. Time of receipt

ICFAT 18 LG PD=WUX BROOKLYN NY 9 315P

CHARLES FERRELL=

BURLINGTON BASEBALL CLUB

BRODIE HOOOD. AL REHM HAROLD ROETTGER =J8CY
SITTING IN THE OFFICER HERE WISH TO ADD OUR
CONGRAULATIONS TO OTHERS ON YOUR IMPENDING MARRIAGE
TONIGHT=

Telegrams to Charlie Ferrell from Branch Rickey, Sr. and Jr. (Eleanor Ferrell Hoover).

go to the Joslyn Clinic for a check-up. So, if the Joslyn Clinic was specified by my grandfather to Charlie it was well after my father had been receiving treatment there for many years."

On July 9, 1945, the day Charlie was married in Durham, the Burlington-Durham game went 15 innings. Immediately after the game ended in

Burlington, Charlie and his teammates sped off for Durham — 30 miles away — arriving 15 minutes before the wedding. A congratulatory telegram was waiting from Branch Rickey, Jr.

Ferrell blew out his arm in Montreal's spring camp in 1946 and required surgery to remove bone chips from his elbow. The operation was performed by Dr. Robert Hyland, the same physician who had examined Wes in 1933. Charlie was sent home to rest before reporting to Brooklyn's affiliate at Cambridge, Maryland, in the Eastern Shore League. In mid-season he was summoned to Branch Rickey's office in Brooklyn, conferring five hours with him before leaving for Montreal, where Ferrell spent the remainder of the year as third-string catcher and pinch-hitter. He batted once that fall in the Junior World Series against Louisville.

That Charlie had potential cannot be denied. A newspaper clipping — one that mentions Carl Furillo, Gene Mauch and Gil Hodges — found in his scrapbook datelined April 6 from Mobile, Alabama (presumably 1946) reads, "Charlie Ferrell, who perhaps is the finest prospect of them all, but at present handicapped by a chronic illness."

Charlie also had a front-row seat for an incredible piece of baseball history, for he was a teammate of Jackie Robinson's at Montreal. "Charlie was high in his praise for the Montreal club," reads another unidentified scrapbook clipping, "and especially Jackie Robinson, the Royals' Negro second baseman. 'Jackie is the best bunter I have ever seen,' Charlie said, 'and it wouldn't surprise me at all to see him stay with Brooklyn next season.'"

Ferrell was in the Brooklyn/Montreal spring camp in 1947, belting a home run on March 5 when he and Robinson played for Montreal against the Cuban Winter League All-Stars in Havana. Ben Chapman gave Charlie a look in the Phillies' camp later that spring and on April 11, when Philadelphia beat the Washington Senators in an exhibition game in Greensboro, Rick Ferrell caught for Washington and Charlie Ferrell handled Dutch Leonard for the Phils.

"A highly capable receiver with a deadly accurate throwing arm and a strong hitter," wrote the Durham paper shortly after Charlie's death in 1966. "Ferrell signed with the Dodgers and was one step away from the majors when hit by diabetes at Montreal. Slowed by his illness, he played for several Carolina League clubs, including the Bulls, before being forced to quit baseball at an age when he should have been blasting major league pitching." Bones McKinney, one of Charlie's pallbearers, said, "If he hadn't been handicapped by his illness, he would have been one of the greatest catchers of all time."

Bev Ferrell passed away in 1998. Deta Ferrell — his widow — lives in

Virginia and graciously provided material on her husband and brother-in-law for this book. "I wish you could have known the Grover Ferrells," she wrote, "especially Grover and Charlie. They were gifted narrators. Charlie never ran out of baseball stories."

* * *

There were three catchers named Ferrell in War Memorial Stadium in Greensboro when Washington played the Phillies on April 11, 1947, for "Big Rick" Ferrell made arrangements for his nephew, "Little Rick," to catch batting practice.

"I wanted to see Rick catch," said Big Rick. "I've never seen him play a game of baseball and I saw him play basketball only once. So this time I told him I wanted him to catch batting practice, and I'll see what he can do. He's young, and it will be a good experience for him."

James R. "Little Rick" Ferrell is now in his seventies and lives in Greensboro. "I signed a contract with the St. Louis Cardinals at the end of 1949 season," he wrote. "I should have signed before that but some of the scouts shied away from me, not wanting to infringe on [Uncle] George. Mace Brown wanted me for the Red Sox organization. George didn't want to take it upon himself to sign me and give me a bonus since I was family. So I went to St. Louis for a couple of weeks to work out there and was signed for a $6,500 bonus.

"Little Rick" Ferrell playing for the Fort Jackson team while in the U.S. Army (James R. "Little Rick" Ferrell).

"I played American Legion and high school ball and then at Guilford College. In the summer of 1948 I played in a very strong semi-pro league on the eastern coast of North Carolina called the Albemarle League. The teams were made up mostly of college players with a mix of pro players. My senior year in high school I played for a semi-pro team in Asheboro sponsored by Lucus Mills that played in the National semi-pro tournament in Wichita, Kansas.

"In 1952 I went into the army and played baseball at Fort Jackson, South Carolina. We had great talent, probably equal to a Triple-A club, with such players as Roger Craig, Frank

House, Haywood Sullivan, Bubba Phillips, Ted Tappe, Joe Landrum, Curt Barclay, Faye Throneberry, Joe Cunningham and other that don't come to mind now.

"After I signed with St. Louis, I played half of my rookie year at Goldsboro, North Carolina and half at Lynchburg, Virginia, in the Piedmont league. Joe Cunningham played first base and Ray Jablonski third base. Whitey Kurowski was our manager.

"After coming out of the service I went to spring training in 1955 with Charlotte, which was a Washington farm club. I was to get a bonus if I made the opening day roster and then was cut one day before. I played the last half of the season with the Greensboro Red Sox. That is about the extent of my years in organized baseball. I should have gone a lot further than I did. I don't know exactly why, unless I was lost in the fold or a lot was my own fault. I do know I had the ability to go higher than I did."

Rick recalls his uncles fondly. "In the early 40s Wes managed Leaksville in the Bi-State League and commuted from his home in Guilford College. One day he picked me up at my home and we went to Leaksville, which was about 35 miles away. I sat in the dugout during the game. The umpiring was bad and by the fourth inning Wes had already broken several bats on the steps. Finally in the fifth inning Wes jumps out of the dugout and waves the entire team to come in. Wes told them all to get dressed. We got in his car and went home with Wes still in his baseball uniform, cussing all the way. He never stopped being a competitor."

Wes was an accomplished golfer who counted the 1943 North Carolina amateur title among his many tournament wins. The National Baseball Golf Tournament was an annual event held each winter in Florida. Play began in the mid-thirties, with the "Powel Crosley, Jr. Trophy" awarded to the winner. Wes won permanent possession of the trophy with his fourth victory in 1940. He maintained friendships with many of the top PGA players of the time; Sam Snead being a frequent golf and fishing partner. George Jacobus, a former PGA president and the longtime director of the baseball player's tournament, said in 1960 that Wes "has the soundest game of any ballplayer" he had observed.

Wes and Rick both brought the same intensity to the links as they did to the diamond, and sportswriters joked about both the distance and accuracy the brothers achieved when firing clubs after errant shots. One story that occurred during the winter of 1936 was often retold whenever a writer needed to fill space. After Wes flubbed a drive during a tight match with Paul Waner, he sat down and started banging his head against a stone distance marker. Suddenly he stopped, looked up at Waner and said, "Paul, if I kill myself, you'll find what I owe you in my hip pocket."

Left to Right
Front Row
Soujas, Munday, Bierschenk, Cave, Ferrell, Baxter, Kennedy, Martin
Back Row
Ballard, Leckrone, Malony, McCall, Thomson, Long, Drews, Williams, Fowler

Little Rick recalls first finding evidence of his uncle's golfing exploits while exploring as a ten year old. "Wes played a lot of golf and was a very good player. One day I was in the basement of the old farmhouse. I saw about 8–10 old fruit baskets with broken clubs jammed in them. I always knew he had a temper on the course, but after seeing this I knew. The summer before Wes died he was visiting this country club I belong to and was in bedroom slippers, suffering from an attack of gout. A friend of mine spotted Wes in the parking lot and asked him to fill out a foursome. My friend didn't know Wes, who told him he would have to play in the slippers because of his feet. Wes went out and shot a 72 — one over par."

Little Rick received a letter from Rick Ferrell in September 1994. The former all-star, just shy of his 89th birthday, was in declining health but still in tune with his game. "I think the strike will be settled for the playoffs and World Series," he wrote. "Both sides are quite firm. However, the owners have never won a point. They usually cave in. The salary cap is a joke. Basketball and football have it and they don't like it. Something has to be done about the salaries, though. They are out of line. I don't blame the players."

* * *

The New York Yankees purchased George Ferrell's contract from Rocky Mount at the end of the 1942 season and assigned him to their International League club in Newark. George, with the uncertainty of the war and being too old for the military draft, was a good insurance policy for the parent club.

Though he was 38 years old, Ferrell was still pulverizing the old pellet, coming off two straight RBI titles in the Bi-State League. Bobby Thomson — a decade before his famous home run — played for George at Rocky Mount in 1942. When asked for his recollections, Thomson recalled long, cold rides in an old bus with broken windows. "I was just an immature, scared kid," he wrote. "I respected George as a leader and he impressed me with his hitting."

Ferrell questioned the sale for, while under contract as a player-manager but being transferred only as a player, he was taking a forced pay cut. When Rick Ferrell heard the story, he urged his brother to file a complaint with Judge Bramham, the minor league commissioner, arguing that the managerial aspect of the contract couldn't be ignored. Bramham agreed with George and declared him a free agent.

Several weeks later, the chairman of the Executive Commission of the

The 1942 Rocky Mount team in the Bi-State League. Bobby Thomson is standing behind manager George S. Ferrell (George W. Ferrell).

National Association of Professional
Baseball Players, Frank Shaughnessy—
who just happened to be the president
of the International League—overruled
Bramham and reinstated George as
Newark/New York chattel.

George appealed to Judge Landis
and traveled to Chicago to argue his
case. He won despite it being George
Weiss—historically recognized as one

Left: George Ferrell managed Lynchburg
in the Piedmont League in 1944. His son,
George Wesley, was the batboy. *Below:*
Jimmy Foxx instructs young George Fer-
rell in 1944. (Both photographs courtesy
George W. Ferrell.)

Working the farm during World War II. From left are George W. (background), George S., Wes and Slats Ferrell. At far right is Everett Johnston, Wes' brother-in-law (George W. Ferrell).

baseball's greatest executives— representing the Yankees. Once free, Ferrell signed to manage and play for Trenton in the Inter-State League.

✶ ✶ ✶

Wes was also having issues with the National Association. The former pitcher won both the home run crown (31) and the batting title (.361) as player-manager of the Virginia League's Lynchburg team in 1942. He was named manager of the All-Star squad at the end of the season, equivalent to "manager of the year" today. Being a major-league celebrity, Wes was a big gate attraction. He happily did his part to put on a show and Lynchburg drew more than 73,000 fans, about twice the population of the city. If he lost a fly ball due to the poor lighting, he returned to the outfield and hung a kerosene lamp on the fence. If he dropped a ball, he appeared toting a bushel basket to his position. Wes had always been able to laugh at himself and the crowds loved his antics. Of course he was still capable of smashing his bat to pieces if he struck out.

With manpower short because of the war, Wes played whatever position the team required, moving from the outfield to second base at mid-season. Lynchburg had but ten available men in a playoff game on September 13 and — due to injury and illness— all three outfield positions were manned by pitchers. When an umpire tossed Lynchburg's shortstop from the game, the only bench player Wes had to replace him with was a left-handed pitcher. Ferrell refused, saying it would make a travesty of the game. The umpire ordered the contest to resume but Wes stood firm. He was suspended on the spot but league president C. R. Williams allowed him to finish the playoffs. Not wanting to make a decision himself, Williams placed the issue in the hands of the National Association. A ruling was handed down in November, suspending Wes for the first 30 days of the 1943 season; a moot point since Ferrell was expected to be in the service by then. He appealed the suspension in January 1943.

When Wes signed to manage Lynchburg for 1946, *The Sporting News* reported the 1942 incident and erroneously, or at least misleadingly, stated that Ferrell had drawn a "suspension for an attack on an umpire."[11] When Wes died in 1976, this "umpire attack" was repeated in his obituary in *The Sporting News.*

The name of Wes Ferrell, wrote Pulitzer Prize winning sportswriter Walter "Red" Smith in 1945, "is good for a hundred stories because, when he was one of baseball's greatest pitchers, he was also one of the fiercest losers." Smith was certainly correct, but while Ferrell's greatness has been forgotten with the passage of time, the stories, often embellished, have not.

◆ 15 ◆

The Executive

The general manager of the Detroit Tigers gave a speech in Grand Rapids, Michigan, in January 1962. It was a routine talk given on the winter banquet circuit, but what he said — at least from a historical point of view — seems quite shocking. "We were pretty close to a deal with the Yankees in 1959," said Rick Ferrell. "We would have traded Frank Lary and Al Kaline for Mickey Mantle and Whitey Ford. There was a lot of discussion about the trade and it wasn't our club that finally backed down on the deal."[1]

George Weiss, GM of the fledgling New York Mets, but running the Yankees in 1959, was sought out by *The Sporting News* to confirm the story and while trying to downplay it, he agreed that discussions had been held. "But a deal such as Rick mentions never came close to being serious. Certainly we talked about all four players involved, and maybe Casey talked with their manager more seriously then I did, but you couldn't say we backed off a deal like that." The Yankees had always liked Kaline, and with Mantle having an off year (for him) coupled with concerns about Ford's arm, the deal seemed a real possibility. It would not have affected the 1959 race had it occurred, opined Weiss, but imagine how it would have changed 1961.[2]

* * *

The Ferrell Brothers were financially astute. Wes had done well in real estate in North Carolina and Florida, so his occasional forays into baseball over the next several decades as a minor league manager and player — he hit .425 to cop the Western Carolina League batting crown in 1948 — had more to do with was his compulsion for the game than it did monetary issues. George spent thirty years managing and scouting for the St. Louis Cardinals and the Detroit Tigers until he retired in 1975. Rick threw all of his energy into mastering the various administrative aspects of running a

Rick Ferrell when he was the general manager of the Tigers.

big league franchise; something, it seems, he had been preparing for his whole life.

"Most of the Nats call Rick Ferrell 'B.B'..." wrote the Washington *Post* in 1947, "because 'B.B.' stands for 'Big Brain,' an appellation Rick won when he was with the St. Louis Browns, who weren't fooling, especially in a baseball way." Ferrell took a coaching position with Washington and remained there through the 1949 season. While still active as a player he served as the club's player rep and was a strong advocate of the proposed pension fund. Writing in the Washington *Post and Times Herald* in 1959, columnist Bob Addie recalled that when Rick held a vote on the plan and ten players balked at the $250 initiation fee, the catcher offered to put up the money for each of the dissenters.

Rick shifted to Detroit at the start of the 1950 season where he and Ted Lyons ran the Tigers' pitching staff for several seasons. He also instructed the catchers, one being 20-year-old bonus baby Frank House. "I'm confident that Manager Red Rolfe and Rick Ferrell are going to show me a lot I never knew before," said House in spring training. In midseason, when by *The Sporting News* inquired how things were progressing, House replied with a thumbs-up. "Rick Ferrell is there — Ferrell, he's the coach Detroit hired to make a catcher out of House."

John McHale was then the Detroit farm director and a rising baseball exec. He was a Notre Dame graduate who played for the Tigers in the 1940s before advancing to various front office jobs, eventually becoming the GM at both Detroit and Milwaukee before accepting the job of chief administrator for baseball commissioner William Eckert in 1967. The following year, when virtually assured of the commissioner position himself, McHale withdrew from consideration to take the job as president and GM of the Montreal Expos.

"Rick was a dear friend," wrote McHale in 2002. "Jim Campbell, whom I hired, and Rick got together at meetings, World Series, All-Star

Tinker Field, Orlando, Florida: Washington Senators catchers get a few point-
ers from coach Rick Ferrell during start of spring training. Left to right: Jake
Early, Al Evans, Leonard Okrie and Coach Ferrell.

Games and Spring Training. He came to the Tigers as coach for Red Rolfe.
It was a very good staff which included Ted Lyons and Charlie Keller. When
Red was fired, I hired Rick to scout the Carolinas and do some cross checking of outstanding prospects. This brought Rick and Jim together. They
became fast friends and mutually dependent on each other.

"Rick was an excellent scout. His judgment on talent as well as sup-
porting people turned out to be very valuable to Jim. I don't think Jim ever
made a move on player and personnel without consulting Rick. As you
may recall, Bill DeWitt came to Detroit as President, 1959-1960. I think
he made the Colavito-Kuenn trade.

"Rick was involved in several good Tiger deals after that. (Norm)
Cash for Demeter; McLain to Washington for three players, including Joe
Coleman, and free agent signings of Jack Morris, Willie Horton, Bill Freehan and several others. Sparky Anderson was also a product of his encouragement to Jim."

Rick scouted college and military teams as well as the Carolinas in
the mid–1950s. The first player he signed that advanced to the big club was

pitcher John Tsitouris. Pitcher Hal Woodeshick was drafted out of the New York Giants chain based on Ferrell's recommendation.

Ferrell's stature in the Detroit chain climbed along with his mentor's and when McHale became director of player personnel in 1956, Rick's territory expanded from the Carolinas to the Southeastern states. McHale called Rick north the next year to cover Big Ten college baseball, and George Ferrell, after almost a decade scouting for the St. Louis Cardinals, moved over to Detroit. "George," said McHale "will work with his brother, Rick, who had become one of the best scouts in the major leagues. Rick did a good job last summer looking at the major league clubs for us. He would have a report for (Jack) Tighe before each series and the information he gathered also went into our file at Briggs Stadium."[3]

* * *

The eighth Ferrell to play professionally was George Wesley Ferrell who signed with the Tigers in 1958. "When I was 16 years old," the younger George recalls, "Walter Rabb, the baseball coach at UNC at Chapel Hill, came to see me play at Guilford High School. He was the first scout to start following me. That was the year Dad, Wes and Rick started really training me to become a professional." Using training methods that were progressive of the then accepted standards, young George hit off a stationary batting tee on the advice of family friend Ted Williams. He also worked with a weight training program established by his father and uncles.

The elder Ferrells were concerned about expectations that would be placed on the youngster because of his name. "Wes told me to expect people to compare me to him and Dad. I had experienced that in high school and at Oak Ridge, but Wes was afraid it would be much worse when I went to the pros. He was concerned that I might overreact and hit someone. He told me over and over, 'You have to be smart and not let anyone get under your skin. Don't ever hit anybody and give them a chance to sue you. You've got to have class for people to respect you.' Rick and Dad agreed with Wes but they were preparing me for the rougher side of baseball that might confront me."

Young George traveled alone to Detroit for a tryout in the summer of 1958. "I was told Dad had to go to Mississippi to scout a prospect. Wes said he couldn't go with me. Rick said he had to be in California on business. That was their way of seeing how I would stand up under the pressure of being with some of the greatest players of the era.

"The first day Ed Katalinas asked me to come to the park at 3:00 PM, two hours before batting practice began. He and Jim Campbell took me to a box seat near the Tigers' dugout. The stadium was empty except for

George W. Ferrell in 1958 as a Tigers minor league outfielder (George W. Ferrell).

a few people who worked there. Mr. Katalinas said he wanted me to sit alone and just look at the stadium and get used to it. He said that being there for the first time could be intimidating.

"After about an hour, a man came to me and said, 'You're Wes Ferrell's nephew, huh? He was the meanest SOB I ever saw, but I loved to watch him pitch.' I never did find out who the man was. Finally Katalinas came and took me to the dressing room. Suddenly I was with Al Kaline, Billy Martin, Harvey Kuenn and all the rest. At that point I understood what Dad meant when he said, 'When you cross the foul line we cannot help you.'

"Wes told me that that if you hit the ball hard enough into the upper deck the wooden seats would shatter like kindling. The Yankees were in Detroit the last few days I was there. My turn to take batting practice came and Mickey Mantle was standing behind me. Al Kaline was on the other side of the cage, Enos Slaughter was about 15 feet behind me and John McHale, the Detroit VP, was standing behind the cage. I hit three or four balls in the upper deck that shattered seats and one on the roof of the stadium. Everybody started hollering approval at me. I don't think my feet touched the ground the rest of the time I was in Detroit.

"Later, when I was warming up with Ozzie Virgil, I heard talking behind me. It was Rick being interviewed by Pee Wee Reese for TV. He had flown in to see how I was doing, but he didn't speak to me or let me see him. A few days later, back in Greensboro, he came out to the house and by phone he and Dad (still in Mississippi) negotiated my contract with John McHale. Rick also handled negotiations with several companies for my endorsements."

Young George was in the Detroit's "Tigertown" spring camp for rookies in 1959 along with such players as Mickey Lolich, Fred Gladding, Phil Regan and Dick McAuliffe. On April 15, he ran into a wall while playing left field in Henley Field and was knocked unconscious. "I hit the corner of the support column of the concrete wall," he recalls. "The entire left side of my body hit the corner with the left side of my face receiving the most serious injury. I had a brain concussion, damage to my left eye, left shoulder, left hip and foot. I was unconscious for 4½ hours. When I woke up Dad and Johnny Pesky were sitting by my bed. Dad would not tell my mother or Wes about the accident in an effort to keep them from worrying."

When his injuries were slow in responding, Rick had his nephew flown to Detroit for addition medical evaluation. One physician told George that had he not been wearing unbreakable glasses he likely would have lost his left eye. Johnny Pesky later saw a red spot on George's eye and recalled that he had received a similar injury when Ted Williams' elbow hit him while they were exiting a dugout. "I don't know if Johnny was trying to make me feel better or not," said Ferrell, "but my spot dissolved and I was happy. Johnny was a good friend to me. He was a patient manager and excellent coach."

Soon after returning to the field that summer, George was hit with a pitch that careened off his left arm and into his face. Several of his teeth where shattered, requiring several hours of dental surgery, and he had to wear an arm cast for several weeks. "With so many injuries in such a short period, my reflexes were not good enough to get out of the way. I kept trying to play and everybody hoped that I would recover, but I did not despite Rick, Wes and Dad's best efforts. They gave me their support and love until they died. No one could have done more for their family than Rick, Wes and Dad."

* * *

Rick Ferrell worked each spring with the Detroit's young catchers. It also wasn't unusual for him to consult on catching issues with other major-league franchises. In 1957, manager Fred

Eddie Waynick — George S. Ferrell's grandson — became the ninth member of the family to play professional ball. He hit 12 home runs in 289 at bats for Winston-Salem in the Carolina League in 1982 (Eddie Waynick).

Hutchinson and GM Frank Lane of the St. Louis Cardinals brought him into their spring camp to instruct their catchers— Hal Smith, Gene Green and Hobie Landrith — on handling knuckleball hurlers Hoyt Wilhelm, Jim Davis and Murry Dickson. "He advised us not to crouch or squat as low when catching knuckleball pitches as we would for others," said Landrith. "He told us that from a half-standing position, I'd guess you call it, we could move laterally better and also drop on a knuckler falling off the table."[4]

By August 1958, McHale had been the GM of the Tigers for nearly 16 months and had his team in place with Jim Campbell as business manager and Ferrell director of minor-league personnel. When McHale resigned in January 1959 to take over the Milwaukee Braves, he nominated Ferrell as interim GM. Asked if Rick was in the running for position on the permanent basis, board chairman John Fetzer responded with "Anything is possible. We will weigh this thing carefully. We will not hurry the matter. The Detroit club is fortunate to have a man like Ferrell in the organization to step into an emergency situation like this." When Ferrell was given the permanent title in April, Fetzer said "Rick has one of the soundest baseball minds I've ever known."

The three-man team that would operate the Detroit club for the next twenty-odd years was shaping up. Fetzer was/would be top man and he believed strongly in the chain of command theory. Ferrell was in charge of the players and farm system, and Jim Campbell directed the business end. *The Sporting News*, noting that players like Hank Greenberg, Ralph Kiner and Marty Marion were holding similar major- or minor-league positions, was quick to praise Rick's elevation to GM. "These men, in the executive branch, know something that no one else could know — the problems of the players because they, too, have worn the uniform. Ferrell and the Tigers both are to be congratulated on the advancement of Rick. The game needs more officials who combine administrative ability with first-hand knowledge of conditions on the playing field."[5]

Though Fetzer had been a member of a multi-partner group that purchased the Tigers in 1956, he was unable to gain complete control of the team until 1961 and in the intervening time, confusion often reigned at Briggs Stadium. The Tigers had not been a factor in an American League pennant race since 1950, and pressure was on to rejuvenate baseball interest in the Motor City. In other words, Fetzer and Ferrell were under the gun. "There were so many owners," Jim Campbell later recalled of the situation, "it looked like most just wanted to be around a major-league team. They wanted to make decisions about things they really knew nothing about."[6] Fetzer was trying to sort through things as well. "None of us were prepared for the problems we faced," he said. "It seemed like every little move we made was scrutinized to the finest details by the press. I didn't mind the scrutiny. But some of the guys writing the stories knew a whole lot less than anyone in our group. And none of us professed to be baseball experts."[7]

The Detroit owners' group caved in under the pressure and hired Bill DeWitt as president late in 1959, giving him absolute power. DeWitt, a former owner of the Browns and assistant GM of the Yankees, was a marquee name in baseball administration, but he alienated most of the organization with his radical restructuring plans and Fetzer quickly realized the tactical blunder he had made in hiring him.

Ferrell, though initially retaining the title of general manager, was in a lame-duck situation. He kept on plugging through the turmoil, scouting the Cuban and Puerto Rican Winter leagues and hiring the organization's first full time Caribbean scouts— his old Washington catching partner Mike Guerra for Cuba and Babel Perez for Puerto Rico. He worked on expanding the Tigers' minor league chain, signing a working agreement with Victoria, Texas. "There may be some GM duties that I will handle," said DeWitt in November 1959. "However, Rick will be in charge of all players from top to bottom." Ferrell also handled contract negotiations. "Rick's doing all right," said DeWitt. "He knows the ballplayer's language when it comes to contracts. After all, Rick signed 18 contracts himself as a player."

DeWitt abolished the GM title in April 1960 and Rick became "special assistant to the president." When Fetzer assumed a controlling interest in the club that fall, he quickly paid off the two remaining years on DeWitt's contract — at $45,000 per year — and placed Ferrell back in the role of GM; although the designation was not being used. Fetzer was then club president, owning 100,000 of the team's 100,400 stock shares. Three men — Ferrell, Campbell and Harry Sisson — held vice-president designations and split the other 400 shares.[8]

Now in total control of the Tigers, the Fetzer-Ferrell-Campbell triumvirate headed to California where they spent several unsuccessful weeks trying to sign Casey Stengel as their new manager. "I feel more hurt about turning the Detroit people down than they do," The Old Professor said. "The offered me a wonderful opportunity. I'll probably regret the day I turned them down, but I just can't make a decision at his time.

"Detroit has some outstanding players like Colavito and Kaline and I honestly feel they could push the club up — and me with them. And Detroit is a wonderful city. It draws amazing crowds. Fetzer and Rick Ferrell were 100 per cent behind me. I'm sorry I couldn't take the job at this time."[9]

The Tigers had one of the finest years in the franchise's history in 1961, winning 101 games but falling short of the mighty New York juggernaut. Kaline, Colavito and Cash had career years, and the pitching staff had a pair of aces in Lary and Jim Bunning. Ferrell made several alterations in the outfield fences before both the 1960 and 1961 seasons. "The right-field fence was taken down for the football season," said Rick. "We may leave it down. We got to thinking how easy it is to hit home runs in the Yankee Stadium. Roger Maris has no more power than Norm Cash. The difference is that Cash has a little farther distance to swing at in his home park. We'd like to even things up a bit."[10]

A photograph of Rick Ferrell and Bill Freehan appeared in an April 1962 issue of The Sporting News. "I can't think of anything I don't like about him." Rick said of the Tigers' young catching prospect. "He's got desire and size and loves to play." Ferrell had often watched Freehan playing college ball at Michigan. "You know, you made that tag the wrong way," Rick told the young catcher after a game. "I know it, but it'll never happen again," agreed Freehan. "He was right," said Rick in spring training camp. "I've never seen him tag a runner that way again."

Detroit, hampered by Kaline's broken collarbone and Lary's elbow tendonitis, finished fourth in 1962 and rumors began late in the season that Ferrell's job as GM was on the line. "Rick is the fall guy for a lot of things that have happened to the Tigers," said Fetzer. "Ferrell is a sound baseball man and is doing a good job in Detroit. Nobody's taking over for him."[11] Several months later Fetzer restructured his command staff, making Campbell the GM and Rick "VP in the area of evaluating talent." Said Campbell, "Rick is the best man at this job of anyone I know." *The Sporting News* referred to Ferrell as "executive scout, in charge of evaluating talent on his and other teams." However the titles were dished out, Detroit's executive team was harmonious, and Rick was still handling trades in 1963 when both Gabe Paul of Cleveland and DeWitt, then with the Cincinnati Reds, approached Detroit trying to obtain Colavito.

The Campbell-Ferrell team was proud of their trading prowess, citing the acquisition of Earl Wilson as one of their best. They were also quick to acknowledge mistakes. "I saw Jim Bunning pitch in Atlanta recently," said Rick late in 1966, "and one paper called him Detroit's biggest mistake since the Edsel." Ferrell referred to the Tito Francona for Larry Doby trade in 1959 as one of his biggest blunders.

While the payoff was long in coming, Rick's forty years of hard work culminated in a World's Championship in 1968. Legendary scribe Bob Broeg penned an article titled "Tomorrow Finally Came for Tigers and Rick Ferrell" that appeared in the St. Louis *Post-Dispatch* on September 29, 1968.

"I'd been nipped at the wire so many times," Rick said citing 1945, 1950, 1961 and 1967 as examples. Ferrell had been scouting the Cardinals for several weeks in preparation for the Series and Broeg put one big question before him. "About Bob Gibson and Denny McLain?" The former catcher, who usually named Grove and Wes as they two best pitchers he handled, was too experienced to step into that trap. "Gibson has more velocity on his fast ball, McLain more variety of pitches. He has a better curve, but Gibson throws a quick slider. They're both strong, good competitors who don't scare and they've got good control. It's silly to say anyone is better than Gibson, and anyone who wins more than 30 games (McLain) is a great pitcher."

Jim Campbell was the general manager of the '68 Tigers, but Ferrell's contribution should not be overlooked. "John Fetzer knows quite a bit about baseball and even more about how to manipulate a front-office team," wrote *The Sporting News* immediately after the World Series. "When Fetzer gained control interest of the Tigers, Rick Ferrell was general manager and Jim Campbell was farm director. Fetzer could sense that Campbell had the aggressive nature needed for a top job and he noted that Ferrell had remarkable baseball instincts and savvy. So he moved Campbell into the endless details of the general manager's office. And he kept Ferrell moving around in baseball as vice-president. Together, they are an effective combination."[12]

Campbell and Ferrell remained at the helm through the 1970s and into the 1980s. Rick continued his scouting and evaluating duties, providing essential support and data to managers like Billy Martin, Ralph Houk and Sparky Anderson.

"I spent five years with Rick when I managed Detroit," wrote Houk in 2002. "He was a great baseball man. He gave me valuable information on players in the league — sometimes as an advance scout. He was vice-president when I was there and I respected him very much. Rick Ferrell is in the Hall of Fame, which he deserves."

Jim Leyland — manager of the 1997 World Champion Florida Marlins — began his career as a catcher in the Detroit chain in 1964, advancing steadily through their system as a manager before taking command of the Pittsburgh Pirates in 1986.

"I was very familiar with Rick Ferrell during my days with the Detroit Tigers," wrote Leyland, also in 2002 when asked to comment for this book. "Rick was a throwback to the old school of baseball and just a wonderful man. He was very articulate and also very brilliant. He assisted as vice president of the Tigers, helping GM Jim Campbell during my minor league days with the organization. Rick was the type of person that when he talked about baseball, everybody listened. I think he was really a shy person and you had to get to know him before he felt comfortable around you.

"I spent several occasions talking baseball with Rick, ranging from handling contract negotiations to baseball strategy. Of course I enjoyed the latter much more. He had a great feel for selecting talent and a tremendous awareness of what it took to be a successful player on a winning team in the big leagues.

"Respected by everyone in the game, my career was certainly affected by having been around Rick. It was an honor to have known him and share baseball thoughts on several occasions."

Bill Hass, a sportswriter for the Greensboro *Daily News*, checked in with Rick in 1981. "I do some scouting and checking out of ball players we're interested in," Ferrell said over the phone. "I look at free agents (high school and college players) that are going to cost a lot of money and double-check to see if they're worth what they're asking. I also scout other teams in the American and National leagues to see players we might be interested in. Then I act as a consultant on trades to Manager Sparky Anderson and General Manager Jim Campbell. I just returned from Pittsburgh where I looked over some players in the National League."

Rick Ferrell never went away, he just faded away. "I guess you should, at my age," he said when asked about retirement. "But I enjoy being close to the club. There's not a lot of pressure in my job and it's not too strenuous. They want me here, so I expect to keep going."

Maureen Ferrell — Rick's oldest daughter — recalls this period as a very happy and content time for her father. "When I walked through the commissary in Tiger Stadium with him I would be so proud," she wrote. "He'd have a nice word for everyone, and everyone from vendors to executives responded to him. He wasn't emotional but was always there and someone you could depend on, and a person people instinctively liked. He just had a great manner about him, sincere and extremely likeable. Although outwardly he was mild and quiet, returnees at the Hall of Fame weekends would mention how competitive he was, and feisty! Those were traits I'd never associated with him since his career was nearly over when I was born."

Rick passed away in 1995. He rests in the family plot in the New Garden Cemetery in Greensboro, along with his parents and brothers Wes (who died in 1976), George (1987), Kermit (1962) and Ewell (1933).

Rick moved his family to Michigan in 1959. A memorial service was held there shortly after his death. "He was a great gentleman and a man of great integrity," said Al Kaline. "He treated everybody the same, whether they were the president of the club or someone working in the concession stand. He spent a lot of years with the Tigers and was very loyal to them. He embodied the spirit of Tiger baseball."

Jim Campbell was also in attendance. "He's one of the greatest friends I ever had," said the former general manager. "In all the years I was with the Tigers, I don't think I ever made a deal without discussing it with Rick. We didn't always agree and if there was a disagreement, Rick usually won.

"When you talk about a guy like Rick, you don't have to search too hard for find nice things to say. He was just a helluva guy."

Epilogue

While this book has attempted to chronicle the baseball history of the Ferrell family, it is really the story of three brothers.

George was the eldest of the trio and the local hero. Before television made the game visual to the nation, Washington, D.C., several hundred miles away, was the closest place for the Carolina folk to see a big league game, and in an era when it wasn't unusual that the first major-league game many players saw was the one they debuted in, it's doubtful that many of the Ferrell kindred and neighbors actually witnessed Wes and Rick in big time action. Being in professional baseball for fifty years, George played, managed and scouted for, with and against the same people that his brothers did, and his stature in Virginia and the Carolinas, especially the Piedmont League, cannot and should not be overlooked.

Rick was the cerebral baseball brother. He devoted sixty years to the game in such capacities as college player, eight-time major league all-star, coach, scout and major league executive. The Veteran's Committee, in what should be regarded as one of their finest moments, elected him to the Hall of Fame in 1984. From John McGraw and Connie Mack to Sparky Anderson and Jim Leyland, there has been nothing but praise for Rick Ferrell.

"This is the ultimate a player can achieve," Rick said regarding his induction. "I always enjoyed trips to Cooperstown, but this trip tops them all. To tell you the truth, I never knew whether I'd make it or not. I was never disappointed when I was passed over and I was never discouraged either. I kept saying 'Maybe next year.' And finally next year came."

His younger brother was never far away in Rick's thoughts, and the former catcher loved to regale listeners with stories about his brother's hitting and pitching feats. "There wasn't a single thing on the baseball diamond that Wes couldn't do," he was fond of saying. "Wes and I used to talk about maybe someday making it to the Hall of Fame, and we talked

273

Rick Ferrell at Tiger Stadium in the late 1980s. He never left the game (Maureen Ferrell).

about how wonderful it would be to get there together. He had great statistics and someday hopefully he will be voted into the Hall of Fame, too. But we wanted to make it together."

Wes was the natural. He was as talented as anyone who ever set foot on a baseball diamond and as good as any pitcher who ever threw a ball.

The only thing that separated him from the upper rank was the duration of his greatness. Take your pick for the best right-handed pitcher of all time, be it Young, Johnson, Alexander, Feller, Gibson, Seaver, Clemens or Maddux. Maybe it was Christy Mathewson — the legend that observers of the day, including managers like

Top: Wes (second from left) at an old-timer's game. Ferrell is wearing a Cleveland uniform that was last worn in 1969. Bob Feller (third from right) is wearing a Cleveland uniform that was first used in 1970 (Gwenlo Ferrell Gore). *Right:* Wes in the den of his Guilford home in 1962 (Wes Ferrell, Jr.).

Huggins, Mack and McCarthy, likened Wes to—who was the greatest. Whoever it was, they had nothing on Ferrell but longevity.

Honus Wagner, writing in the *Saturday Evening Post* in 1940 about sore arms, began his article using the former ace as his example, saying, "Once a pitcher gets a sore arm, there's nothing he won't do to try and get it repaired. Wes Ferrell, who came a cropper when he should have been tops...."[1]

As time passes and players fade away, statistics are all that remain to measure baseball greatness, but mere numbers will never capture the Ferrell fortitude. Cooperstown has never called Wes' name, and without him the institution lacks a glowing star. How can a man who was recognized by his peers as having both the ability to pitch like Matty and hit like the Babe not be enshrined in the Hall of Fame?

The last words belong fittingly to Ferrell—a man who never conceded an inch in any competitive endeavor—for it was these words he said to historian Donald Honig in *Baseball When the Grass Was Real* that inspired this book.

"I played against a lot of great stars," Wes said. "You name 'em. Ruth, Gehrig, Greenberg, Gehringer, Simmons, Foxx, Grove, DiMaggio, Cochrane, Feller. I saw them all. And they saw me. You bet they did."

Appendix

Ferrell, Richard Benjamin (Rick)

Born, October 12, 1905, at Durham, North Carolina. Died, July 27, 1995, at Bloomfield Hills, Michigan. Batted right. Threw right. Height, 5' 10". Weight, 170. Brother of pro baseball players George and Wes Ferrell. Elected to Baseball Hall of Fame, 1984.

Year	Club	League	Pos	G	AB	R	H	TB	2B	3B	HR	RBI	SB	PCT
1926	Kinston	Virginia	C	64	192	24	51	63	6	0	2	20	1	.266
	Columbus	American Association	C	5	14	4	4	5	1	0	0		0	.286
1927	Columbus	American Association	C	104	345	42	86	114	14	4	2	44	2	.249
1928	Columbus	American Association	C	126	339	51	113	160	31	5	2	65	4	.333
1929	St. Louis	American	C	64	144	21	33	41	6	1	0	20	1	.229
1930	St. Louis	American	C	101	314	43	84	113	18	4	1	41	1	.268
1931	St. Louis	American	C	117	386	47	118	165	30	4	3	57	2	.306
1932	St. Louis	American	C	126	438	67	138	184	30	5	2	65	5	.315
1933	St. Louis/Boston	American	C	140	493	58	143	184	21	4	4	77	4	.290
1934	Boston	American	C	132	437	50	130	170	29	4	1	48	0	.297
1935	Boston	American	C	133	458	54	138	189	34	4	3	61	5	.301
1936	Boston	American	C	121	410	59	128	189	27	5	8	55	0	.312
1937	Boston/Washington	American	C	104	344	39	84	98	8	0	2	36	1	.244
1938	Washington	American	C	135	411	55	120	157	24	5	1	58	1	.292
1939	Washington	American	C	87	274	32	77	92	13	1	0	31	1	.281
1940	Washington	American	C	103	326	35	89	111	18	2	0	28	1	.273
1941	Washington/St. Louis	American	C	121	387	38	99	130	19	3	2	36	3	.256
1942	St. Louis	American	C	99	273	20	61	69	6	1	0	26	0	.223
1943	St. Louis	American	C	74	209	12	50	57	7	0	0	20	0	.239
1944	Washington	American	C	99	339	14	94	107	11	1	0	25	2	.277
1945	Washington	American	C	91	286	33	76	93	12	1	1	38	2	.266
1946	Washington	American	[Coach, did not play]											
1947	Washington	American	C	37	99	10	30	41	11	0	0	12	0	.303

Ferrell, Wesley Cheek (Wes)

Born, February 2, 1908, at Greensboro, North Carolina. Died, December 9, 1976, at Sarasota, Florida. Batted right. Threw right. Height, 6' 2". Weight, 195. Brother of pro baseball players George and Rick Ferrell.

PITCHER

Year	Club	League	G	CG	IP	W	L	PCT	H	BB	SO	R	ER	ERA
1927	Cleveland	American	1	0	1	0	0	.000	3	2	0	3	3	27.00
1928	Terre Haute	Three-I	33	23	240	20	8	.714	218	46	122	81	73	2.74
	Cleveland	American	2	1	16	0	2	.000	15	5	4	5	4	2.25
1929	Cleveland	American	43	18	243	21	10	.677	256	109	100	112	97	3.59
1930	Cleveland	American	43	25	297	25	13	.658	299	106	143	141	109	3.30
1931	Cleveland	American	40	27	276	22	12	.647	276	130	123	134	115	3.75
1932	Cleveland	American	38	28	288	23	13	.639	299	104	105	141	117	3.65
1933	Cleveland	American	28	16	201	11	12	.478	225	70	41	108	94	4.21
1934	Boston	American	26	17	181	14	5	.737	205	49	67	87	73	3.63
1935	Boston	American	41	31	322	25	14	.641	336	108	110	149	126	3.52
1936	Boston	American	39	28	301	20	15	.571	330	119	106	160	140	4.19
1937	Boston/Washington	American	37	26	281	14	19	.424	325	122	123	177	153	4.90
1938	Washington/New York	American	28	10	179	15	10	.600	245	86	43	144	125	6.28
1939	New York	American	3	1	19	1	2	.333	14	17	6	10	10	4.74
1940	Brooklyn	National	1	0	4	0	0	.000	4	4	4	3	3	6.75
1941	Boston	National	4	1	14	2	1	.667	13	9	10	8	8	5.14
	Leakesville-Spray-Draper	Bi-State	7	3	42	3	1	.750	56	9	26	31		
1942	Lynchburg (Manager)	Virginia	[Played 123 games at 2B and OF]											
1943/44	[Did not play]													
1945	Greensboro (Manager)	Carolina	[Played 8 games at 1B and OF]											
1946	Lynchburg (Manager)	Piedmont	2	0	7	0	2	.000	2	1	6	2		
1947	[Did not play]													
1948	Marion (Manager)	Western Carolina	3	0	8	1	1	.500	13	1	9	5		
1949	Greensboro	Carolina	[Played 20 games in the outfield]											
	Tampa	Florida International	1	0	1	0	0	.000						

Non-playing Manager: 1963 Rock Hill (Western Carolinas); 1965 Shelby (Western Carolinas).

Wes Ferrell, cont'd

BATTER

Year	Club	League	Pos	G	AB	R	H	TB	2B	3B	HR	RBI	SB	PCT
1927	Cleveland	American	P	1	0	0	0	0	0	0	0	0	0	.000
1928	Terre Haute	Three-I	P	49	105	12	28	37	1	1	2	19	1	.267
	Cleveland	American	P	2	4	0	1	1	0	0	0	0	0	.250
1929	Cleveland	American	P	47	93	12	22	36	5	3	1	12	1	.237
1930	Cleveland	American	P	53	118	19	35	49	8	3	0	14	1	.297
1931	Cleveland	American	P	48	116	24	37	72	6	1	9	30	0	.319
1932	Cleveland	American	P	55	128	14	31	46	5	2	2	18	0	.242
1933	Cleveland	American	P-OF	61	140	26	38	66	7	0	7	26	0	.271
1934	Boston	American	P	34	78	12	22	38	4	1	4	17	1	.282
1935	Boston	American	P-OF	75	150	25	52	80	5	1	7	32	0	.347
1936	Boston	American	P-OF	61	135	20	36	59	6	1	5	24	0	.267
1937	Boston/Washington	American	P-OF	71	139	14	39	49	7	0	1	25	0	.281
1938	Washington/New York	American	P	31	61	7	13	19	3	0	1	7	0	.213
1939	New York	American	P	3	8	0	1	2	1	0	0	1	0	.125
1940	Brooklyn	National	P	2	2	0	0	0	0	0	0	0	0	.000
1941	Boston	National	P	4	4	2	2	5	0	0	1	2	0	.500
1942	Leakesville-Spray-Draper	Bi-State	OF-P	74	263	58	84	161	13	2	20	70	0	.332
1942	Lynchburg (Manager)	Virginia	2B-OF	123	410	92	148	277	18	9	31*	99	4	.361*
1943/44	[Did not play]													
1945	Greensboro (Manager)	Carolina	1B-OF	8	29	11	7	17	1	0	3	9	0	.241
1946	Lynchburg (Manager)	Piedmont	OF-P	18	36	2	3	4	1	0	0	2	0	.083
1947	[Did not play]													
1948	Marion (Manager)	Western Carolina	OF-P	104	381	99	162	292	30	14	24	119	3	.425*
1949	Greensboro	Carolina	OF	20	69	8	25	36	2	0	3	9	0	.362
	Tampa	Florida International	1B-OF-P	30	92	9	23	28	2	0	1	8	0	.250

Non-playing Manager: 1963 Rock Hill (Western Carolinas); 1965 Shelby (Western Carolina)
*Led or tied for league lead

Ferrell, Isaac Marvin (Marvin)

Born, December 1, 1910, at Greensboro, North Carolina. Died, October 3, 1969, at Newport News, Virginia. Batted right. Threw right. Height, 6'1". Weight, 170. Home address in 1932: Guilford, North Carolina. Brother of former professional baseball players, George S., Richard B. and Wesley C. Ferrell. Played semi-pro baseball at Williamson, West Virginia, in 1930.

PITCHER

Year	Club	League	G	CG	IP	W	L	PCT	H	BB	SO	R	ER	ERA
1931	Milwaukee	American Association	16	0	40	0	1	.000	41	31	13	38	29	6.53
	Wichita Falls	Texas	5	1	27	2	3	.400	23	16	17	22	16	5.33
1932	Wichita Falls	Texas	4	0	9	0	2	.000						
	Burlington	Mississippi Valley	1	1	8	0	1	.000						
1933	Scranton	New York-Pennsylvania	24		129	4	8	.333	136	87	39	80	75	5.23
1934	Asheville	Piedmont	4		20	1	3	.250	25	10	2	17		
1935	Reidsville	Bi-State	2	0	6	0	2	.000	18	0	4	11		
1936	[Out of organized baseball]													
1937	Landis	North Carolina State	[Fewer than ten games— no pitching record]											
1938	Trenton	Eastern	19	13	138	12	4	.750	128	47	90	51	43	2.80
	Greenville	South Atlantic	19	7	104	4	9	.308	134	50	47	88	77	6.66
1939	Greenville	South Atlantic	6	5	47	2	3	.400	42	14	22	30	16	3.06
	Landis	North Carolina State	3	1	12	1	1	.500	20	4	8	11		
1940	New Bern	Coastal Plain	[Ten games— no pitching record]											

*Led or tied for league lead

Marvin Ferrell, cont'd

BATTER

Year	Club	League	Pos	G	AB	R	H	TB	2B	3B	HR	RBI	SB	PCT
1931	Milwaukee	American Association	P	16	15	1	3	5	2	0	0	0	0	.200
	Wichita Falls	Texas	P	5	9	2	4	5	1	0	0	0	0	.444
1932	Wichita Falls	Texas	P	4	[Statistics unavailable]									
	Burlington	Mississippi Valley	P	[Fewer than ten games]										
1933	Scranton	New York–Pennsylvania	P-OF	52	137	12	39	52	7	3	0	19	1	.285
1934	Asheville	Piedmont	P	[Fewer than ten games]										
1935	Reidsville	Bi-State	P	[Fewer than ten games]										
1936	[Out of organized baseball]													
1937	Landis	North Carolina State	OF-P	56	171	22	54	69	10	1	1	24	4	.316
1938	Trenton	Eastern	P	23	58	4	11	11	0	0	0	5	1	.190
	Greenville	South Atlantic	P	10	29	3	4	4	0	0	0	1	0	.138
1939	Greenville	South Atlantic	P	[Fewer than ten games]										
	Landis	North Carolina State	P	[Fewer than ten games— no pitching record]										
1940	New Bern	Coastal Plain		10	37	2	9	9	0	0	0	4	0	.243

*Led or tied for league lead

Ferrell, George Stuart

Born, April 14, 1904, at Greensboro, North Carolina. Died, October 6, 1987, at Greensboro, North Carolina. Batted right. Threw right. Height, 6'. Weight, 180. Brother of Rick, Wes and Marvin Ferrell, all pro baseball players. Played semi-pro baseball in 1925.

Year	Club	League	Pos	G	AB	R	H	TB	2B	3B	HR	RBI	SB	PCT
1926	Monroe	Cotton States	OF	103	355	67	126	229	35*	6	20*		2	.355
	Memphis	Southern Association	OF	12	28	3	5	6	1	0	0	2	0	.179
1927	Memphis	Southern Association	OF	120	408	70	119	174	22	9	5	65	6	.292
1928	Memphis	Southern Association	OF	69	191	27	56	76	11	3	1	30	2	.293
1929	Memphis	Southern Association	OF	142	500	82	148	206	27	11	3	71	9	.296
1930	Winston-Salem	Piedmont	OF	141	530	113	175	277	42	12	12	105	17	.330
1931	Greensboro	Piedmont	OF-3B	119	464	93	155	237	33	5	13	94	5	.334
	Buffalo	International	OF	5	9	0	1	1	0	0	0	0	0	.111
1932	Buffalo	International	OF	14	36	6	11	18	4	0	1	1	0	.306
	Wilkes-Barre/Scranton	New York-Pennsylvania	OF-3B	98	374	48	123	174	26	5	5	65	4	.329
1933	Scranton	New York-Pennsylvania	OF-3B	134	491	74	148	189	25	5	5	85	9	.301
1934	Asheville	Piedmont	OF-3B	90	341	82	125	216	25	3	2	82	9	.367
	Reading	New York-Pennsylvania	OF	43	160	25	48	68	11	3	20	31	7	.300
1935	Richmond	Piedmont	OF	129	462	101	174	297*	36	6	25	110	5	.377*
1936	Richmond (Manager)	Piedmont	OF	142	540	94	181	288	32	6	21	114	7	.335
1937	Richmond	Piedmont	OF	138	508	92	163	245	26	1	18	110	7	.321
1938	Richmond	Piedmont	OF	135	524	87	157	232	21	0	18	110	5	.300
1939	Richmond	Piedmont	OF	143	506	103	174	297*	25	1	32	129*	4	.344
1940	Richmond	Piedmont	OF	139	507	86	147	218	28	2	13	89	4	.290
1941	Martinsville (Manager)	Bi-State	OF-3B	112	419	86	147	241	41*	4	15	114*	7	.351
1942	Rocky Mount (Manager)	Bi-State	OF-3B	124	455	93	143	248	33	3	22	105*	5	.314
1943	Trenton (Manager)	Inter-State	OF-3B	70	246	42	84	118	21	2	3	47	5	.341
1944	Lynchburg (Manager)	Piedmont	OF	136	482	62	139	181	29	5	1	73	4	.288
1945	Lynchburg (Manager)	Piedmont	OF	51	192	19	58	81	15	1	2	33	2	.302
	Winston-Salem (Manager)	Carolina	OF	64	239	28	69	91	11	1	3	41	3	.289
1946—48 and 1950 [Out of organized baseball]														
1949	Winston-Salem (Manager)	Carolina	[Did not play, managed part of season]											
1951	Goldsboro (Manager)	Coastal Plain	[Fewer than ten games]											

*Led or tied for league lead

Ferrell, George Wesley

Born, March 20, 1937, at Greensboro, North Carolina. Batted left. Threw right. Height, 6' 3". Weight, 183. Graduate Oak Ridge Military Institute, 1957. Attended Guilford College. Son of George Stuart Ferrell, pro baseball player 1926–1951.

Year	Club	League	Pos	G	AB	R	H	TB	2B	3B	HR	RBI	SB	PCT
1958	Montgomery	Alabama-Florida	OF	15	48	5	8	9	1	0	0	6	0	.167
	Erie	New York-Pennsylvania	OF	30	110	15	32	43	5	0	2	18	0	.291
1959	Decatur	Midwest	OF	2	1	0	0	0	0	0	0	0	0	.000
	Erie	New York-Pennsylvania	OF	51	176	26	34	45	1	2	2	30	3	.193
1960	Duluth-Superior	Northern	OF	18	40	6	10	12	2	0	0	3	3	.250
	Forest City	Western Carolina	OF	73	279	42	82	109	10	1	5	36	4	.294
1961	Raleigh	Carolina	OF	10	38	4	6	7	1	0	0	3	1	.158
1962	[Out of organized baseball]													
1963	Rock Hill	Western Carolina	OF	10	28	1	3	3	0	0	0	2	0	.107

Ferrell, Charles DeWitt

Born, July 10, 1921, at Durham, North Carolina. Died, May 14, 1966, at Durham, North Carolina. Batted right. Threw right. Height, 6' 2". Weight, 185. Attended Durham, North Carolina, High School. Home address in 1949: Highland Ave., Durham, North Carolina. First-cousin of pro baseball players George, Marvin, Rick and Wes Ferrell. Played semi-pro baseball for Wright's Automatic Machine Company, Durham, NC, 1944.

Year	Club	League	Pos	G	AB	R	H	TB	2B	3B	HR	RBI	SB	PCT
1941	New Bern/Williamston	Coastal Plain	C	96	334	37	72	92	9	1	3	35	4	.216
1942	Petersburg	Virginia	C	1	4	1	1	1	0	0	0	1	0	.250
1943/44	[Played semi-pro baseball]													
1945	Montreal	International	C	19	47	8	14	14	0	0	0	9	1	.298
1946	Burlington	Carolina	C	73	300	50	104	157	15	7	8	56	4	.347
	Montreal	International	C	6	13	3	5	5	0	0	0	1	0	.385
	Cambridge	Eastern Shore	C	64	236	38	73	102	11	3	4	39	8	.309
1947	Durham	Carolina	C	64	208	34	61	85	12	3	2	34	0	.293
1948	Albemarle	North Carolina State	C	33	128	20	41	51	8	1	0	25	3	.320
1949	Raleigh	Carolina	C	72	243	35	60	78	12	0	2	26	1	.247
1950	Reidsville	Carolina	C	101	334	43	84	126	28	1	4	48	1	.251
	Pulaski	Appalachian	C	[Fewer than ten games]											
	Raleigh	Carolina	C	30	73	4	17	19	2	0	0	10	1	.233
1951	Hagerstown	Inter-State	C	20	61	5	13	18	5	0	0	4	0	.213
	Danville	Carolina	C	73	207	14	57	70	10	0	1	24	0	.275

Ferrell, James Richard (Little Rick)

Born, June 9, 1928, at Greensboro, North Carolina. Batted right. Threw right. Height, 5' 10". Weight, 165. Graduate Greensboro, NC, High School, 1947. Attended Guilford College. Home address in 1955: 1509 Fairmont, Greensboro, North Carolina. Nephew of Rick and Wes Ferrell, former Major League players.

Year	Club	League	Pos	G	AB	R	H	TB	2B	3B	HR	RBI	SB	PCT
1950	Goldsboro	Coastal Plain	C-OF	74	213	25	46	62	10	0	2	25	7	.216
	Lynchburg	Piedmont	C	10	18	2	2	3	1	0	0	3	0	.111
1951	Albany	Georgia–Florida	[Fewer than ten games]											
	Johnson City	Applachian	C-OF	37	103	14	23	26	1	1	0	7	3	.223
1952–54	[In military service]													
1955	Greensboro	Carolina	C	2	5	0	0	0	0	0	0	0	0	.000

Ferrell, Beverly Graydon (Red)

Born, July 22, 1915, at Durham, North Carolina. Died, December 22, 1998, at Charlottesville, Virginia. Batted right. Threw right. Height, 5' 11". Weight, 180. Home address in 1939: 310 S. Boulevard, Charlotte, North Carolina. Resided in Charlottesville, Virginia, for many years prior to his death. First cousin of former Major League players, Rick and Wes Ferrell. Played semi-pro ball at Durham, North Carolina, in 1933.

Year	Club	League	Pos	G	AB	R	H	TB	2B	3B	HR	RBI	SB	PCT
1933	Baltimore	International	OF	2	2	0	0	0	0	0	0	0	0	.000
	Johnstown	Middle Atlantic	OF	3	8	0	0	0	0	0	0	0	0	.000
	Hartford	Northeastern	OF	31	108	13	28	46	7	4	1		0	.259
1935	Thomasville	Georgia-Florida	OF	115	407	83	122	198	29	7	11		6	.300
1936	Thomasville	Georgia-Florida	OF	112	402	86	136	219	19	11	14	77	31	.338
1937	Charlotte	Piedmont	OF	143	512	93	141	234	30	9	15	94	11	.275
1938	Charlotte	Piedmont	OF	139	507	106	152	230	30	3	14	92	8	.300
1939	Charlotte	Piedmont	OF	133	448	97	134	222	31	3	17	88	11	.299
1940	Greenville	South Atlantic	OF	143	514	102	143	247	29	6	21	103	10	.278
1941	Springfield	Eastern	OF	31	93	4	19	25	1	1	1	8	0	.204
	Greenville	South Atlantic	OF	63	225	38	61	104	15	2	8	47	0	.271

Chapter Notes

Chapter 1

1. *The Sporting News.* December 21, 1933.
2. *Richmond Times-Dispatch.* April 18, 1936.
3. *The Sporting News.* July 4, 1935.
4. Ibid.
5. *Boston Post.* July 15, 1935.
6. *Richmond Times-Dispatch.* July 16, 1935.
7. Ibid.
8. *The Catcher Was a Spy.* Page 100.
9. *The Sporting News.* August 1, 1935.
10. *Baseball When the Grass Was Real.* Page 33.
11. *The Sporting News.* July 25, 1935.
12. Data provided by David Vincent and SABR's Home Run log.
13. Unidentified clipping in Ferrell's HOF file.
14. *Boston Globe.* April 8, 1935.

Chapter 2

1. *The History of Guilford County, North Carolina.* Page 13.
2. *Lefty Grove: American Original.* Page 37.
3. *Baseball When the Grass Was Real.* Page 15.
4. Cone Mills Park was often referred to as just Cone Park.
5. *Richmond Times-Dispatch.* April 4, 1936.
6. Ibid.
7. *Greensboro Daily News.* Dated 1948 but not specific to issue.
8. Primary documentation of the Ferrell's boxing career was never located.

9. *Greensboro Daily Record.* January 22, 1925.
10. Transcript of interview between George Ferrell and his son.
11. *Greensboro Daily News.* March 23, 1926.
12. Ibid. May 25, 1926.
13. *The Sporting News.* April 7, 1927.
14. *Greensboro Daily News.* August 28, 1926.
15. Some references refer to him as Henry White.
16. American League Service Bureau release. January 2, 1932.
17. *The Sporting News.* June 23, 1938.
18. Ibid. January 31, 1929.
19. *Baseball Between the Wars.* Page 186.
20. *The Sporting News.* November 10, 1932.
21. *Baseball: The People's Game.* p. 241.
22. *Cleveland Plain Dealer.* August 16, 1931.
23. *The Sporting News.* July 28, 1932.
24. Rufus Frazier Smith entry. *Historical Catalogue of Brown University.* 1934 . Page 948.
25. *Baseball When the Grass Was Real.* Page 16.
26. *Hank Greenberg: The Story of My Life.* Page 16.
27. *The Sporting News.* December 14, 1960.
28. *Baseball When the Grass Was Real.* Page 16.

Chapter 3

1. *The Sporting News.* April 12, 1928.
2. Ibid. September 13, 1928.

3. Based on a minimum of 100 games played.

4. *Diamond Gems*. Pages 164–6.

5. Ibid.

6. Unidentified newspaper clipping provided from Ferrell family scrapbooks.

7. *The Sporting News*. November 15, 1928.

8. Newspaper clipping in Ferrell's Hall of Fame file. Marked "November 15, 1928 — Telegram."

9. *The Sporting News*. November 22, 1928.

10. Ibid. July 5, 1945.

11. Prior to his death in 1987, George S. Ferrell sat down and reminisced about his career. His son, George W. Ferrell, recorded those conversations. Transcripts of those talks are used throughout this book.

12. *The History of the Texas League of Professional Baseball Clubs, 1881–1951*. Page 312.

13. *The Sporting News*. August 11, 1932.

14. Unidentified newspaper clipping in Ferrell's HOF file. Dated April 17, 1935. Frank Graham.

15. *Cleveland Plain Dealer*. September 29, 1928.

Chapter 4

1. Ibid. March 21, 1929.

2. Ibid. April 14, 1929.

3. This was League Park. In the late '20s it was called Dunn Field.

4. *Cleveland Pain Dealer*. April 18, 1929.

5. Ibid. April 27, 1929.

6. Ibid. April 27, 1929.

7. *The Sporting News*. June 13, 1929.

8. Ibid. July 25, 1929.

9. *New York Times*. July 20, 1929.

10. *Cleveland Plain Dealer*. July 28, 1929.

11. *The Sporting News*. August 15, 1929.

12. Unidentified newspaper clipping in Ferrell's HOF file.

13. *Cleveland Plain Dealer*. September 30, 1929.

14. *The Sporting News*. October 10, 1929.

15. *Forgotten Fields*. 1984.

16. *The Sporting News*. July 4, 1929.

17. Ibid. August 22, 1929.

18. Ibid. August 29, 1929.

19. Ibid. August 15, 1929.

20. Detroit led the American League in runs scored in 1929 with 926. Boston was last with 605.

21. *Greensboro Daily Record*. August 13, 1925.

22. Ibid. September 23, 1925.

23. *Baseball When the Grass Was Real*. Page 16.

24. *The Sporting News*. July 25, 1929.

25. Ibid. October 24, 1929.

26. Ibid. October 24, 1929.

27. Ibid. December 26, 1929.

28. Ibid. December 5, 1929.

29. Ibid. October 24, 1929.

30. *Cleveland Plain Dealer*. August 27, 1929.

Chapter 5

1. *Baseball Magazine*. March 1930. P 455.

2. American League Service Bureau press release. January 26, 1930.

3. *Cleveland Plain Dealer*. April 28, 1930.

4. Ibid. May 3, 1930.

5. Ibid. May 24, 1930.

6. Ibid. May 31, 1930.

7. Ibid. June 9, 1930.

8. *The Sporting News*. March 29, 1945.

9. *Cleveland Plain Dealer*. June 23, 1930.

10. Ibid. July 20, 1930.

11. Ibid. July 23, 1930.

12. Ibid. July 28, 1930.

13. Ibid. August 15, 1930.

14. *The Sporting News*. August 21, 1930.

15. *Cleveland Plain Dealer*. August 21, 1930.

16. Ibid. September 7, 1930.

17. *Baseball When the Grass Was Real*. Page 122.

18. *The Sporting News*. September 11, 1930.

19. *Cleveland Plain Dealer*. September 13, 1930.

20. Ibid.

21. *The Sporting News*. September *28, 1933*.

22. *Lefty Grove: American Original*. Pages 139–40.

23. *You Can't Steal First Base*. Page 31.

24. *The Sporting News*. March 29, 1945.

25. Ibid. February 20, 1930.

26. *Boston Globe*. June 8, 1937.

27. *Cleveland Plain Dealer*. September 14, 1930.

28. *Award Voting*.

Chapter 6

1. *Cleveland Plain Dealer.* April 14, 1931.
2. *Cleveland Press.* April 30, 1931.
3. Unidentified newspaper clipping in author's file. Dated May 27, 1963. Thought to be a Boston paper.
4. Unidentified newspaper clipping in Ferrell's HOF file.
5. *New York Times.* May 1, 1931.
6. Ibid. May 5, 1935.
7. *Greensboro Daily News.* May 5, 1931.
8. *Cleveland Plain Dealer.* May 18, 1931.
9. Ibid. May 24, 1931.
10. *The Sporting News.* June 11, 1931.
11. *Baseball* Magazine. October 1931.
12. *Cleveland Plain Dealer.* June 3, 1931.
13. Ibid. June 5, 1931.
14. *New York Times.* June 9, 1931.
15. *Cleveland Plain Dealer.* June 9, 1931.
16. Ibid. June 13, 1931.
17. Ibid. June 17, 1931.
18. Ibid. June 18, 1931.
19. *New York World-Telegram.* June 10, 1931.
20. *Cleveland Plain Dealer.* June 29, 1931.
21. Ibid. July 2, 1931.
22. Ibid. July 22, 1931.
23. Ibid. July 26, 1931.
24. Ibid. July 30, 1931.
25. Ibid. August 3, 1931.
26. Ibid. August 9, 1931.
27. Ibid. August 28, 1931.
28. Ibid. September 13, 1931.
29. Ibid. September 17, 1931.
30. *Baseball Magazine.* October 1931.
31. *The Man in the Dugout.* Page 261.
32. *Cleveland Plain Dealer.* September 22, 1931.
33. Ferrell hit 38 home runs in his career. One came as a pinch-hitter.
34. *Greensboro Daily News.* May 31, 1931.
35. *Baseball Magazine.* August 1931.
36. *The Sporting News.* September 17, 1931.
37. *Greensboro Daily News.* May 8, 1931.

Chapter 7

1. *The Sporting News.* May 26, 1932.
2. *Cleveland Plain Dealer.* April 10, 1932.
3. *The Sporting News.* March 3, 1932.
4. Ibid. April 7, 1932.
5. *The Man in the Dugout.* Page 226.
6. *Cleveland Plain Dealer.* April 14, 1932.
7. Ibid. April 19, 1932.
8. Ibid. April 24, 1932.
9. Ibid. April 28, 1932.
10. Ibid. May 2, 1932.
11. *Philadelphia Public Ledger.* May 6, 1932.
12. *Cleveland Plain Dealer.* May 10, 1932.
13. Ibid. May 18, 1932.
14. Ibid. May 26, 1932.
15. *New York World-Telegram.* June 14, 1932.
16. *Cleveland Plain Dealer.* May 29, 1932.
17. Ibid. May 31, 1932.
18. Ibid. June 4, 1932.
19. Ibid. June 6, 1932.
20. *New York World-Telegram.* June 14, 1932.
21. *Cleveland Plain Dealer.* June 16, 1932.
22. Ibid. July 1, 1932.
23. Ibid. July 5, 1932.
24. *The Sporting News.* July 28, 1932.
25. *Cleveland Plain Dealer.* July 9, 1932.
26. Ibid. July 11, 1932.
27. *Baseball: When the Grass Was Real.* Pages 25–26.
28. *Cleveland Plain Dealer.* July 20, 1932.
29. Ibid. August 2, 1932.
30. Ibid. August 7, 1936.
31. Ibid. August 8, 1932.
32. *New York World-Telegram.* August 17, 1932.
33. *Cleveland Plain Dealer.* August 22, 1932.
34. *Cleveland Press.* August 17, 1932.
35. *Cleveland Plain Dealer.* August 27, 1932.
36. Unidentified clipping in Ferrell's HOF file.
37. *The Sporting News.* September 8, 1932.
38. Ibid. September 15, 1932.
39. Ibid. April 14, 1932.
40. Ibid. January 26, 1933.
41. *Cleveland Plain Dealer.* September 12, 1932.
42. Ibid. September 18, 1932.
43. Ibid. September 24, 1932.
44. *New York Times.* November 21, 1932.
45. *Baseball Between The Wars: Memories of the Game by the Men Who Played It.* Page 13.

Chapter 8

1. *Greensboro Daily News.* March 6 and 7, 1933.

2. *Boston Globe*. May 10, 1933.
3. Ibid. May 17, 1933.
4. *The Sporting News*. April 13, 1933.
5. *New York Times*. March 16, 1933.
6. *Boston Globe*. May 24, 1933.
7. *Cleveland Plain Dealer*. March 18, 1933.
8. *Baseball Magazine*. June 1933.
9. *The Sporting News*. April 27, 1933.
10. *Cleveland Plain Dealer*. April 25, 1933.
11. Ibid. April 30, 1933.
12. Ibid. May 23, 1933.
13. Data complied by L. Robert Davids.
14. *Cleveland Plain Dealer*. May 28, 1933.
15. Ibid. June 2, 1933.
16. Ibid. June 18, 1933.
17. Ibid. June 24, 1933.
18. Ibid. June 26, 1933.
19. *Boston Globe*. July 6, 1933.
20. Five of Ferrell's seven errors in 1933 came in September.
21. *The Sporting News*. July 13, 1933.
22. *Washington Post*. July 8, 1933.
23. *Greensboro News-Record*. July 13, 1993.
24. *The Sporting News*. January 1, 1934.
25. *Cleveland Plain Dealer*. July 9, 1933.
26. Ibid. July 15, 1933.
27. Ibid. July 20, 1933.
28. Ibid. July 24, 1933.
29. *Cleveland Press*. August 16, 1933.
30. *Cleveland Plain Dealer*. August 16, 1933.
31. Ibid. August 21, 1933.
32. Ibid. September 4, 1933.
33. Ibid. September 9, 1933.
34. *The Sporting News*. October 12, 1933.
35. *Cleveland Plain Dealer*. September 10, 1933.
36. Ibid. September 19, 1933.

Chapter 9

1. *Greensboro Daily News*. April 10, 1934.
2. Ibid. March 3, 1934.
3. Unidentified newspaper clipping in Ferrell's HOF file. Written by Gordon Cobbledick.
4. *The Sporting News*. January 31, 1934.
5. Ibid. April 5, 1934.
6. Ibid. April 12, 1934.
7. Ibid. April 12, 1934.
8. *Greensboro Daily News*. April 5, 1934.
9. Ibid. April 13, 1934.
10. Ibid. May 1, 1934.
11. Ibid. May 15, 1934.
12. *Baseball When the Grass Was Real*. Pages 30–31.
13. *Boston Globe*. May 26, 1934.
14. Ibid. June 6, 1934.
15. *Boston Post*. June 17, 1934.
16. *Baseball When the Grass Was Real*. Page 23.
17. *New York World-Telegram*. June 21, 1934.
18. *Boston Globe*. July 2, 1934.
19. Ibid. June 26, 1934.
20. Ibid. July 14, 1934.
21. *St. Louis Post-Dispatch*. July 14, 1934.
22. *Boston Globe*. August 9, 1934.
23. *Memories of a Ballplayer: Bill Werber and Baseball in the 1930s*. Page 31. Werber described this action as happening in the sixth inning, not the third.
24. *The Sporting News*. November 16, 1944.
25. *New York Times*. August 12, 1934.
26. *Memories of a Ballplayer: Bill Werber and Baseball in the 1930s*. Page 31.
27. *Boston Globe*. August 23, 1934.
28. Ibid.
29. *The Sporting News*. June 21, 1945.
30. *Boston Globe*. July 9, 1934.
31. *The Sporting News*. August 30, 1934.

Chapter 10

1. *Boston Globe*. April 10, 1935.
2. *Richmond Times-Dispatch*. March 8, 1935.
3. Unidentified newspaper clipping in Ferrell's HOF file.
4. *New York World-Telegram*. April 18, 1935.
5. *Boston Post*. May 5, 1935.
6. Ibid. May 10, 1935.
7. *Boston Globe*. May 14, 1935.
8. Ibid. May 23, 1935.
9. Ibid. May 24, 1935.
10. Ibid. May 25, 1935.
11. Ibid. May 31, 1935.
12. Ibid. June 5, 1935.
13. *Boston Post*. June 12, 1935.
14. *The Sporting News*. June 20, 1935.
15. *Boston Globe*. June 20, 1935.
16. *Richmond Times-Dispatch*. August 23, 1935.
17. Unidentified newspaper clipping from Beverly Ferrell's scrapbook.

18. Ferrell's actual record at that time was 18–10.
19. *The Sporting News.* August 15, 1935.
20. *Boston Globe.* August 6, 1935.
21. *The Sporting News.* August 22, 1935.
22. *Boston Globe.* August 17, 1935.
23. Ibid. August 22, 1935.
24. Ibid. August 30, 1935.
25. Ibid. September 6, 1935.
26. *Boston Post.* September 9, 1935.
27. *Boston Globe.* September 17, 1935.
28. Ibid. September 19, 1935.
29. Ibid. September 25, 1935.
30. Ibid. September 26, 1935.
31. *The Sporting News.* January 2, 1936.
32. Ibid. May 14, 1931.
33. Ibid. March 3, 1938 and May 12, 1938.
34. *New York Times.* August 8, 1935.

Chapter 11

1. *The Sporting News.* March 5, 1936.
2. *Richmond Times-Dispatch.* February 28, 1936.
3. Ibid. March 5, 1936.
4. Unidentified clipping in Ferrell's HOF file.
5. *Boston Globe.* April 15, 1936.
6. Ibid. April 18, 1936.
7. Ibid. April 24, 1936.
8. Ibid. May 4, 1936.
9. Ibid. May 8, 1936
10. Ibid. May 11, 1936.
11. Ibid. May 13, 1936.
12. Ibid. May 19, 1936.
13. *The Sporting News.* May 28, 1936.
14. *Boston Globe.* May 21, 1936.
15. Ibid. May 27, 1936.
16. *Boston Post.* May 31, 1936.
17. *Boston Globe.* June 4, 1936.
18. Ibid. June 5, 1936.
19. Ibid. June 11, 1936.
20. Ibid. June 13, 1936.
21. *Greensboro Daily News.* September 7, 1981.
22. *Boston Globe.* June 22, 1936.
23. Ibid.
24. *Sleeper Cars and Flannel Uniforms.* Page 161.
25. *The Sporting News.* June 11, 1936.
26. *What's the Matter with the Red Sox? The Saturday Evening Post.* March 23, 1946.
27. Ibid.
28. *Boston Globe.* July 2, 1936.

29. Ibid. July 7, 1936.
30. Ibid. July 11, 1936.
31. Ibid. July 17, 1936.
32. Ibid. July 17, 1936.
33. Ibid. July 27, 1936.
34. *Teenagers, Graybeards and 4-F's. Volume 2: The American League.* Page 20.
35. *Boston Globe.* July 31, 1936.
36. *Boston Globe.* August 8, 1936.
37. Ibid. August 13, 1936.
38. Ibid. August 17, 1936.
39. *New York Times.* August 23, 1936.
40. *Boston Globe.* August 22, 1936.
41. Ibid.
42. *New York Times.* August 23, 1936.
43. *Boston Globe.* August 22, 1936.
44. Ibid.
45. *The Sporting News.* September 3, 1936.
46. *Boston Globe.* August 27, 1936.
47. Ibid. September 4, 1936.
48. Ibid. September 7, 1936.
49. *New York Times.* September 7, 1936.
50. *Boston Globe.* September 12, 1936.
51. Ibid. September 14, 1936.
52. *Boston Post.* September 20, 1936.
53. *Boston Globe.* September 30, 1936.
54. *The Sporting News.* October 22, 1936.
55. Unidentified newspaper clipping from Beverly Ferrell's scrapbook.

Chapter 12

1. *Boston Globe.* April 5, 1937.
2. Ibid. April 12, 1937.
3. Ibid. March 30, 1937.
4. Ibid. May 5, 1937.
5. Ibid. May 14, 1937.
6. Ibid. May 18, 1937.
7. *Baseball, The Fan's Game.* Page 127.
8. *Boston Globe.* May 27, 1937.
9. *Washington Post.* June 11, 1937.
10. *The Sporting News.* October 15, 1936.
11. *Washington Post.* June 13, 1937.
12. Ibid. June 21, 1937.
13. *Baseball When the Grass Was Real.* Page 34.
14. *Washington Post.* July 21, 1937.
15. Ibid. July 25, 1937.
16. Ibid. July 30, 1937.
17. Ibid. August 4, 1937.
18. Ibid. August 8, 1937.
19. Ibid. August 12, 1937.
20. *Baseball When the Grass Was Real.* Page 33.

21. *Washington Post*. August 25, 1937.
22. Ibid. August 29, 1937.
23. Ibid. September 2, 1937.
24. Ibid. September 16, 1937.
25. Ibid. September 22, 1937.
26. *Richmond Times-Dispatch*. July 23, 1937.

Chapter 13

1. *Washington Post*. April 24, 1938.
2. Ibid. April 29, 1938.
3. Ibid. May 19, 1938.
4. Ibid. June 4, 1938.
5. *Baseball When the Grass Was Real*. Page 45.
6. *Hank Greenberg: The Story of My Life*. Pages 99–100.
7. *Washington Post*. June 27, 1938.
8. Ibid. July 16, 1938.
9. Ibid. July 21, 1938.

Chapter 14

1. Ibid. April 18, 1944.
2. *The Sporting News*. August 12, 1943.
3. *Washington Post*. March 4, 1944.
4. *The Sporting News*. March 9, 1955.
5. Ibid. April 6, 1944.

6. Ibid. June 14, 1945.
7. *The Man in the Dugout*. Page 165.
8. *The Sporting News*. July 5, 1945.
9. Unidentified newspaper clipping from Bev Ferrell's scrapbook.
10. *New York Times*. April 5, 1945.
11. *The Sporting News*. December 20, 1945.

Chapter 15

1. Ibid. January 31, 1962.
2. Ibid. February 14, 1962.
3. Ibid. November 6, 1957.
4. Ibid. March 27, 1957.
5. Ibid. April 22, 1959.
6. *John Fetzer: On a Handshake*. Page 50.
7. Ibid. Page 51.
8. *The Sporting News*. November 22 and December 27, 1961.
9. *New York Times*. November 11, 1960.
10. Ibid. October 25, 1961.
11. *The Sporting News*. August 8, 1962.
12. *The Sporting News*. October 12, 1968.

Epilogue

1. *Saturday Evening Post*. July 13, 1940.

Bibliography

Books

Alexander, Charles. *Breaking the Slump: Baseball in the Depression Era*. New York: Columbia University Press. 2002.

Armour, Mark L., and Daniel R. Levitt. *Paths to Glory: How Great Baseball Teams Got That Way*. Virginia: Brassey's. 2003.

Auker, Elden, and Tom Keegan. *Sleeper Cars and Flannel Uniforms*. Chicago: Triumph Books. 2001.

Bevis, Charles. *Mickey Cochrane: The Life of a Baseball Hall of Fame Catcher*. North Carolina: McFarland. 1998.

Cantor, George. *The Tigers of '68: Baseball's Last Real Champions*. Texas: Taylor. 1997.

Chrisman, David F. *The History of the Piedmont League*. Oregon: Maverick. 1986.
_____. *The History of the Virginia League*. Oregon: Maverick. 1988.

Crissey, Harrington E. *Teenagers, Graybeards and 4-F's. Volume 2*. New Jersey: White Eagle Printing. 1982.

Cochrane, Gordon S. (Mickey). *Baseball: The Fan's Game*. Ohio: The Society for American Baseball Research. 1992. Originally printed in 1939.

Dawidoff, Nicholas. *The Catcher Was a Spy: The Mysterious Life of Moe Berg*. New York: Pantheon Books. 1994.

Deane, Bill. *Award Voting*. Missouri: The Society for American Baseball Research. 1988.

Dreisewerd, Edna. *The Catcher Was a Lady: The Clem Dreisewerd Story*. New York: Exposition Press. 1978.

Dykes, Jimmie, and Charles O. Dexter. *You Can't Steal First Base*. Philadelphia: J. B. Lippincott. 1967.

Ewald, Dan. *John Fetzer: On a Handshake*. Illinois: Sagamore Press. 1997.
_____. *They Call Me Sparky*. Michigan: Sleeping Bear Press. 1998.

Gaunt, Robert. *We Would Have Played Forever: The Story of the Coastal Plain Baseball League*. North Carolina: Baseball America. 1997.

Golenbock, Peter. *Fenway: An Unexpurgated History of the Boston Red Sox*. New York: G.P. Putnam's. 1992.

Green, Paul. *Forgotten Fields*. Wisconsin: Parker. 1984.

Greenberg, Hank, and Ira Berkow. *Hank Greenberg: The Story of My Life*. New York: Times Books. 1989.

Gregory, Robert. *Diz: Dizzy Dean and Baseball During the Depression*. New York: Viking. 1992.

Hirshberg, Al. *The Red Sox: The Bean and the Cod*. Boston: Waverly House. 1947

_____. *From Sandlots to League President: The Story of Joe Cronin*. New York: Julian Messner. 1962.

Holaday, J. Chris. *Professional Baseball in North Carolina*. North Carolina: McFarland. 1998.

Honig, Donald. *Baseball When the Grass Was Real*. New York: Coward, McCann and Geoghegan. 1975.

_____. *Baseball Between the Lines*. New York: Coward, McCann and Geoghegan. 1976.

_____. *The Man in the Dugout*. Chicago: Follett. 1977.

Johnson, Lloyd. *The Minor League Register*. North Carolina: Baseball America. 1994.

Kaplan, Jim. *Lefty Grove: American Original*. Ohio: The Society for American Baseball Research. 2000.

Karst, Gene, and Martin J. Jones, Jr. *Who's Who in Professional Baseball*. New York: Arlington House. 1973

Kerr, Jon. *Calvin: Baseball's Last Dinosaur*. W. C. Brown. 1990.

McConnell, Bob, and David Vincent. *The Home Run Encyclopedia*. The Society for American Baseball Research. New York: Simon and Schuster Macmillan. 1996.

Murdock, Eugene. *Baseball Between the Wars: Memories of the Game by the Men Who Played It*. Connecticut: Meckler. 1992.

_____. *Baseball Players and Their Times: Oral Histories of the Game, 1920–1940*. Connecticut: Meckler. 1991.

Overfield, Joseph M. *The 100 Seasons of Buffalo Baseball*. New York: Partner's Press. 1985.

Parker, Al. *Baseball Giant Killers: The Spudders of the 1920s*. Texas: Nortex Press. 1976.

Pattison, Mark, and David Raglin. *Detroit Tigers. Lists and More. Runs, Hits, and Eras*. Detroit: Wayne State University Press. 2002

Ruggles, William B. *The History of the Texas League*. 1951.

Seymour, Harold. *Baseball: The People's Game*. New York: Oxford University Press. 1990.

Smith, Myron J., Jr. *Baseball: A Comprehensive Bibliography*. North Carolina: McFarland. 1986.

Stockard, Sallie W. *The History of Guilford County, North Carolina*. Tennessee: Gaut-Ogden Company. 1902. Re-published by the Guilford County Genealogical Society 1983.

Stout, Glenn, and Richard A. Johnson. *Red Sox Century*. Boston: Houghton Mifflin. 2000.

Upward, Geoff. *Ernie Harwell's Diamond Gems*. Michigan: Momentum Books. 1991.

Werber, Bill. *Circling the Bases*. Privately published. 1978.

_____, and C. Paul Rogers. *Memories of a Ballplayer*. Ohio: The Society for American Baseball Research. 2001.

Wright, Marshall D. *The American Association*. North Carolina: McFarland. 1997.

_____. *The International League*. North Carolina: McFarland. 1998.

_____. *The Southern Association in Baseball*. North Carolina: McFarland. 2002.

Magazines

Baseball Digest
Falls, Joe. *Bill Freehan: The Game's Next Super Star.* May 1965.
Lardner, John. *Wes Ferrell, Home Run King.* November 1942.
Ruark, Bob. *Catcher Killer — The Story of Dutch Leonard.* September 1946.
Sampson, Arthur. *The Day Ferrell Met Weatherly.* May 1954.

Baseball Magazine
Bloodgood, Clifford. *Rick Ferrell, Brother of Wes.* August 1931.
_____. *The Steady and Dependable Rick Ferrell.* January 1939.
Lane, F. C. *The Phenomenal Ferrell.* March 1930.
_____. *Our All-America Baseball Team for 1930.* December 1930.
_____. *Ferrell, the Coming Mathewson.* October 1931.
_____. *Baseball's Greatest Pitcher in 1932.*
_____. *Wes Ferrell's Ambition.* June 1933.
_____. *That Contradictory Character, Wes Ferrell.* September 1935.
Rumill, Ed. *That Unsung Catching Star, Rick Ferrell.* February 1945.

Collier's
Rice, Grantland. *Under Study.* June 20, 1931.

Esquire
Gerstenzang, N. M. *Sit-Down Strikes and Balls.* June 1937.

Labor's Heritage
Reynolds, Doug. *Hardball Paternalism, Hardball Politics: Blackstone Valley Baseball, 1925–1955.* April 1991.

Oldtyme Baseball News
Carroll, Bob. *Mitt-Igating Circumstances.* 1995. Volume 7, Issue 3.
Hershberger, Chuck. *Rick Ferrell: Baseball's First Free Agent.* 1993. Volume 5, Issue 1.

Sport Magazine
Katz, Fred. *Rick Ferrell: Free Thinking Front Office Man.* May 1962.
Orr, Jack. *Lefty Grove: Best of His Era.* November 1963.

Sports Scoop
Eichmann, J. K. *Wes Ferrell — Good, Great or Immortal?* November 1973.

The Saturday Evening Post
Kaese, Harold. *What's the Matter with the Red Sox?* March 23, 1946.
Wagner, J. Honus, and George Kirksey. *Help! Help! — Help for the Pitchers.* July 13, 1940.

The Sporting News
Broeg, Bob. *Ferrell Was a Blue-Chip Redneck: A Marvel on Mound.* January 22, 1977.
_____. *Ferrells a Blue-Ribbon Battery.* January 29, 1977.

Brundidge, Harry. *Ferrell Brothers Make Game Profitable Family Business*. October 27, 1932.

Enright, James. *Tigers' No. 1 Fan? Prexy Fetzer's Wife*. October 26, 1968.

Lang, Jack. *Vets Committee Taps Reese, Ferrell for Hall*. March 12, 1984.

Shannon, Paul. *Wesley Ferrell and Lefty Grove Prove Critics Wrong by Staging Brilliant Comebacks on Mound for Boston*. August 1, 1935.

Spoelstra, Watson. *Freehan Earns No. 1 Mitt Label, Bengals Assert*. November 4, 1967.

_____. *Boss Fetzer "Regular Guy" to Tigers Players*. October 12, 1968.

_____. *Campbell Shrewd Boss—Tigers Prove It*. November 30, 1968.

_____. *Joe Niekro, Robertson Buttress Tigers on Hill*. September 20, 1969.

Newspapers

Boston Globe

Boston Post

Cleveland Plain Dealer

Cleveland Press

Greensboro Daily News

Greensboro Daily Record

Greensboro News & Record

Greensboro Patriot

Milford Daily News

New York Times

New York World-Telegram

Philadelphia Public Ledger

Richmond Times-Dispatch

St. Louis Post-Dispatch

The Sporting News

Washington Post

Websites

Ancestry.com

Baseball-almanac.com

Baseballindex.org

Baseballlibrary.com

Paperofrecord.com

Baseball-reference.com

Genealogy.com

Proquest.com

Retrosheet.org

Rootsweb.com

Sabr.org

Index